To Mother
w

Christmas 1974.

The Stewart Kingdom
of Scotland 1371–1603

The Stewart Kingdom of Scotland 1371–1603

Caroline Bingham

Weidenfeld and Nicolson
London

ISBN 0 297 76808 5

Printed in Great Britain by
Richard Clay (The Chaucer Press), Ltd,
Bungay, Suffolk

Contents

To my daughter
Frances Bingham

Illustrations

The author and publishers would like to thank the following photographers: Annan of Glasgow, Tom Scott of Edinburgh, Photo Studios Ltd, Arnold, and A. C. Cooper Ltd of London.

Acknowledgements

First of all I should like to acknowledge my debt of gratitude to Mrs Mary McKerrow and Mr Harold Elborn for their translation of Ferrerius' *Chronicle of the Reign of James III*.

Johannes Ferrerius, a sixteenth-century Piedmontese cleric, expressed 'a great desire to learn about the deeds done among the Scots in the period just before our own'. He became the historian of the Abbey of Kinloss, and wrote his chronicle, which was appended to the second edition of Hector Boece's *Chronicles of Scotland*, published in Latin in 1574. The Scottish Text Society Boece, which is an edition of John Bellenden's translation of 1531, therefore does not include Ferrerius. The quotations from Ferrerius in chapter five are from Mrs McKerrow and Mr Elborn's translation.

I should like to thank Dr Anne Robertson of the University of Glasgow for her information on Scottish coinage, and for kindly providing me with the photographs of coins which appear in this book. The photographs were taken by Mr H. Forbes.

I should also like to express my gratitude to Mrs Stirling of Keir for most kindly supplying me with a photograph of the portrait of James IV, and to Colonel William Stirling of Keir for his permission to reproduce it. I am most grateful to Dr Duncan Thomson of the Scottish National Portrait Gallery for informing me of the existence of the *Book of Hours* of James IV. I should also like to thank Mr James T. Kelman for having the portrait of Bishop Elphinstone photographed for me.

I should like to have had an opportunity to thank the late Sir James Fergusson of Kilkerran for telling me that I and numerous other writers have inherited and inadvertently propagated an error first made by the historian John Pinkerton in 1797 – that of killing too many earls at Flodden. The number was nine: Argyll, Bothwell, Caithness, Cassillis, Crawford, Errol, Lennox, Montrose and Rothes. Sir James Fergusson's correction is incorporated in this book.

Caroline Bingham
11 June 1974

I

Scotland before the Stewarts

We were a tribe, a family, a people . . .
Courage beyond the point and obdurate pride
Made us a nation . . .

(Scotland 1941, Edwin Muir)

In 1603 James VI, King of Scots, the ninth sovereign of the Scottish
Royal House of Stewart, succeeded to the English throne. This Union
of Crowns marked the first stage of the process by which the government of Scotland was merged with that of England; the process was
completed just over a century later by the Union of Parliaments in
1707.

The decisive moments of history are not always conveniently
marked by an accession, an Act of Parliament, a battle or a death. The
Union of Crowns marks the end of Scotland's separate existence as a
fully sovereign state; it is less easy to assign a date to the beginning of
Scotland's existence as a kingdom.

Archaeologists who study the prehistory of Scotland tell us that the
north of Britain was inhabited, from perhaps as early as 5000 BC, by
invaders who came immediately from northern Europe, perhaps originally from the lands around the Mediterranean. Hunters, pastoralists
and agriculturalists successively established themselves. Their weapons,
personal adornments, artifacts and even rubbish heaps, and their various
methods of burying their dead, provide a certain amount of evidence
about the quality of their life, and their preoccupation with life after
death, but give away very little concerning their history.

Prehistory and history connect at the point when the tribes inhabit-
ing north Britain came into contact with the might of the Roman
Empire. The temporary coalescing of some of the tribes to resist

Roman imperialism was the beginning of the process which forged the many peoples of the north into one people, and the land which they inhabited into the kingdom of Scotland.

Between AD 80 and 84 the Roman governor Gnaeus Julius Agricola attempted to expand the province of Britannia to the northernmost limits of the island. By 84 he had provoked against himself a confederation of tribes which, according to Tacitus, had mustered an army of 30,000 men under the leadership of the first man to be named in Scottish history, Calgacus.

Tacitus, the biographer of Agricola, puts into the mouth of Calgacus a speech, presumably apocryphal, but well worth quoting as a perpetually relevant condemnation of any imperialism: 'A rich enemy excites their cupidity, a poor one their lust for power. . . . To robbery, butchery and rapine they give the lying name of "government"; they create a desolation and call it peace.'

To William Wallace and Robert the Bruce Calgacus would have spoken with the voice of a contemporary.

Calgacus and his tribal confederation were defeated at the Battle of Mons Graupius in 84. Agricola's victory may almost have justified Tacitus's assertion that Britain was 'thoroughly conquered'; but there was no Roman occupation of north Britain as there was of the south, for the north of the island was no sooner conquered than troubles in more strategically important parts of the Empire caused it to be abandoned. Despite later efforts at conquest, in the reigns of Hadrian, Antoninus Pius and Severus, the Romans ultimately contented themselves by containing the northern tribes behind an artificial barrier, Hadrian's Wall, which links the Tyne and the Solway.

The Romans were not the last invaders of Scotland, nor were the tribes who resisted them the only components of the nation which eventually came into being. Later Roman writers, though they knew the names of about seventeen northern tribes, tended to refer to them generally as 'Caledonii' or 'Picti'. Picti they used as a collective name for all the inhabitants of north Britain; but by the sixth century the historic kingdom of the Picts was specifically the eastern area of the country, extending lengthwise from Orkney to the Forth.

Other small kingdoms were established. The Scots, who like the Picts were of Celtic origin though divergent history had led to their developing a different version of the Gaelic language, came from

Ireland and established the kingdom of Dalriada, in the area which is now Argyll. Their leader was a chief named Fergus Mor mac Erc, from whom the later Kings of Scots claimed descent.

Most of the south-west comprised the kingdom of Strathclyde, which was inhabited by Welsh-speaking Britons. The south-east was settled by Anglians from Northumbria, who occupied it partly by colonization, and later by attempted conquest.

The expansion of Northumbria, which for a time bid fair to establish its power throughout the whole of Britain, was checked in 685 when Brude or Bridei, King of the Picts, defeated the Northumbrians at the Battle of Nechtansmere, near Dunnichen in Forfarshire.

Nechtansmere can truly be called a decisive battle, for it ensured that north Britain would not fall under the sway of a kingdom whose geographical position could have permitted it to dominate both the north and the south of the island. Some writers have gone so far as to say that Brude's victory made the future development of Scotland possible.

The next stage in the development of the kingdom can be dated very neatly in the year 843, when Kenneth mac Alpin, King of Scots, succeeded to the throne of the Picts, and united the two dominant peoples of the country. Sometime after this the Picts tacitly and mysteriously disappear from history. Their disappearance is the more complete in that although they left some sophisticated sculpture and metalwork they left no written records, with the exception of certain alarmingly consonantal inscriptions which have hitherto defied translation.

The disappearance of the Picts may be due partly to a slaughter of Pictish nobility carried out by Kenneth mac Alpin to ensure the future dominance of the Scots (such an event is referred to by Giraldus Cambrensis, who admittedly was writing many years later, in the reign of Henry II of England), or it may have been caused by a great defeat of the Picts at the hands of the Norsemen. Whatever the cause the dominance of the Scots was the consequence. The myths and legends of the Scots became the common tradition of the whole people, and the name of the Scoto-Pictish kingdom, which at first was called 'Albainn', became 'Scocia'.

The Norsemen, who first crossed the North Sea only to raid the island of Britain, began in the ninth century to make permanent settlements. They occupied Shetland and wrested Orkney from the Picts. They made mainland settlements on the coasts of Sutherland and

Inverness-shire, and colonized the Western Isles as far south as the Isle of Man.

In the meantime the internal unification of the kingdom of Scots had progressed. The most potent of unifying influences had been that of Christianity. It had been introduced, though by no means universally established, by St Ninian, who late in the fourth century built his church at Whithorn, on the coast of Galloway. In 563 St Columba sailed from Ireland and founded his monastery on the Isle of Iona. Thence he went to the mainland, and lent the immense strength of his moral authority to the royal house of Dalriada, to which he was related. The Scots of Dalriada may have been Christian upon their arrival in Scotland, having come from Ireland as converts of St Patrick. Tradition attributes the conversion of the Picts to St Columba, but more probably he began it and later missionaries continued it in the course of the ensuing century.

The Norsemen arrived to commit their depredations on a Christian population. Archaeology has revealed that whatever atrocities they may have committed upon the living, they showed respect for Christian burial places. Presently, as they formed settlements, they conformed to local custom and became Christian themselves.

By the second half of the eleventh century the King of Scots was the ruler of an area which comprised the old kingdoms of Pictland, Dalriada and Strathclyde. The most recent accession of territory was the Anglian-inhabited area of the Lothians. The Norsemen retained Orkney, Shetland and the Western Isles, and still held some settlements on the mainland. To the south of Scocia, now a recognizable kingdom though its limits were still undefined, lay Anglo-Saxon England, in its last days and about to fall victim to the conquering energy of William, Duke of Normandy.

In the meantime there occurred an event which has been made common knowledge by Shakespeare: Duncan 1, King of Scots, was slain by his kinsman Macbeth. This was not in actuality the murder committed for motives of ambition which Shakespeare represents, but the outcome of a disputed succession. Succession disputes were complicated by the fact that the Kings of Scots had inherited the Pictish law of matrilineal succession, which meant that succession went from uncle to nephew or from cousin to cousin rather than from father to son. (It was presumably in accordance with this law that Kenneth mac

Alpin had become King of the Picts.) Duncan I may have intended to alter the arrangement to that of succession by primogeniture, in favour of his eldest son Malcolm. Macbeth, asserting the old rule of succession, was victorious (in battle, not by murder), and ruled successfully for seventeen years, before he himself was slain by Malcolm, who in 1057 became King Malcolm III.

Therefore it was Malcolm 'Ceann Mor' or Big Head (we do not know if the nickname referred to a physical feature, or to a great brain) who faced the responsibility of deciding how the kingdom of Scots should meet the problems posed by the Norman Conquest of England.

Hitherto the kingdom of Scots had been forged by successive processes of resistance: resistance to the Romans, resistance to the Anglians, resistance to the Norsemen. The accompanying process of internal unification had aided resistance and sometimes permitted expansion.

While William of Normandy was consolidating his conquest of England, Malcolm III pursued an expansionist policy which aimed at pushing his southern frontier further south towards the river Tees. However, by 1072 William had established himself sufficiently securely as William I of England to feel able to turn his attention to the Scots. He marched north with a great army and was received by Malcolm at Abernethy. Possibly Malcolm had realized that his resources were insufficient to resist the might of William, for he received him peaceably, acknowledged William as his overlord and took an oath to be 'his man'. That politic submission perhaps prevented William I from hammering the Scots as Edward I was to do just over two centuries later, in attempts to enforce the English claim to overlordship. Malcolm saved the situation for the time being, but sowed the seeds of future trouble.

The Norman conquest of Scotland was effected not by force from without, but by peaceful means from within. It was brought about first by the religious and cultural reforms initiated by Malcolm's second wife, St Margaret, and was completed by the reforms in governmental and social organization carried out by their youngest son King David I.

St Margaret, the kinswoman of Edward the Confessor, though an English princess by birth, was essentially a European by upbringing, and had received her education at the court of Hungary. What she brought to Scotland was not the dying culture of Anglo-Saxon England but the burgeoning culture of medieval Europe.

5

St Margaret's innovations affected chiefly the religious and cultural life of the country. Her achievement has sometimes been represented as the negative one of uprooting the native 'Celtic Church' and planting the 'Roman Church' in its place. The Celtic Church, however, had a separatism that consisted only in the fact that monastic life predominated, since a system of dioceses and parishes had not been developed in either Ireland or Scotland, and that long separation from the Roman source had resulted in curious local developments such as a different method of calculating the date of Easter and a different shape for the clerical tonsure. In the basic matter of doctrine there were no divergences. St Margaret, with Malcolm's support, brought local custom into line with European practice.

As far as cultural life was concerned St Margaret was responsible for bringing European scholarship and European court life to her husband's country. The court of Malcolm had been more like that of a great tribal chief than that of a European king; the increased luxury and the greater use of ceremonial introduced by St Margaret enhanced the prestige of the court of Scotland in its relationship with the other courts of Europe. Her own sanctity, and her canonization which took place in 1251, equally served to add lustre to the Scottish Royal House.

David I, who succeeded in 1124, extended the work of his mother into the political organization of the kingdom. He had spent his youth at the English court and had been impressed by the efficiency of the feudal system imported by the Norman Kings. Simply expressed, the underlying theory was that all land was held of the King; the tenants-in-chief held their lands directly of the King in return for political advice and military service; the sub-tenants held their land of their lord upon the latter condition; and the peasantry worked the land of their lord and received in return security and protection. This simple but comprehensive system of mutual service and benefit, though imperfect in practice as are all human institutions, provided a framework of society which under a strong King could bring a kingdom efficiency and prosperity.

David I admired this system to the extent of importing it into his own kingdom, which he effected partly by transporting Norman and Breton barons and knights as the feudal superiors of existing small landowners (the fortunes of the great families of Bruce and Stewart were founded by this means), and partly by converting the Celtic aristocracy of

'Mormaers' and 'Toiseachs' into Earls and Barons. The process was assisted by his endeavour to create a universal system of law.

David I likewise introduced into Scotland the great offices common to the courts of Europe: Constable, Chamberlain, Steward and Marischal. He founded the first Royal Burghs, towns which were granted the privilege of foreign trade in return for dues paid directly to the King. He imported European monasticism, and established Cistercians at Melrose, Dundrennan, Newbattle and Kinloss, Tironensians at Kelso, and Premonstratensians at Dryburgh, Cluniacs on the Isle of May, and Augustinian canons regular at Holyrood, Jedburgh, Cambuskenneth and St Andrews, and on St Serf's Island in Lochleven. Indeed, as the chronicler Andrew of Wyntoun summed it up

> *He illumynyd in his dayis*
> *His landys wyth kyrkys and wyth abbayis.*

Those who for reasons of sentiment or heredity are attached to the idea of the ancient Celtic kingdom, and who write resentfully of the Norman conquest effected by St Margaret and David I, may perhaps fail to consider what would have been the destructive alternative to their work. The fate of a loosely organized Celtic society faced with the military power of an efficient feudal kingdom can be read in the unhappy histories of the relations of Wales and Ireland with England. The achievement of St Margaret and her son was to ensure that Scotland did not suffer that fate, by bringing to their country the culture and organization of a European kingdom.

The capacity of the kingdom of Scotland to maintain its status was severely tested during the successive reigns of David's grandsons, Malcolm IV ('the Maiden') and William the Lion.

William, who derived his nickname from the heraldic device of the lion rampant which he adopted as his arms, deserved that name equally for his qualities of character. In 1173 he invaded England in an attempt to regain the county of Northumberland, which had already changed hands a number of times. He was captured and forced by Henry II to acknowledge the English overlordship asserted by William the Conqueror over Malcolm III. William the Lion, however, was a King equally ready to take advantage of a good opportunity. When Henry's successor Richard Cœur-de-Lion was raising funds for his participation in the Third Crusade, in 1189, William bought back the full sovereignty of his kingdom for a cash payment of 10,000 marks. The purchase of one Lion King's independence from the other might reasonably have been expected to end the question of English overlordship once for all. Unhappily for Scotland it did not do so, but before the kingdom's independence was put to its greatest test there ensued a tranquil century which some historians have been disposed to see as the Golden Age of Scotland.

Golden ages are perhaps golden only in retrospect, but Scotland in the thirteenth century, during the successive reigns of Alexander II and Alexander III, was in the main a fortunate kingdom. The work of the preceding Kings was consolidated, internal peace and the rule of law steadily increased and the Kings were able to hold the balance between the different peoples over whom they ruled, and whose racial identity had remained differentiated. By the end of the thirteenth century all the subjects of the Crown of Scots were usually content to be called 'Scots', except at moments of particularly self-conscious awareness. But as Scots they were also aware of another racial identity: Norman, Anglian or Celtic. Linguistically, these racial identities remained sharply defined. Norman-French, indeed, the language of the incomers of the reign of David I, gradually went out of use in the course of the thirteenth century. It was never, in any event, the language of court and nobility in Scotland to the extent that it was in England. In the Anglian-inhabited Lothians and in the towns of the east coast the Anglian speech which eventually became known as 'Scots' predominated; and with the development of more towns, inhabited by communities of Anglian-speaking merchants, it became the dominant language of all the Lowlands. In the north and west, inhabited in the main by Celts, who have never been town-builders or willing town-dwellers, the Gaelic language continued dominant.

Alexander II and Alexander III, strong Kings, to whom the extension of law and order over the geographically inaccessible areas of the north-west, and the internal unity of the whole kingdom, were matters of profound concern, kept the balance between the different cultures of the south-east and the north-west, as later Kings, for reasons which came about in the next century, were to fail to do.

The coronation of Alexander III in 1249, the first coronation of which detailed descriptions have survived, serves very well to illustrate

8

the successful balance which was held between the cultures. It took place at Scone, the traditional place of coronation. The King was ceremonially seated upon the Stone of Destiny, the ancient throne of the Celtic Kings, he was crowned and he took a coronation oath in the manner common to European Kings, and at the conclusion of the ceremony a Gaelic-speaking 'seannachie' or bard recited his genealogy, beyond Fergus Mor mac Erc, through a line of legendary forbears to a probably mythical progenitor who also bore the name of Fergus. Alexander's title, derived from his forbears and handed on to his successors, 'King of Scots', enshrined the concept that he was thought of as the King of the peoples who had come to be called 'the Scots', rather than as a territorial ruler.

Territorially, indeed, Scotland was still a kingdom with undefined frontiers. The King of Scots undoubtedly regarded Shetland, Orkney and the Western Isles as *Scotia irredenta*, even though they had been under Norse rule since before the kingdom had possessed internal unity. Alexander III regained the Western Isles from the Crown of Norway in 1266, partly by fighting and partly by bargaining, but Orkney and Shetland were not brought within the kingdom until the fifteenth century.

The frontier of Scotland and England was likewise undefined, and doubtless its history of fluctuation was in part due to the fact that nothing more geographically noticeable than the beds of rivers and the ridges of hills too gentle to form barriers suggested what line it should follow. It had been, and was to be, much fought over; but in the thirteenth century its history was not a bloody one. Alexander II and Alexander III were strong enough rulers not to tempt the ambition of English Kings. Alexander III married as his first wife a sister of Edward I of England. He paid homage to his brother-in-law for lands that he held in England (just as the English King paid homage to the French King for lands that he held in France) without jeopardizing his sovereign status.

The end of a century of stability came in 1286 when Alexander III died without heirs male. A very well-known fragment of poetry laments the passing of his times:

> *When Alexander our King was dede*
> *That Scotland held in love and le,*[1]

[1] law.

Away was sons[2] of ale and brede,
Of wine and wax, of game and glee:
Our gold was changit into lede –
Christ, born into Virginité,
Succour Scotland, and remede
That stad is in perplexité.

Upon Alexander's death the leading nobles of the kingdom felt sufficiently confident of its stability to acknowledge as their sovereign the late King's three-year-old granddaughter, the child of his daughter who had married the King of Norway. The 'perplexité' referred to in the poem followed the death of the little 'Maid of Norway', who died in Orkney on her way to her kingdom.

There were many claimants to the Crown of Scots. Some of the claims were ingenious and far-fetched. For example, the King of Norway claimed by ascent, as the father of the rightful sovereign, the Maid of Norway, instead of by descent in the normal fashion. However, there were two claimants whose relationship to the Royal House effectually left the other claims out of count. These were two descendants of David I, both in the female line: John Balliol and Robert the Bruce (grandfather of the namesake who eventually became King). These claims can best be understood from genealogical table I on p. 267.

It was perhaps not irrational that the nobles who had been elected the 'Guardians' of Scotland decided to bring the succession dispute before Edward I for arbitration. He had been, after all, the brother-in-law and ally of their late King. However, Edward I was quick to see the opportunity offered by a situation which placed him in so advantageous a position. He demanded that the nobles who were desirous to defer to him as arbitrator should also defer to him as feudal superior. He was a King; they were not. It was entirely in accordance with the spirit of feudalism that they agreed.

Edward I's decision, after long deliberation, was in favour of John Balliol, from whom he demanded another acknowledgement of English overlordship in his new capacity as King of Scots. John Balliol was not a strong character yet, had he been twice the man he was, he had been manoeuvred into an almost impossible position. He could not refuse

² plenty.

Edward the homage which he had already received, without making a gesture of enmity which might not gain the support of a sufficient number of his nobility. Many Scottish nobles held lands in England which would be forfeited if they showed enmity to the English King.

In these unenviable circumstances, John Balliol was crowned King of Scots, at Scone on St Andrew's Day, 30 November 1292.

Edward I had already subjugated Wales, and he did not leave long in doubt his intention to do the same to Scotland. With a brutal assumption of superiority, calculated to provoke a man whose position demanded that he should be a ruler as well as a vassal, Edward goaded John Balliol to rebellion and at the same time prepared to conquer him and his kingdom.

Balliol's response was not altogether undignified. He formally repudiated his allegiance to the King of England, and in 1295 formed with France an alliance which was to be renewed so many times that it earned at last the name of the 'auld alliance', and formed an enduring affinity between Scotland and France.

The following year, however, Edward I brought a great army north, sacked Berwick with much bloodshed, and defeated Balliol in a battle near Dunbar. The disputed succession, which had split the Scottish nobility into Bruce and Balliol factions, ensured that John Balliol did not command the full support of the nobility in this battle. For this reason alone his defeat was almost inevitable, the more so as his opponent was one of the most distinguished soldiers of his age, with all the prestige he had won by the conquest of Wales to put fear into the hearts of those who mustered against him.

The short reign of John Balliol ended on 10 July 1296, when he was forced to abdicate and go south to captivity in the Tower of London. Later he was permitted to retire to France, where he died free but unregarded in 1313. Edward I took back with him to England the Crown of Scots and the Stone of Destiny, though legend persistently relates that the latter object was a supposititious stone. However, since he had demoted and imprisoned the King whom he had originally set up, and had removed the symbols of sovereignty, it must have appeared to him and to all observers that he had reduced Scotland to the condition of Wales.

Nonetheless, Wales had lacked the degree of internal unity and the sense of nationhood which in Scotland had been long developing. If

Edward presupposed a similarity of condition between the disunited Celtic principality of Wales and the fairly well integrated and feudalized kingdom of Scotland, that error was fatal to his ambitions.

In 1297 Edward I was occupied with an inconclusive campaign against Philip IV of France, who was determined to increase his authority over the French lands which Edward held as his vassal. Edward drew no analogy between the much resented activities of Philip IV and his own very much more extreme measures to assert his authority over Scotland. Between 1298 and 1307 he earned for himself the title 'Scotorum Malleus' – 'The Hammer of the Scots' – which is inscribed upon his tomb. 'Hammer', it may be observed, but not 'Conqueror'. In Scotland his memory is much hated, but perhaps he should receive a little backhanded gratitude, for his hammering forged the nationhood of Scotland into something which is probably indestructible.

Opposition to Edward I was initially led by Sir William Wallace, whose name in its earlier form 'le Waleys' means 'the Welshman'. Possibly he came of the old stock of Welsh-speaking Britons of Strathclyde; or possibly, since his family were vassals of the Stewarts, who came to Scotland from Shropshire in the reign of David I, in circumstances which will be related in the next chapter, the progenitor of the Wallaces was actually a Welshman. Whatever his origins, the resistance which he inspired against Edward's attempted conquest was essentially nationalistic.

In 1297 Wallace inflicted a totally unexpected defeat upon an English army, commanded during Edward's absence in France by the Earl of Surrey, at Stirling Bridge. The following year Edward returned to defeat the Scots once again at the Battle of Falkirk. But Wallace's victory had proved to his countrymen that the English were not invincible, and his naming the cause for which he fought 'the liberty of the kingdom' defined an idea which had come into existence before it had been given a form of words.

Many of the greater nobles, as feudatories of both the King of England and the King of Scots, faced in ti   years a conflict of personal loyalties which for a time stood in the way of their developing a sense of loyalty to the kingdom. Wallace, whose lower position in the feudal hierarchy enabled him to see the position in very much more clear-cut terms, emerged as the first exponent of a new sense of nationhood, of which Scotland soon became intensely and passionately aware.

From the deposition of John Balliol to the coronation of Robert the Bruce, a period of just on ten years, Scotland was without a King. During this time the 'Guardians' who attempted to defend the kingdom against Edward I described themselves as acting on behalf of 'the Community of the Realm of Scotland' (in other words the sum of the politically conscious free men of the kingdom), and declared that their allegiance was given to 'the Lion', that is, to the device of the lion rampant borne by the Kings of Scots. The idea had come into being that it was possible to give loyalty to a concept of impersonal sovereignty in the absence of a sovereign. This was a new concept in political thought, brought to definition in the Scottish Wars of Independence; a concept which has led at least one historian to claim for Scotland the title of 'first of the nations' ('nations' as opposed to 'kingdoms of Christendom').

The death of Wallace, who was captured and executed by the English as a traitor in 1305, strengthened the cause of Scottish Independence by giving it a martyr. Wallace was not a traitor, since he had given no allegiance to Edward I, but a prisoner of war.

After the martyr came the King. Some admirers of Robert the Bruce have made embarrassed attempts to explain away the vacillations of his early career. They need not. Robert the Bruce, like many members of his class, held lands in England and experienced the unavoidable conflict of loyalties. Furthermore, it was scarcely to be expected that he, whose family represented the rival claim, would have been a very willing supporter of so uninspiring a King as John Balliol. More than once Robert the Bruce made his submission to Edward I. His final decision to stake his all upon making good his claim to the Crown came as a result of his murderous quarrel with John 'the Red' Comyn, Lord of Badenoch, the nephew and supporter of Balliol, who had given his allegiance to Edward. Comyn's murder branded Bruce as the enemy of Edward, and left him no choice but the great gamble of asserting his claim to the Crown of Scots.

In the event, that gamble was gloriously justified, and he became not only a King but a great King; he not only saved Scotland from conquest, but re-established his country as a fully sovereign state.

His coronation took place, in the most inauspicious circumstances, in March 1306. He was indeed crowned in accordance with tradition, at Scone; but lacking both Crown and Stone of Destiny, he was placed on a makeshift throne and crowned with a golden 'coronella' hastily made for the occasion. Furthermore, the coronation was that of a fugitive, and after flight came years of guerilla warfare, during which King Robert won back the kingdom piecemeal from the English occupying forces.

King Robert was fortunate in one thing: in 1307 Edward I died. During his struggle to regain and consolidate his kingdom King Robert's opponent was not the formidable Hammer of the Scots, but his son Edward II, whose reign was largely occupied with domestic discord and civil strife. Edward II did indeed give his full attention to Scotland in 1314, when he marched north with an army of 20,000 men, only to be resoundingly defeated at the Battle of Bannockburn.

Bannockburn, as decisively as the long-ago Battle of Nechtansmere, freed Scotland from the imminent prospect of control from the south. Robert the Bruce, who immediately after his coronation had been scornfully referred to by the English as 'King Hob', was from the time of Bannockburn, in the words of a contemporary English chronicler, 'commonly called King of Scotland by all men, because he had acquired Scotland by force of arms'.

It was some years before the recovered independence of Scotland was officially recognized. In 1320 the nobility of Scotland sent a letter to Pope John XXII, on behalf of the Community of the Realm, declaring the King's achievement and stressing the reality of the situation. The letter has come to be called 'the Declaration of Arbroath', and it contains these words:

'To him [Robert] we are obliged and resolved to adhere on account both of his rights and of his merits as the man who has restored the people's safety and will defend their freedom. But if he should turn aside from the work he has begun, wishing to subject us or our kingdom to the King or people of England, we should at once set ourselves to expel him as the betrayer of his own rights and ours and would make another King capable of defending us.

'For so long as one hundred men remain we shall never submit under any conditions to the domination of the English. It is not for glory, riches or honours that we fight, but only for that liberty which no good man will abandon but with his life.'

The Declaration of Arbroath illustrated clearly enough that while Robert the Bruce was given the credit for having regained the independence of the kingdom, the concept of national sovereignty (as opposed to the King's personal position at the apex of a feudal system which might overlap the frontier of his own kingdom and underlie the frontier of another) had come into being as a permanent element in political thought.

England was forced to recognize the reality of the situation in 1328, the year following the death of Edward II, when the Treaty of Northampton, negotiated on behalf of the boy-King Edward III, acknowledged the title and sovereignty of Robert the Bruce and the full autonomy of Scotland. In 1329 the King of Scots died, having lived to see his life's work crowned with success.

By his first wife, Isabella of Mar, King Robert had no sons. His only daughter, Margery, married Walter the Stewart, the sixth hereditary High Steward of Scotland, by whom she had one son, Robert, who was recognized as the heir presumptive in 1318. Ultimately he became Robert II, the first King of the House of Stewart. In the meantime, however, Robert the Bruce had married as his second wife Elizabeth de Burgh, daughter of the Earl of Ulster; she bore him a son who succeeded at the age of five as David II.

Had Robert the Bruce lived longer certain wounds inflicted on the kingdom during the Wars of Independence, wounds which required the treatment of strong rule, might have been successfully healed. But a long minority with its concomitant troubles left those wounds untended to weaken the kingdom in the future.

The Western Isles, which had become subject to the Crown of Scots as recently as the reign of Alexander III, had enjoyed under the attenuated Norse overlordship a degree of independence which the nobility of the Isles relinquished unwillingly. Some of the chiefs had seen the advantage of giving their allegiance to the remote Kings of England rather than to Robert the Bruce, and some of the nobility of the north-west, the kindred of King Robert's murdered enemy the Red Comyn, had chosen the same course. King Robert possessed the strength, had he been granted the time, to continue the unifying work of Alexander III. He crushed the Comyn kindred by force of arms, and subsequently won both respect and support from the Isles and the north-west; but such respect and support was offered to King Robert personally, not to the Crown. During the minority of David II and the weak rule of his two successors the policy of separatism followed by some of the Western Isles chiefs was permitted to develop almost unchecked. In 1354 John of Islay of the clan MacDonald possessed sufficient power to arrogate to himself the title of Lord of the Isles, and the status almost of a King. During the same period the Highlands were scarcely less neglected, and the cultural separatism of the northwest which had always existed led gradually to the development of a dichotomy, at best suspicious and at worst inimical, between Highland and Lowland, which has existed ever since.

There would have been no necessity for the Celtic and Anglian cultures to have become mutually inimical had not the troubled relations of Scotland and England led the Kings of Scots to concentrate their power near the vulnerable frontier of the country, inevitably neglecting the Highlands, until in the sixteenth century the dwellers in the southeast could refer to their countrymen of the northwest, beyond the Highland Line, as 'the Wild Scots'. During the earlier Middle Ages Scotland, like other medieval kingdoms, had no capital. In the thirteenth century, while relations with England were amicable, the Kings of Scots had held their court at Perth, Abernethy or Inverness as frequently as at Stirling or Edinburgh. It was largely the strategic necessity of safeguarding the Border which fixed the centre of power ultimately at Edinburgh.

Trouble with England recurred after the death of Robert the Bruce. Edward, the son of John Balliol, attempted to recover his father's throne on the same terms, as the vassal of the King of England. With the support of old Balliol and Comyn partisans who had been disinherited of their Scottish lands by Robert the Bruce he was temporarily successful, and was crowned King of Scots, while David II was sent to France for safety. However, after a reign of only a few months, Edward Balliol was ignominiously driven from the country with 'one leg booted and the other naked'.

The expulsion of Edward Balliol was only the beginning of a long war to combat renewed English aggression and recover the country for David II. It seemed as though the work of Robert the Bruce had been undone. The Scots, however, had not lost their determination to enjoy 'the liberty of the kingdom', and during the 1330s Sir Andrew Moray of Bothwell, the 'Guardian', and Robert the Stewart the young heir presumptive, fought for it with a resolution which equalled that of their fathers' generation. By 1341, when Edward III had begun his country's involvement in the Hundred Years War with France, it was possible for David II to return.

David II has not received a good press. Perhaps, inevitably, he has been compared with his father to his detriment. In 1346, in support of his French allies, he led an invasion of England which resulted in his defeat and capture at Neville's Cross, after which he spent eleven years in English captivity before he was ransomed for the huge sum of 100,000 marks. By the Treaty of Northampton he had been married to Joan of the Tower, a sister of Edward III. His brother-in-law had attempted to reassert English overlordship, breaking that same treaty, and had attempted to supplant David II with his vassal Edward Balliol. Yet David remained on amicable terms with him, and would even have been willing to permit one of Edward's sons to inherit the throne of Scotland, subject to certain conditions safeguarding the independence of the kingdom.

For this reason it is natural enough that David II should have been accused of betraying his father's achievements. Recently, however, he has found some defenders, who have seen in his dissimulated friendship with Edward III a defence of his country conducted by a means less expensive than warfare. Certainly, while money for the ransom was collected little of it was paid, so that the finances of the Crown were built up, increasing the strength of the monarchy. Certainly the King extended his authority until it was said that 'nane durst well wythstand his will'. But, when he has been given the credit for these achievements, it must still be admitted that he was prepared to undo his father's work to the extent of advocating the succession of an English prince. That such an arrangement would have placed Scotland in a subordinate relationship to England, despite constitutional safeguards, cannot be doubted. Not surprisingly, David's proposal was unacceptable to the Community of the Realm, for whom the Declaration of Arbroath had spoken so eloquently.

The explanation of David II's policy lies in his own inability to produce an heir and in his enmity to his nephew Robert the Stewart. Robert's attitude was reciprocally inimical, naturally enough, since the birth of David had foiled him of his expected inheritance. He had fought for David loyally in the 1330s, preferring his cause to Edward

Balliol's; but basic resentment, and David's policy, caused an attrition of his loyalty in later years.

The years passed, and neither Joan of the Tower nor David's second Queen Margaret Logie produced a child. David II died in 1371, at the age of forty-six, to be succeeded by his nephew, who was eight years older than himself, and already an elderly, ailing man. Robert II became King of Scots fifty-three years after he had been recognized the heir presumptive of Robert the Bruce.

2
The Early Stewarts

Robert II: A tenderer heart might no man have
(Andrew of Wyntoun)

Robert III: The worst of Kings and the most miserable of
men
(Of himself)

Robert, Duke of Albany: He semyt to be a mychty King
(Andrew of Wyntoun)

The tragedy of *Macbeth*, Shakespeare's only play with a Scottish theme, was written in 1606 as a compliment to the Scottish sovereign who had recently succeeded to the English throne. Shakespeare found the story of Macbeth in Holinshed's *Chronicles*, his main source for the plots of his history plays. One of the principal characters in Holinshed's version of the story was 'Banquo, the Thane of Lochquhaber, of whom the house of the Stewards is descended, the which by order of lineage hath now for a long time enjoyed the Crown of Scotland, even till these our days.' (Holinshed died just over twenty years before the Union of Crowns.)

Shakespeare's dramatization of Holinshed's story of the meeting of Macbeth and Banquo with the three weird sisters, 'that is, as ye would say, the goddesses of destiny', is faithful to the original. To Banquo they said, in Holinshed's words:

'We promise greater benefits unto thee than unto him [i.e. Macbeth], for he shall reign indeed but with an unlucky end; neither shall he leave any issue behind him to succeed in his place, where contrarily thou indeed shall not reign at all, but of thee those shall be born which shall govern the Scottish kingdom by long order of continual descent.'

19

Shakespeare made good use of this promise further to compliment James VI and I, in the entirely fictitious scene in which Macbeth, having murdered Banquo but failed to kill his son Fleance, visits the weird sisters' cave to learn more secrets of the future. In the cave he is shown a vision of Banquo's kingly descendants, some carrying 'treble sceptres' symbolizing their sovereignty over three kingdoms: Scotland, England and Ireland. 'What,' cries Macbeth in horror, 'will the line stretch out to the crack of doom?' James VI and I was doubtless as gratified as he was intended to be by the reference to the great antiquity of the House of Stewart, and by the prognostications of an endlessly glorious future.

James was doubtless familiar with the story of his descent from Banquo, which most likely he would have read not in Holinshed, but in the Latin *Historia* of Hector Boece, published in 1526. Holinshed himself may have taken the story from Boece, or from John Bellenden's translation of the *Historia* which was published in 1530. Boece in turn probably derived his information concerning the Stewart pedigree from *The Stewartis Original*, a lost work by John Barbour, the author of the great epic poem *The Bruce*. It appears that Barbour traced the ancestry of the Stewarts back to Ninus, the legendary founder of Nineveh.

The most imaginative genealogies of the old Royal House of Scotland, which had ended in the male line with Alexander III, had traced the ancestry of the Kings of Scots beyond the mythical Fergus to a hero named Gaythelos who had married Scota, daughter of the Pharaoh who had ruled Egypt in the time of Moses. Their descendants, named Scots in honour of the matriarch, ultimately became the people of Dalriada. This myth, and the myth of the descent of the succeeding Royal House of Stewart from the probably equally mythical Ninus, was perhaps elaborated in the period following the Wars of Independence to stress that the origins of the Scots were entirely separate from those of the English, whose mythology, as set down by Geoffrey of Monmouth, claimed for the early British Kings descent from Brutus, great-grandson of Aeneas. The House of Stewart, Barbour would have his readers believe, was yet more ancient and illustrious.

Twentieth-century historians and their readers may smile at the absurdity of these genealogies. But, though the prestige-seeking inclusion of mythological heroes may be absurd, within the genealogies is enshrined in simplified form the story of the wanderings of some of those races which came at last to inhabit the island of Britain.

Since Barbour's work was lost, the information it contained is known only from references made to it by Andrew of Wyntoun, in his *Original Chronicle*. If Ninus was forgotten as the progenitor of the Stewarts Banquo was remembered, and held general credence until historians of the eighteenth century began to approach traditional history in a more critical spirit than that of their predecessors.

David Dalrymple, Lord Hailes, in his *Annals*, published in 1775, was the first historian to cast doubt on the Banquo legend. Then, in 1800, Andrew Stuart in the *Genealogical History of the Stewarts* mentioned Banquo, Fleance, Walter and Alan as Stewart ancestors of four successive generations, but added 'there is no satisfactory evidence concerning any of them'. It looked as though such evidence might be forthcoming when a Shropshire historian, E.W.Eyton, writing in 1858, discovered that Walter, the High Steward of Scotland in the reign of David I, who had been brought to Scotland by King David from Shropshire, was the son of Alan, Lord of Clun and Oswestry, who in turn was the son of a man named Flaald, Fléald or Flahault. Eyton reached the apparently obvious conclusion that Fleance and Flaald must have been the same person.

It was the research of Dr J.Horace Round, at the end of the nineteenth century, which gave Banquo the status of a fictitious or at least a legendary character, separated once more the identities of the legendary Fleance and the historical Flaald, and divulged the truth about the earliest known ancestors of the Royal House of Stewart.

In the late eleventh century, when Malcolm *Ceann Mor* ruled Scotland, Rhiwallon, Count of Dol, a town in Brittany south-west of St Malo, had a *dapifer* or steward whose name was Alan. The steward of Dol had three sons, Alan, Flaald and Rhiwallon. Alan succeeded his father as dapifer; Rhiwallon became a monk; Flaald's fortunes took him to Britain, and he settled at Monmouth in 1101 or 1102. Flaald's son Alan in turn had three sons, Jordan, William and Walter. Jordan succeeded his uncle Alan as dapifer of Dol; William became the ancestor of the English FitzAlans, later Earls of Arundel; Walter, the High Steward of David I, was the ancestor of the Royal House of Stewart.

Although the ancestors of the Stewarts owed their fortunes in

Scotland to the Normanizing King David I, they were not themselves Normans but Bretons, and the Bretons, like the Scots, were Celts. Breton knights were initially granted lands in England by King Henry I, to whom they had given aid against his brothers, William II (Rufus) and Robert, Duke of Normandy, with whom Henry was at war before he became King of England. Flaald, it appears, owed his lands on the Welsh Marches to the favour of Henry I, and it was at Henry's court that David I must have made the acquaintance of Flaald's grandsons William and Walter.

After the death of Henry I, King David espoused the cause of Henry's daughter the Empress Maud against the rival claimant to the English throne, her cousin Stephen of Blois. The lords and knights of Shropshire likewise supported Maud, and it was doubtless under these circumstances of alliance that Walter FitzAlan came increasingly to enjoy the favour of the King of Scots. In due course King David appointed Walter his High Steward.

The first holder of this newly created office in David's reign had been Ailred, who is better known in history as the chronicler Ailred of Rievaulx. He had been brought up at the Scottish court as the companion of David's son Earl Henry, who predeceased his father. In 1134 Ailred made a journey to York, and on his way home lodged at the great Yorkshire Abbey of Rievaulx. There he discovered a vocation to the monastic life, and accordingly he abandoned his promising career to become a Cistercian novice. Years later he recorded in his chronicle his love and respect for King David, 'now flourishing in hale old age, whom I have loved beyond all mortals'.

Ailred's place in the political life of Scotland was filled by Walter FitzAlan some time between 1134 and 1140. Walter also received from the King a grant of the barony of Renfrew, though it appears from a later charter that neither the office nor the barony was in the first place granted heritably. The heritable grants followed in the reign of King David's grandson, Malcolm IV.

In 1162, after his position at Renfrew had been secured by the grant of King Malcolm, Walter the High Steward brought from the priory of Wenlock in Shropshire a colony of Cluniac monks, whom he established beside the existing church of St Mary and St James on the King's Inch near Renfrew. A few years later he transferred them to Paisley, where he founded the Abbey 'for the souls of King Henry of England,

King David and King Malcolm', an endowment which provides a perfect illustration of the trans-national nature of a feudal noble's loyalties.

In 1177 Walter died, leaving his estates and office to his son, Alan FitzWalter, who in 1204 was succeeded by his son Walter FitzAlan, who died in 1246. The fourth High Steward, Alexander, had command of the Scottish army under King Alexander III at the Battle of Largs in 1263, which broke the Norse power in the Western Isles. James, the fifth High Steward, followed the fortunes of Robert the Bruce in the Wars of Independence. He married Cecilia, daughter of Patrick, Earl of Dunbar and March, and their son was the sixth High Steward, Walter 'the Stewart', who married Margery, daughter of Robert the Bruce. Their son, Robert the Stewart, as previously recounted, became King of Scots on the death of David II, in 1371.

While the kingdom of Scots progressed towards nationhood the family of the High Stewards progressed towards kingship. Throughout the early Middle Ages theirs was a history which could have been paralleled by that of many another noble family; a history of high office honourably occupied, of increasing reputation gained by fighting on the winning side, of the acquisition of more estates and of greater wealth and power. From the reign of Malcolm IV the family of the High Stewards had ranked among the greatest of the Scottish nobility, and the marriage of King Robert's daughter to Walter the Stewart was no *mésalliance*.

Despite the prominent position of the family there is little personal information, still less anecdote, concerning any individual earlier than Walter the Stewart. Walter was born in 1292. He appears in the pages of Barbour's *The Bruce* as a brave and generally admired young man, who was knighted on the morning of the Battle of Bannockburn by King Robert himself. In that battle he shared with the King's great captain 'the good' Sir James Douglas the command of one of the four Scottish divisions. Barbour wrote, in a dramatic 'historic future':

> *The lad is young, but none the less*
> *Shall bear himself with such prowess*
> *And show such manliness in war*
> *That tutelage he'll need no more.*

After Bannockburn he married Margery Bruce, who died within a year after having been thrown from her horse while heavily pregnant,

23

though her child survived the tragic accident. Walter himself won great renown by his defence of Berwick against the English in 1319; but he died in 1326 at the age of thirty-four. By this time his son Robert, named heir presumptive in 1318, had been displaced from his position in the succession by the King's late-born son David.

The early career of Robert the Stewart has been the subject of much controversy. Was he a loyal subject of David II, or was he a time-server, always waiting upon the opportunity which might give him the Crown? The answer to these questions is not a simple one. Certainly he showed loyalty while David was in his safe exile in France. In 1346 he accompanied King David on the invasion of England which resulted in the defeat of Neville's Cross. Robert had command of the left wing of the army, which, after the defeat, he managed to withdraw in good order. His action has been subject to differing interpretations: either he behaved as a competent and responsible soldier, or he treacherously deserted his King, leaving him to be taken prisoner. Which is the correct interpretation cannot be known, and either, if presented as un-qualified fact, merely reflects the personal opinion of the historian.

Robert acted as Regent during King David's captivity in England. He seems to have attempted to serve his country's best interests during a very difficult period, and to have done nothing to impede the release of the King, even though it would end his own tenure of power. After David's return his pro-English policy, whatever justifications can be found for it, could not have been expected to commend itself to Robert, who was heir presumptive only for so long as David II remained child-less and for so long as the succession of an English prince remained unacceptable to his people.

In 1362 David's first wife died, and he planned to marry his mis-tress, Margaret Logie. Robert and his sons headed a half-hearted rebellion which was easily crushed. In April 1363 David made Margaret Logie his Queen, and forced Robert to take a renewed oath of fealty to him.

David doubtless hoped that his new Queen would bear him a son. But, whether she did so or not, the rebellion had increased his dislike of his heir presumptive and stiffened his resolve to exclude him from the succession by whatever means available. Therefore, either as an in-terim measure or as a *pis aller*, in March 1363 King David presented to the Scottish Parliament his proposals for an English succession. The greatest bait which he had to offer was the automatic cancellation of the residue (still by far the greater part) of his ransom, if the proposals were accepted.

The Scottish Parliament was a unicameral assembly consisting of representatives of the Three Estates: nobility, clergy and burgesses. It was the prosperity of the burgesses which had won them the right to be consulted in Parliament; their presence and consent were especially necessary in the business of arranging the taxation to raise the ransom payments. This fact is of some significance, since the Parliament steadfastly rejected the King's proposals, preferring to bear the burden of the ransom and leave Robert's position unimpaired.

There is little doubt that hope long deferred, desire for the Crown and fear lest it should be snatched from him at last, led Robert the Stewart into an equivocal position. It is only fair to add that for most of the reign he seems to have been unenthusiastically loyal to David; and that in the rebellion of 1363 his two elder sons, looking ambitiously to the future, played a more active part than he did.

John of Fordun, writing of Robert in his youth, described him as 'tall and robust, modest, liberal, gay and courteous; and for the innate sweetness of his disposition generally beloved by true-hearted Scotsmen', a pleasant description, though couched in conventional terms. Andrew of Wyntoun, writing of him in later life, said simply, 'a tenderer heart might no man have'. As an illustration of this quality Hector Boece recounted how 'he would not suffer the people to sustain the damage done to them through stamping down of their corn by the multitude of people that was at his coronation, but paid the same with large money'. Such kindly impulses naturally endeared him to his people. Scotland acquired an amiable, elderly King, well-liked for the very qualities of character which would least aid him in his task of governing.

Robert II was crowned at Scone on 26 March 1371. He had many problems to face. Not least was that of establishing the succession, which was complicated by his matrimonial history. In 1336 Robert had married Elizabethan Mure of Rowallan, to whom he was related within the 'forbidden degrees' of kinship, a situation which demanded that a papal dispensation be obtained before the marriage could be considered lawful. The forbidden degrees were not only those which are still generally recognized as a bar to marriage; they were many and ramifying, and included distant connections by marriage and god-parentship. It is possible that Robert the Stewart and Elizabeth Mure may have been unaware of an existing connection, for as heir presumptive Robert would not have wished to risk the position of his children in the succession, by permitting them to be born in unlawful wedlock. As it was, four sons were born in 'canonical incest', and were therefore illegitimate. The situation was regularized in 1347, possibly upon discovery of the forbidden degrees connection, when Robert tardily obtained the necessary papal dispensation, which both regularized the marriage and legitimatized the children. After the death of Elizabeth Mure Robert married a second wife, Euphemia of Ross, by whom he had two sons. It was arguable that these younger children, born in irreproachable circumstances, had a better claim to the succession than the children of Elizabeth Mure.

Robert II, however, stood by the rights of his firstborn and the efficacy of the papal dispensation to establish them. After his coronation a declaration was issued that the heir to the throne was the King's eldest son, John, Earl of Carrick. This declaration incidentally established in Scottish law the principle that children are legitimatized by the subsequent marriage of their parents.

Two years later the succession was laid down in greater detail, with the evident intention of obviating future disputes. It was declared again that the Crown should pass to John, Earl of Carrick and his heirs male. If that line should fail, it should pass to his brother Robert, Earl of Fife and his heirs male (Walter, the King's second son, being already dead), and if that line should fail to Alexander, Lord of Badenoch, and his heirs male. Only if all these lines should fail was the Crown to pass to David, Earl of Strathearn, the King's elder son by Euphemia of Ross, and his heirs male, and if that line should fail, to the younger son Walter, later Earl of Athol.

These provisions set out strictly and elaborately the principle of primogeniture, which had been established in Scotland with great firmness by David I, who had nominated his son Earl Henry his successor, and upon Henry's death had insisted that the succession should pass to his grandson, Malcolm IV. Thereafter the rule had been firmly adhered to until Robert the Bruce, representative of a junior line, had taken the place of John Balliol. King Robert himself, anxious to avoid the weakening of the national position which could result from the accession of a Queen, obtained the consent of his daughter Margery that his brother Edward Bruce and his heirs should have precedence over Margery in the succession. But upon the death of Edward Bruce without issue King Robert reverted to the principle of strict primogeniture. Under this principle Robert II had ultimately succeeded, and he was anxious to assert it on behalf of his eldest son.

The Stewarts, unfortunate in many other respects, were fortunate in being able to maintain the line of succession in unbroken primogeniture in the male line until the birth of Mary, Queen of Scots in 1542. Robert II's provisions specifically excluded the succession of an heiress, who was to be passed over in favour of the nearest heir male. However, by 1542 the Royal House was so long and firmly established that the accession of Mary was accepted without question.

The succession problem was perhaps the only problem to which Robert II found a firm solution; difficult as it was, the economic condition of Scotland, and the political situation, domestic and foreign, presented greater difficulties still.

The country was exhausted and impoverished by the long and expensive struggle of the Wars of Independence, and the reign of David II had not provided the conditions necessary for recovery. David himself had spent two long periods out of the country, and even when he was in it his presence had not automatically brought the return of peaceful conditions. He had, indeed, begun to enforce respect for his authority before the end of his reign, but he had not lived long enough to consolidate his achievement.

The collection and partial non-delivery of the ransom payments had served to build up his own finances, but only at the cost of draining yet further the resources of his subjects. In another effort to ameliorate the impoverished condition of the Crown, David had depreciated the currency by increasing the number of pennies minted from the pound of silver from 252 to 352. The result of the depreciation was that the value of the pound Scots dropped to about one quarter that of the English pound, which adversely affected national prestige as well as money transactions.

There were other and profounder causes of economic troubles. David's reign had seen two outbreaks of the Black Death, in 1349–50 and in 1361–2. Since Scotland was sparsely populated and the towns were small and scattered, the loss of population was probably proportionately much less than in more densely populated parts of Europe. Loss and distress were certainly experienced, but the effect of the Black Death was probably felt in Scotland most keenly in terms of economic hardship resulting from a drop in demand for Scotland's exports, which were her natural products: wool, hides, salted fish and pearls.

Twentieth-century experience has made familiar the fact that wars are followed by periods of social unrest, of casual violence and disregard for law. Such conditions were experienced in Scotland in the period following the Wars of Independence. To attain the related objects of peace and prosperity was the task which Robert II attempted, but the problems were too complex for his failing energy, too great for his unsure authority. Success eluded him.

As King of Scots Robert II possessed theoretical prestige; the King was the symbol of Scotland's nationhood. Robert II was the hundredth successor of Fergus Mor mac Erc, the latest embodiment of an institution of awesome antiquity. But the strength of monarchy as an institution has a perpetually renewed dependence upon the strength of character of the King. A strong King creates a strong monarchy, but a weak successor speedily dissipates that strength. David II could not be classified as a strong King, though he had shown himself fairly astute in some respects. His successor had nothing much to build upon, and few resources with which to build at all. He suffered from the disadvantages of being fifty-four years old, at a period in which the rigours of life allowed few men the expectation of reaching a healthy old age, and of having contracted a complaint which caused him to have 'red, bleared eyes, the colour of sandal-wood, which showed him to be no valiant man, but one who would rather remain at home than march to the field'.

His peaceable nature was not shared by the mass of his subjects; long necessity had made the Scots a martial people. In 1369 a fourteen-year truce with England had been concluded, but unofficial warfare continued in spite of it. Robert II endeavoured to strengthen Scotland's position, in the manner which had already become traditional, by renewing the alliance with France in 1371. France was once again on the offensive against England, for Edward III's victorious period was now past; the warrior King was an old man with only six more years to live.

In 1385 a French force of one thousand knights, commanded by the

Admiral of France, Jean de Vienne, was sent to Scotland. The French knights were eager for a full-scale invasion of England and hopeful of winning chivalric glory. They were disgusted to discover that their allies expected them to participate in the guerilla warfare by which the Scots habitually gained their best successes against the English. The arrival of Vienne's force may indeed have done more harm than good, since it provoked an English invasion led by Richard II. The second Earl of Douglas restrained Vienne from offering battle, while the English King burnt the Abbeys of Melrose, Dryburgh, Newbattle and Holyrood, and devastated the town of Edinburgh. Richard II's resources were sufficient to permit his marching north to spread destruction, but insufficient to permit his attempting conquest in the manner of Edward III, much less of Edward I. The Scots watched him retire, and cleared out the English occupying force which had held Teviotdale since the days of Edward Balliol.

The reign of Robert II has been recounted frequently enough as a narrative of Border episodes. The endemic condition of frontier strife provided many dramatic incidents, such as the 'Battle of Otterburn' in 1388, which was a clash between the Douglases and the Percys of Northumberland, not an international battle, and which might not have been remembered any more than a dozen other such clashes had it not inspired two memorable ballads. In one of them the Earl of Douglas, who won the battle and met his death, is made to say

> *But I have dreamed a dreary dream*
> *Beyond the Isle of Skye;*
> *I saw a dead man win a fight,*
> *And I think that man was I.*

Fine poetry has bestowed immortality on an incident of little consequence.

What was of consequence was the internal condition of Scotland. In forthright words of contemporary complaint, the kingdom was 'nocht governit', and the reason was the tenuous hold upon affairs maintained by the ailing King. In 1384 Robert II gave his heir John, Earl of Carrick full authority to enforce the law 'everywhere throughout the realm', because he himself was too enfeebled to travel around his kingdom as energetically as the disturbed conditions demanded. In 1388, however, the Earl of Carrick was kicked by a horse, and received an injury from which he never fully recovered. He in turn deputed his authority to his next brother, Robert, Earl of Fife, who was to dominate the Scottish political scene for the next thirty years.

In 1390 Robert II died, and the semi-invalid John of Carrick succeeded him. The name John was considered ill-omened for a King: the reigns of John of England, John Balliol and John of France, who had been captured by the English at the Battle of Poitiers, offered sufficient basis for such a superstition. Furthermore, John Balliol had reigned as the vassal of the King of England. What was his status as King of Scots? Should John of Carrick be styled John I or John II? The new King solved the problem by assuming the name of Robert III.

The change of name, however, did not serve to change the omens. The reign was inaugurated by an act of violence which set the pattern for much that was to follow. The King's brother Alexander, Lord of Badenoch, had won for himself by his ruthlessness and savagery the name of 'The Wolf of Badenoch'. The Bishop of Moray ventured to reproach him for his violent deeds, whereupon he burnt down the Bishop's Cathedral of Elgin, shortly before the coronation of his brother. Robert III obliged Alexander to perform a public penance; but it was generally recognized that the punishment in no way paid for the crime. It was small wonder that the chronicler of the *Register of Moray* wrote:

> 'In those days there was no law in Scotland, but he who was stronger oppressed him who was weaker, and the whole kingdom was a den of thieves; murders, herschips [ravagings] and fireraising, and all other misdeeds remained unpunished; and justice, as if outlawed, lay in exile outwith the bounds of the kingdom.'

One of the most notorious scenes of slaughter of the whole reign, the 'Battle of the Clans' in 1396, was in fact an attempt to settle a Highland feud by judicial combat. The Exchequer Rolls record that £14 2s 11d was spent on building a wooden enclosure for 'sexaginta personarum pugnacium in Insula de Perth' – sixty persons fighting upon the Inch of Perth. The thirty champions from each clan met in mortal combat, presided over by Robert III, who ended the combat by casting down his baton when only twelve men survived. Contemporary chroniclers were divided in their opinions as to whether the slaughter ended the feud or not.

At the beginning of the reign Robert III had retained his brother the Earl of Fife in office as Governor of the Realm. In 1393, however, he had decided to take the government into his own hands, and at the time of the Battle of the Clans he was still vainly attempting to keep order. In 1399 he decided to abrogate his authority once more, and this time he appointed as his deputy his elder son David, to whom he gave the title of Duke of Rothesay and the style of Lieutenant of the Kingdom. The Earl of Fife was compensated for his loss of status with the title of Duke of Albany.

The rest of the reign passed in a power struggle between Rothesay and Albany, in which the King was little more than a helpless spectator. Perhaps the most unhappy aspect of Robert III's situation was his own awareness of failure. He is recorded as having told his Queen that she need give him no epitaph other than 'Here lies the worst of Kings and the most miserable of men'. The Queen to whom he uttered this painful *cri du cœur* was Annabella Drummond, the niece of David II's second Queen Margaret Logie. She was a strong-minded woman who endeavoured in the absence of any real monarchical authority to strengthen the position of her son the Duke of Rothesay as best she could.

The Queen had no easy task, for Rothesay was an extraordinarily insouciant young man, and one who made enemies with utter disregard for his own future, or for the ambitious enmity of his uncle Albany. Rothesay had been appointed Lieutenant of the Kingdom initially for a period of three years, and throughout those years he acquitted himself with discredit. In 1401 he refused to resign his office, and the King was persuaded to order his arrest. It seems most likely that the instigator of the arrest was Albany, for Rothesay was placed in his custody. The unfortunate young man had no friend, since his mother had recently died and his father's mind had been turned against him. In 1402 he himself died, in Albany's castle of Falkland.

If Rothesay died from natural causes it was unfortunate but inevitable that Albany's reputation suffered; if, on the other hand, Albany was unscrupulous enough to murder him, he was also strong enough to get away with it. He was indeed obliged to appear for interrogation before a General Council which met two months after Rothesay's death, but the official verdict was that Rothesay had 'departed this life by divine providence and not otherwise'. Ugly rumours circulated that he had been starved to death, but Albany, having been exonerated, was able to ignore them. More than that, he stepped into Rothesay's place and assumed the title of Governor of the Realm.

Albany was, moreover, the heir presumptive. Between him and the succession was his younger nephew, the King's younger son, Prince James, who had been born in 1394. It is possible that at the time of Rothesay's death Robert III did not suspect Albany of having caused it, or of having designs upon the throne. Perhaps the suspicion grew gradually in his mind, or was suggested to him, for in 1406, when he himself was greatly enfeebled and Albany's power had commensurately grown, Robert decided to send his surviving son to France.

James spent a month on the Bass Rock in the early part of the year, awaiting a vessel which would take him to safety. In March he boarded a ship of Danzig, named the *Maryenknyght*, and on the 22nd of the month the ship was seized by English pirates off Flamborough Head. A truce was in force between Scotland and England at the time, but pirates had little regard for truces; neither, as it turned out, had Henry IV of England, when so great a prize as the Prince of Scotland was brought before him. Henry is said to have remarked that the King of Scots had no need to send his son to France to learn French, he could learn it equally well at the court of England. James was imprisoned in the Tower of London, and news of his capture may have added one last sorrow to the many which had afflicted 'the most miserable of men'. Robert III died on 4 April.

The Scottish Parliament recognized the imprisoned Prince as King James I, but he was too valuable a prisoner to be relinquished readily. Besides, his captivity ministered admirably to Albany's ambition. As Governor Albany assumed a quasi-royal style. A fine Great Seal was struck for him which bore the inscription 'Sigillum Roberti ducis Albanie Gubernatoris Scocie' – 'The Seal of Robert Duke of Albany Governor of Scotland' – and an image of himself enthroned, flanked by his own arms and the arms of the kingdom, holding in his right hand the Sword of State, and wearing a chain-like coronet, symbolic perhaps of the bonds of duty. Documents issued under this Great Seal were issued in the name of the Governor and not of the King, and dated by the year of the Governorship and not of the reign. Furthermore, Albany was wont to refer to 'his' subjects, not those of the King.

In 1409 he made a 'band' or bond of mutual support with the fourth

Earl of Douglas, which contained the words 'and if it happens the said Lord the Duke [of Albany] to grow in time to come to the estate of King, this band, as touching even [i.e. equal] fellowship and estate shall expire from thenceforth, but all kindness and friendship shall be kept between them in time to come'.

These words betray clearly enough the direction of Albany's ambitions; but he did not pursue them with direct efforts to supplant the King. His policy seems rather to have been one of patience and passivity; one of hoping that he might 'grow' to the estate of King rather than have need to seize the Crown. As a politician he showed a certain astuteness. Henry IV of England held a valuable pawn in the captive King of Scots; but Henry himself wore his crown uneasily, for he had supplanted and imprisoned his cousin Richard II, who had subsequently died in captivity. Almost equally damaging to Henry were tales of his murder and rumours of his escape. At Stirling Albany entertained a guest who was treated with royal honours: some men scornfully called him 'the mammet' – the scarecrow – but the Governor chose to regard him as the late King of England.

Andrew of Wyntoun wrote respectfully of Albany, 'he semyt to be a mychty King'. Had he indeed been king he could well have been mighty; but since he lacked the prestige of kingship he lacked the means to enhance his authority.

'If,' one chronicler commented, 'any enormities perchance were committed in the realm by the powerful, he patiently temporized, knowing how to reform them prudently enough at an opportune time.' He temporized with skill, awaiting the opportune time, and making no attempt to redeem the young King from his English captivity.

In the course of Albany's governorship many enormities were committed in the realm, perhaps the most memorable being a bloody battle long remembered as 'Red Harlaw', fought near Aberdeen in 1411 between Donald, Lord of the Isles, who was Albany's nephew (the son of his sister Margaret by her husband John, Lord of the Isles), and Alexander Stewart, Earl of Mar, also Albany's nephew (the son of his brother 'The Wolf of Badenoch'). The occasion of the battle was a dispute concerning the earldom of Ross, claimed by the Lord of the Isles; it was not, as it has often been called, a clash between the Highland and Lowland cultures. Its true significance is perhaps that it illustrates the waning of the supreme authority: even in the reign of

Robert III a great dispute could be submitted to judicial combat, but under Albany's governorship the solution was private war.

In 1413 Henry IV died, and was succeeded by his son Henry V, the last of England's spectacular warrior Kings who attempted the conquest of France. Henry V was desirous to obtain the neutrality of Scotland, for which he might well have used the release of the King as a bargaining counter. In his negotiations with Henry V, Albany showed his hand more clearly than he had done before. His own son Murdoch had been a prisoner in England since 1402; in 1416 Albany ransomed him for £10,000, leaving the King still a prisoner.

The release of Murdoch, however, did not secure the neutrality of the Scots. Albany's younger son, John, Earl of Buchan, took a force of 6,000 or 7,000 men to France in 1419, and defeated the English at the Battle of Baugé in 1421. The following year Henry V died, and the Regency Council which took over the government of England on behalf of the infant King Henry VI was even more eager than Henry V had been to prevent the Scots from fighting for the enemy. Accordingly, negotiations were opened upon these terms for the release of King James I.

In the meantime the Duke of Albany had died in 1420. He was eighty years old, and had retained a vigour of mind and body which neither his father Robert II nor his brother Robert III had possessed when each in turn had succeeded to the throne in his middle fifties. Albany was succeeded both in his dukedom and in his governorship by his son, the recently ransomed Murdoch.

Murdoch lacked the political astuteness of his father. In his dealings with the nobility of Scotland he showed an unhappy blend of arrogance and weakness. His attempts to assert authority were greeted with contempt. How completely would-be authority was ignored was illustrated in 1422, when only £50 out of a total of £1,150 collected from the customs of Edinburgh reached the Governor's exchequer. This was but one example of a widespread occurrence. Financial failure was probably the most basic cause of the collapse of Murdoch's regime.

Lawlessness and self-seeking were not, however, characteristic of the nobility of Scotland as a whole. The Earl of Douglas, whose power had been illustrated by the 'band' he had signed with the old Duke of Albany in 1409, had been responsible for the pillaging of the customs; but naturally enough not all the nobility wished to see one of their number able to act in a fashion so unrestrained. The rule of tooth and claw benefits only the strongest; those whose teeth and claws do not permit them to prevail react by demanding protection. Under these circumstances the return of the King came greatly to be desired. In December 1423 his release was at last arranged, and he returned to his kingdom in the spring of the following year.

3
James I,
1406–1437

A King such as Scotland had never yet had
(*Scotland the Nation*, Rosaline Masson)

THE CAPTIVE

Hard is myn aventure
(*The Kingis Quair*, James I)

James I, though not the founder of the Royal House of Stewart, was the founder of the greatness of that House; yet the beginning of his reign, like the beginning of the dynasty, was inauspicious. He became King of Scots a few days after his capture by the English pirates, and he remained a prisoner in England for eighteen years. He was approaching the age of thirty when he returned at last to his kingdom.

He was born in the later part of the month of July 1394, probably on the 25th, the feast of St James the Great. Little is known of his childhood, except that he was created Earl of Carrick in 1404, and that his education was entrusted to Henry Wardlaw, Bishop of St Andrews, a learned and statesmanlike prelate, whose excellent influence he was permitted to enjoy for two years before his despatch to France and his capture at sea.

At least educationally the capture of James was not disastrous, and King Henry's jibe concerning the relative educational facilities of the French and English courts was true enough. The reputation of the Lancastrian court as a centre of culture has suffered through its having been compared, to its detriment, with the brilliant and civilized court of Richard II. But the court of England was still an excellent training ground for an aspiring and teachable prince, and James was a royal captive, honourably entertained, not an ill-used prisoner.

36

At first, indeed, James and his retinue were lodged in the Tower of London, which was both royal residence and state prison; but subsequently James was permitted to share in the life of the court, under moderate restraints. From time to time he was taken back to the Tower, usually at moments of political instability; but at other times he resided at the royal castles of Windsor or Nottingham, and during the later part of his captivity, for a time at Pevensey.

He was taught horsemanship, swordplay, and archery, the 'gentlemanlie activity' which was considered both appropriate and necessary for him. He also practised wrestling and throwing the hammer. Captivity, even the relatively mild captivity imposed by Henry IV, did not give James the scope that he might have wished for the enjoyment of outdoor sports and the practice of knightly skills. He was vigorous and athletic, and, as his later life illustrated, full of restless energy. Perhaps the restraints upon his freedom made him a more apt scholar than he might otherwise have been, by forcing him to seek a mental outlet for his energy when a physical one was denied him.

It is possible, despite King Henry's remark on the subject, that James had learnt French in his early childhood. Both his parents knew the language. Indeed, a letter survives written in French by his mother Queen Annabella to Richard II, announcing James's birth. However, if he had not learnt French in Scotland, assuredly he would have learnt it in England, where it was still the language of the court, though English, gaining ground as a literary language and lately made fashionable by Chaucer, was rapidly superseding it.

James learnt Latin, which was still and for a long time was to remain the common language of European culture, of religion, and of much diplomacy. He retained, as some of his correspondence and his poetry proves, the language of his youth, the northern dialect of English which may now conveniently be termed 'Scots'. The Lowland Scots still considered that they spoke 'Ynglis' and the Highlanders 'Scottis'. It was the late-fifteenth-century poet William Dunbar who referred to the Gaelic speech of the Highlanders as 'Erse', and Gavin Douglas who followed in the early sixteenth century by calling the Lowland speech 'Scottis'. By the beginning of the fifteenth century, however, Scots had come into its own as a language distinct from the English of the time. James I's use of it was automatically fostered by the Scottish household which surrounded him throughout the years he spent in

England, and by the many visitors from Scotland who came and went with increasing frequency as the years passed and James worked more and more earnestly to obtain his freedom.

James's education had other aspects than the basic acquisition of languages. His correspondence, either because he lacked a confidential secretary, or because he desired secrecy, was written with his own hand, in exquisitely beautiful handwriting, legible and modestly decorated. He had been taught the art of speaking well, and was 'so good an orator that nothing might be more artificial than that which he spake'. 'Artificial' denotes the product of artistry; oratory was an art to be cultivated by a King for purposes of diplomacy.

Knightly pastimes, languages, and the allied arts of writing and speaking with eloquence and effect were the practical aspects of his education. For his pleasure James studied music, and a contemporary chronicler set on record that he played the harp and sang 'like another Orpheus'. All his life he must have taken pleasure in poetry, for he became one of the most distinguished of the Scottish courtly poets. When he returned to his kingdom, his pleasure in literature and delight in making music were looked upon with approval as 'honest solaces of grete pleasance and disporte', since he was sufficiently a man of action for them to carry no stigma of dilettantism.

From 1412, when he reached the age of eighteen, the regaining of his freedom and his kingdom became the main purpose of James's life. It had become obvious to him that the Duke of Albany had little interest in redeeming him from his captivity, and he began to write urging him to do so, 'that . . . we be nouch send to sek remede of our deliverans otherqware in tyme to cum'. At the same time he attempted to implement this threat of seeking 'otherqware' by negotiating with the powerful Douglas family to assist him. To one of them he wrote 'the delay of our hamecome standis alanely in thaim that sowlde persue for us'. Albany made no move. Possibly, as James's biographer E.W.M. Balfour-Melville has suggested, James 'by showing the promise of a capable personality, only made Albany the more anxious to keep him out of Scotland'. Doubly so, since he had begun to blame Albany for that very reason.

From the confines of the English court James attempted to participate in the affairs of his country as best he could.

James was, of course, legally the King of Scots, since he had been recognized by Parliament after his father's death. As a captive it was impossible for him to exercise sovereign powers; but he made an occasional gesture to illustrate that at least he possessed sovereign rights.

At the end of November 1412 he issued letters confirming Sir William Douglas of Drumlanrig and his brother Archibald in their lands of Drumlanrig, Hawick, Selkirk and Cavers. The letters were sealed with his personal signet, but contained his undertaking that he would issue them under the Great Seal 'in tym to come', in other words, when he returned to his kingdom.

He associated himself with Bishop Wardlaw's foundation of the University of St Andrews, adding his name to the petition which was sent to the Avignonese Pope Benedict XIII for a bull of foundation. The University was founded at the beginning of 1412, though the Papal bull did not arrive until 1414.

That same year the Council of Constance met to attempt to heal the Papals Schism, which had lasted almost forty years, and greatly weakened the moral prestige and the political influence of the Papacy. For political reasons England had acknowledged the Roman Popes and Scotland had joined with France in acknowledging the Avignonese Popes. The Council of Constance found a solution to the problem in 1417, by displacing the existing pontiffs and electing a new and truly universal head of the Church, Oddo Colonna, who assumed the name of Martin V.

The Duke of Albany remained obdurately loyal to Benedict XIII, even though the latter was reduced to taking refuge in a fortress in Aragon. James, who combined intense orthodoxy with a strong sense of political advantage, offered his obedience to Martin V. No doubt he was aware of the potential power of his gesture to weaken Albany's position and strengthen his own. However, in 1418 the new University of St Andrews, more orthodox than its patron, adhered to the new Pope, and the following year the Duke of Albany, whose position as the only remaining head of state to support the anti-Pope could be regarded as schismatic, reluctantly gave Martin V the obedience of Scotland. James's politic gesture may not have been wholly wasted; but he was still a prisoner.

In their orthodoxy James and Albany had one thing, possibly the only thing, in common. In praise of Albany, Andrew of Wyntoun wrote:

He was a constante Catholyk
All lollaris he laythit and herrotyk.

In 1407 he burnt James Resby, an English Lollard, at Perth, an act
which his royal nephew would have considered praiseworthy, since he
himself was to burn a heretic at St Andrews in 1433.

In England James had ample opportunity to study the obverse and
reverse of religion, orthodoxy and heresy; for Lollardry flourished in
the reigns of Henry IV and Henry V, and the government was ruthless
in enforcing religious conformity.

John Wycliffe, reformer and translator of the Scriptures, founded in
the fourteenth century an informal missionary order of Poor Priests;
but his followers, lacking the exacting discipline of their Franciscan
and Dominican predecessors, developed a religious and political
radicalism undreamed of by their founder.

The Lollards, as they were popularly named, extended the holy
poverty of the Franciscans to a denial of private rights of property.
They advocated sexual communism, which, as Agnes Mure Mackenzie
rightly observed, has 'a quite remarkable habit of invading the creeds of
unbalanced enthusiasts'. They denounced the irreligious lives of many
churchmen, and argued that no man could be Pope or priest unless he
led a holy life. Furthermore, those of them who admitted the per-
missibility of ownership argued that the possession of material goods
was, or should be, dependent upon 'grace'. When they advocated such
disruptive, possibly explosive, doctrines, it was small wonder that the
Lollards were 'laythit' by the Duke of Albany and by the kings of
England.

Henry IV had inaugurated his reign by passing the statute *De
Heretico Comburendo*, and his son Henry V followed his example as a
ruthless persecutor of heretics. He was called 'the most virtuous and
wise of all Christian princes who reigned in his time', and there is no
reason to suppose that as far as his religious attitudes were concerned
James I thought otherwise of him. His political attitudes were another
matter.

Henry IV died in 1413. In character he seems to have been not unlike Shakespeare's Bolingbroke: a victorious pragmatist, and a man
with a bad conscience. His bad conscience concerning the long detention of the King of Scots showed itself towards the end of his life in

a 'graciousness' which led James to hope that he had fair expectations of release. Henry IV is even said to have urged his son, on his deathbed, to release the prisoner without demanding any payment. But Henry V had no intention of so doing, and his accession indeed had a detrimental effect upon James's situation. On the day of Henry IV's death both James and his cousin Murdoch, who it will be remembered had endured an even longer captivity, were sent to the Tower. There they experienced conditions both of hardship and neglect. James, suffered the humiliation of being unable to maintain a decently kingly wardrobe. Murdoch's condition, it appears, was even worse; for Humphrey, Duke of Gloucester, in his capacity as Chamberlain, wrote to the King his brother to complain that whereas in the late King's time Murdoch's bedding used to have 'change convenable' it was now two years since the sheets had been changed.

That year, 1415, James was removed from the Tower again, and sent to Pevensey Castle, under the care of Sir John Pelham, who was to receive £700 a year for his maintenance. Meanwhile, Murdoch's release was negotiated, and the following year he returned to Scotland, a free man who was soon referred to by his father as 'our lieutenant'. Murdoch's release must have made James's captivity doubly bitter, and his resentment against Albany must have been increased by the realization that he was associating his son with himself in the work of government in the manner of a King and his heir. The contrast between Albany's obvious aspirations and his own helplessness might well have brought James pardonably near to despair.

1415 was the year of Henry V's great victory of Agincourt. Upon his return to England he sent James back to the Tower, where he was joined by another royal prisoner, Charles of Orleans, who had been taken at Agincourt and was to remain a prisoner in England for twenty-five years.

If Charles of Orleans, himself a distinguished poet, was not a direct literary influence upon James as a poet, at least he was probably a stimulating and congenial companion in captivity. Their common misfortunes and shared pleasure in literature would have done much to make a bond of sympathy between them.

The King of Scots, however, soon ceased to be a neglected captive. The military aid sent to France under John Stewart, Earl of Buchan, Albany's younger son, made James a political pawn of great importance in the possession of the English King. Buchan's arrival in France in 1419 did much to raise the morale of the French, and the following year Henry sent for the King of Scots to join him in France, so that the Scottish troops could be accused of being in arms against their sovereign. James was brought to the siege of Melun, and forced to command the Scottish garrison to surrender to the English. Fully appreciating their King's situation the Scots refused, and when Henry succeeded in taking the town James was forced to witness the hanging of his subjects for their 'rebellion'.

At the beginning of the following year James returned to England with Henry and his newly married Queen Catherine of Valois. On 23 February he attended Catherine's coronation, and at the coronation banquet he sat at the left hand beneath a Cloth of State, dressed in a scarlet doublet and a cape of fur which had been issued to him by the royal wardrobe for the occasion.

1421 was the year of the Franco-Scottish victory of Baugé, the first indication of the turn of the tide against the victorious English. Once again James was taken to France, with a great retinue and with banners and pennons and a surcoat emblazoned with his arms. In the character of Henry's ally and 'carissimus consanguineus Rex Jacobus Scotiae', he was made to serve at the siege of Meaux the same purpose as he had served at Melun.

Meaux surrendered on 10 May 1422, but it was Henry's last victory, for he died on 31 August. It is usually said that Henry died of dysentery, but the malady which caused his death was then popularly called 'St Fiacre's Evil'. A story, probably apocryphal, circulated concerning his death. It was told how, during the siege of Meaux, Henry had ordered the burning of lands which were dedicated to St Fiacre, and which it was said no man could harm without incurring the vengeance of the saint, who had been a Scottish Prince. When Henry was told the name of the disease of which he was dying, he said bitterly, 'Wherever I go, I am bearded by Scots, dead or alive.'

Henry v was, like most men, inconsistent. Fanatical in the pursuit of his ambitions and capable of terrible cruelty, he was also 'a conscious imitator of the champions of an earlier heroic age', and of their virtues. With his ill-deeds forgotten he established himself in the mind of posterity, partly with Shakespeare's help, as a hero-king.

James accompanied Henry's funeral cortège back to England, and attended his burial in November as chief mourner. It cannot be supposed that he felt any sorrow for the man who had held him captive, and had inflicted upon him in France humiliations as great as a King could be called upon to endure.

So ended 1422. The following year was the last of James's captivity, and one which brought him singular happiness, apart from the joyous expectations which he must have felt in the first serious negotiations for his release.

In 1423 James fell in love with Lady Joan Beaufort, the daughter of John, Duke of Somerset, grand-daughter of John of Gaunt, and great-grand-daughter of King Edward III. Rarely in the Middle Ages was love expected to have any part in marriage; James was fortunate that the object of his love was also a suitable candidate to share his throne. He described his experience in his great poem *The Kingis Quair*, i.e. The King's Book, which is supposed to have been written during the last year of his imprisonment, though upon internal evidence it was completed after his release and marriage.

The Kingis Quair is the only surviving poem definitely attributable to James I, but it is not the work of an occasional versifier, or even of a man who wrote once and well under the influence of passionate emotion. Its technical excellence alone suggests long practice in the art of verse-making, and its style and content are eloquent of close acquaintance with contemporary and earlier poetry. Drummond of Hawthornden, in the seventeenth century, said that 'He wrote many verses both Latin and English, of which many yet are extant'. It is sad to reflect that, if they were correctly attributed, so many have perished in the intervening time.

As a type of poem *The Kingis Quair* belongs to a well-established medieval literary tradition, and its formative influences can be found in Chaucer, and ultimately in the great medieval love-allegory *Le Roman de la Rose*. James's poem, however, differs from its predecessors in that it is no allegory or dream-vision but a retelling, within the terms of contemporary poetic convention, of an actual experience. Whether or not it happened precisely as James described is beside the point; the fact is that he fell in love, and employed the poetic convention to celebrate the event. If, however, it did indeed happen as described, the supposition is that the setting was Windsor Castle, where James resided after the death of Henry V.

James begins his poem by describing himself suffering from insomnia, and consoling himself first by reading Boethius and then by meditating upon the mutability of fortune. He then describes his resolve to write a poem, which he begins with an account of his own misfortune, his capture at sea. He goes on to lament his life as a prisoner:

> *Quhare as in ward ful of I wold bewaille*
> *My dedely lyf, full of peyne and penance,*
> *Saing ryght thus, Quhat have I gilt to faille[1]*
> *My fredome in this warld and my plesance?*
> *Sen every wight has thereof suffisance,*
> *That I behold, and I a creature*
> *Put from all this – hard is myn aventure!*

His lamentation ends when he goes to the window to look down upon the garden below. There, nightingales are singing, and in one of the most delightful verses of the whole poem, he sets down the imagined words of their song:

> *Worshippe, ye that loveris bene, this May,*
> *For of your bliss the kalendis ar begonne,*
> *And sing with us, away, winter, away!*
> *Cum, somer, cum, the suete sesoun and sonne!*
> *Awake for schame that have your hevynnis wonne,*
> *And amorously lift up your hedis all,*
> *Thank lufe[2] that list you to his merci call.*

The meditation upon love which follows leads up to the appearance in the early morning of the lady with whom James falls in love at first sight:

> *And therwith kest I doun myn eye ageyne,*
> *Quhare as I sawe, walking under the tour,*
> *Full secretly new cummyn hir to pleyne,*
> *The fairest or the freschest younge floure*
> *That ever I saw, me thoght, before that houre,*
> *For quhich sodayn abate, anon astert*
> *The blude of all my body to my hert . . .*

[1] 'What have I done that I should deserve to lose'.[2]

And in my hede I drewe ryght hastily,
And eftsones I lent it forth ageyne,
And saw hir walk, that verray womanly,
With no wight mo bot ouely women tueyne.
Than gan I studye in myself and seyne,
Ah suete, ar ye a wardly creature,
Or hevinly thing in likeness of nature?

His joy at seeing her is changed to despair when she passes out of sight.

Then follows the conventional dream portion of the poem, in which James describes how he is transported in sleep to the court of Venus, who promises to assist him in his love. She gives him Good Hope as a guide to lead him before Minerva, who tells him that it is needful to love with truth and virtue. Good Hope then takes him on a journey to seek the goddess Fortune. He describes the country through which he journeys with a delicacy and precision reminiscent of the little glimpses of landscape in the background of the miniatures which adorn the illuminated manuscripts of the fifteenth century:

Quhare, in a lusty plane, tuke I my way,
Endlang a ryver, plesant to behold,
Enbroudin all with fresche flouris gay,
Quhare, throu the gravel, bryght as ony gold,
The cristall water ran so clere and cold,
That in myn ere maid contynualy
A maner soun, mellit with armony;

That full of lytill fischis by the brym,
Now here, now there, with bakkis blewe as lede,
Lap and playit, and in a rout can swym
So prattily, and dressit tham to sprede
Thair currall fynnis, as the ruby rede,
That in the sonne on thair scalis bryght
As gesserant[1] *ay glitterit in my sight . . .*

He wanders through the countryside, seeing all around him beasts of 'mony divers kynd', all described with the same exactness of observation: 'The lytill squerell, full of besyness'; 'The chalk-quhite ermyn, tippit as the jete'; and many more. Fortune, when at last he finds her,

---

[1] burnished armour.

bids him climb upon her wheel; and, at this hopeful moment, he awakes. The poem ends with a reference to his recovery of freedom, which brings him

To bliss with her that is my soveraigne.

Fortune may have presided over James's release and marriage to Lady Joan Beaufort; but despite Fortune's favour a hard bargain had to be driven.

As previously recounted, English reverses in France, and the weakening of England's position through the loss of her strong King, made the Regency Council which ruled in the name of the infant Henry VI willing to negotiate James's release.

On the Scottish side, Murdoch may have entered the negotiations in a willing spirit, having found his own position increasingly untenable as his authority underwent a process of attrition. Not only the nobility of Scotland but even his own sons held his attempted authority in contempt. The following anecdote, in Drummond's version, though it over-simplifies the situation, may convey Murdoch's mental processes accurately enough:

> 'Murdoch . . . having neglected all discipline at home, suffered his sons to come to that petulancy, that they were not only offensive to all the people, but withal disobedient to their father, who having a brave falcon, which his son Walter had often begged, but in vain, he snatched it out of his father's hand and wrung off her neck, which his father being angry at, "Well," says he, "since I cannot govern thee, I will bring in one shall govern us both." And from that day he ceased not to further the redemption of the King. . .'

In December 1423 it was arranged by the Treaty of London that the King of Scots should be set free for the price of 60,000 marks, which was to be paid in six annual instalments. Since James had been seized during a time of truce the price of his release could not be called a ransom, as in the case of David II, who had been a lawful prisoner of war. The polite fiction was that the 60,000 marks was the cost of his education and maintenance in England; in fact the annual expenditure of Henry IV and Henry V upon their prisoner had never exceeded £700. Twenty-one hostages were to be sent to England as sureties for the payment of the instalments.

The English wished to make it a further condition of James's release that the Scots who were fighting for the French should be recalled, and that no more Scottish soldiers should be sent to France. James's position *vis-à-vis* the English was now strong enough for him to be able to refuse this condition; at the same time he probably doubted that his authority would extend to his calling home those of his subjects who were beyond the sea. He conceded only that no more military aid would thenceforward be sent to France. Upon these conditions James's release was finally agreed, and on 13 February he married Lady Joan Beaufort in the Church of St Mary Overy, which is now Southwark Cathedral. James wore a robe of cloth of gold which was presented to him as the gift of Henry VI. 10,000 marks, one sixth of the price of his deliverance, was remitted as Lady Joan's dowry.

It is sometimes suggested that this financial concession may have influenced James's choice of a bride more than his glimpse of Lady Joan's beauty from his prison window. This is not convincing, for *The Kingis Quair* is sufficiently eloquent of genuine passion, besides which it was a notorious fact that royal ransoms were seldom paid in full. One or two instalments was the best that the intending recipients could usually expect to receive. It was not James who gained by the dowry concession, but the Beaufort family who gained the appearance of having been generous, at no cost to themselves. All in all, both parties to the arrangement could be well satisfied.

In 1424, 'betuene Mersh and Averill', James I, a free King at last, rode north to take possession of his kingdom, accompanied by his beloved queen, whose place in his affections was never contested.

THE KING

Noster legifer Rex [Our law-giver King]
(Contemporary epithet of James I)

The subjects of James I soon learnt that their King was a formidable personality, but even the first sight that they had of him was sufficiently impressive. James I looked what he was: a King, an athlete and a man of strong mind and high intelligence. He was of middle height and well made, 'broad shulderitt and small waistitt' in the words of Hector Boece. A much damaged portrait, which may be the ruins of a good likeness, shows James as a handsome man with dark auburn hair, thick-growing shapely brows, fine eyes and an expression of both strength and sensitivity. When he returned to his kingdom, a few months short of his thirtieth birthday, though he was still a young man he had been matured by the hard discipline of imprisonment. He had, wrote Agnes Mure Mackenzie, 'a passionate sense of himself as King', nurtured no doubt by the necessity of sustaining his belief in himself in captivity. He had 'a profound and mystical sense of one man who is set by God to stand for the people, holding his kingdom as a trust . . .'. To the task of kingship as he conceived it he brought a dedicated will.

When James returned to his kingdom he put behind him to a very large extent those pleasures of the mind which had sustained him while he was in England. There is no need to see an inexplicable dichotomy of character between James the poet and James the law-giver. Music and poetry became merely the 'honest solaces' of his few hours of leisure, for having become a ruler he gave his attention where it was due.

The full revelation of the supine incompetence of Murdoch was swift in coming to him, and he learnt with mounting disgust of all the concomitant miseries: the crimes of violence which went unpunished because they were committed by the very men whose place in the social structure designed them to be the custodians of law and order; the existence of a large criminal class which preyed upon a helpless population. He learnt of the erosion of the royal finances, the pillaging of the customs and the waning of the central authority which would make his task so much the more difficult. The words traditionally attributed to him, when he had grasped the magnitude of that task, sum up precisely the intentions of his policy: 'If God grant me life, though it be but the life of a dog, there shall be no place in my realm where the key shall not keep the castle and the bracken-bush the cow.'

On 2 May 1424 James was crowned at Scone in the traditional manner. Murdoch exercised the privilege which pertained to him as Earl of Fife of setting the King upon the throne. The crowning itself was performed by Bishop Wardlaw. James was gracious to the erstwhile Governor and his family: Murdoch was accorded his privilege, and witnessed the knighting of his youngest son, Alexander.

However, in the very month of the coronation his eldest surviving son, Walter, was arrested. Walter, whose unpleasant gesture of wring-ing the falcon's neck was recounted as the occasion of his father's recognizing the consequences of his own misgovernment, had been Keeper of the Castle of Dumbarton. Since ships from Dumbarton sailed regularly to France, and since Walter supported the activities of the Scots who were in the service of France under the command of his uncle the Earl of Buchan, it seems likely that the immediate reason for his arrest was to prevent a violation of the recent treaty with England.

With Walter out of the way, and Murdoch given good opportunity to meditate upon the implications of his son's arrest, James held the first Parliament of his reign, at Perth.

Peace, the enforcement of order and the protection of private rights of property were the principal themes of James's first legislation. His Acts of Parliament decreed

'That firm and sure peace be kept and held throughout the realm among all subjects of the King; and if any man presume to make war against another, he shall suffer the full penalties of the law.

'That if any man presume to rebel against the King he shall suffer the pain of forfeiture of life, lands and goods.

'That any man who refuses to help the King against his rebels shall himself be accounted a rebel.

'That no men shall ride throughout the country with excessive followings; and all who move through the land shall make full and ready payment for all they need.

'That officers of the law shall be appointed who can and may hold the law to the people; that they shall be persons of substance who can be punished in their own goods if they fail to do their duty; and that any now holding office who are incapable shall be replaced by others.

'That the sheriffs shall arrest any men who move about the country in bands squatting upon other men's lands and demanding sustenance.'

It need not be supposed that these enactments were easily, or perhaps ever completely, put into effect. But they show wise and well-intentioned legislation, and they mark the beginning of a much-needed improvement in the lot of the ordinary people.

James was aware of the importance above all else of strengthening the authority of the Crown, otherwise his legislation was doomed to remain a dead letter. He was equally aware that the Crown could never be strong without adequate resources, for the simple reason that the finances of the Crown furnished the costs of government. Accordingly he commanded an inquiry 'as to the lands and rents which pertained to the Crown in the reign of David II'. In the instances of 'those lands and rents which have fallen into other hands', tenants could be required to 'give proof of their rights to their holdings'. The intention was clearly that the Crown should repossess its lands wherever possible.

Further to recoup his finances James forbade the payment of any grants or pensions out of the revenue of the customs, with the exception of a few long-established grants to religious foundations. It appears that James also made very much more efficient arrangements for the collection of the customs than Murdoch had been able to do; for there were no further examples of such pillaging of the customs as had occurred under Murdoch's governorship.

In addition to these provisions, James claimed for the Crown any gold or silver mines which should be discovered, 'as is usual of other realms', forbade the export of bullion, and ordered a new coinage 'in like weight and fineness to the money of England'. This last measure, an attempt to put the currency on a parity with that of England, was unsuccessful.

Ostensibly to raise money for the instalments of his 'costage in England' James levied a tax of twelve pence in the pound on land-rents and goods. But, like David II, James retained more of the proceeds of this tax than he passed on. However, whether because the taxation itself was an unpopular innovation, or whether because the dichotomy between pretext and use was generally recognized, the tax was so much resented that it was soon discontinued. The King, it was said, 'after the first collection . . . remitted what was unpaid . . . for he would gently strain milk, and not wring blood, from the breast of his country'.

The first Parliament of the reign also passed assorted legislation for the public good. Wolves were to be hunted and rookeries destroyed. There was to be a close season for certain types of game. Persons between the ages of fourteen and seventy were forbidden to beg unless they could prove that they could not 'win their living other ways'. Landless men were to do agricultural work or 'pass to crafts for winning of their living, under pain of burning on the cheek and banishing of the country'. All men were to learn and practise archery, and if they persisted in playing football instead, were to be fined four pence for each offence. They were to acquire weapons suitable to their rank – and what was considered suitable for every stratum of society was minutely described – and there were to be 'wapinshaws' (i.e. weapon inspections) four times a year.

The King was determined that his subjects should be peaceable and industrious, but able to defend their country in time of need. No doubt some of his enactments were unpleasing to the work-shy, and to those addicted to sport. Archery never superseded football as a popular occupation among the Scots, but the wapinshaws became quarterly festive occasions.

The vigour with which James had initiated his reign, and his determination that the country should be run efficiently, inevitably aroused resentment in those who had been responsible for the previous state of affairs. According to Balfour-Melville, Murdoch's family was 'disposed to resist the royal policy of law and order, and able from its wealth, its rank and the prestige of recent office to lead an opposition which might have overthrown the King'. Whether resentment gave rise to actual plotting is not certain, but it may well have been to forestall a coup d'état that in 1425 Murdoch was arrested, together with his wife, their son Alexander and Murdoch's father-in-law, Duncan, Earl of Lennox. Arrested with them was Sir Robert Graham of Kincardine, who escaped to nourish against the King an implacable hatred, which ultimately played a great part in bringing the reign to its tragic conclusion.

In the meantime the one son of Murdoch who remained at liberty, who was named James, decided to save himself by fleeing to Ireland. But before he left he made an ill-judged gesture of defiance on behalf of his family by burning Dumbarton and killing Sir John Stewart, 'The Red Stewart of Dundonald', a base-born uncle of the King, who had succeeded Walter as the Keeper of Dumbarton Castle.

This deed of violence, far from assisting Murdoch's cause, probably sealed his fate, and that of the rest who shared his imprisonment. In May 1425 Murdoch, his sons Walter and Alexander, and the Earl of Lennox were all beheaded at Stirling.

Whether James acted justly or vindictively in executing Murdoch and his family has remained a matter of controversy. The best justification of his action is probably that he followed a policy of 'strike or be stricken'. The executions have sometimes been represented as a shock to the Scottish nobility and as detrimental to the King's popularity. But this can hardly have been the case, as Murdoch and the rest were condemned to death by an assize of twenty-one noblemen, with James's uncle the Earl of Athol, the youngest son of Robert II, as the foreman of the assize. It is possible that Athol may have been far from impartial, for he was the son of Euphemia of Ross, and he may have been very well satisfied to assist in the elimination of descendants of Elizabeth Mure. A contemporary chronicler described him, indeed, as an 'old serpent and ancient of many evil days' and as 'a seeming innocent lamb'. For most of the reign he appeared in the latter role, but at the end of it in the former.

The populace of Stirling which witnessed the executions likewise showed no perturbation at the fate of the ex-Governor and his family. On the contrary, the people 'flowted at their fall' and 'delighted in their execution', reactions which clearly showed a preference for the King's policy of law and order over Murdoch's lack of any recognizable policy, and his permissive disregard for the welfare of kingdom and people.

The executions greatly strengthened the King's position, for not only was he rid of troublesome and potentially dangerous relations, but the Crown acquired the earldom of Lennox and Murdoch's two earldoms of Fife and Menteith. Indeed, in the course of a few years the King acquired the earldom of Buchan, which reverted to the Crown when the Earl was killed in France; the earldom of Mar, which James annexed upon the death of the Earl, to the exclusion of other claimants; and the earldom of Strathearn, which he gained by depriving the Earl, Malise Graham, of his title and estates. However, he bestowed the earldom of Menteith upon him in compensation.

Malise Graham was the grandson of David, Earl of Strathearn, the elder son of Robert II and Euphemia of Ross. Earl David's daughter Euphemia had married Sir Patrick Graham, and Malise their son had therefore a place in the succession, though only through the female line. James deprived him of his earldom on the grounds that it could not be transmitted through the female line, the implication being that neither could the royal succession. Nonetheless, James thought good to send Malise to England as one of the hostages required under the Treaty of London. James's dealings with the earldom of Strathearn added another dimension to the enmity between himself and Sir Robert Graham of Kincardine, for the latter was Malise's uncle and guardian, styled therefore 'Tutor of Strathearn'.

If James showed himself less than scrupulous in this matter, he appeared less scrupulous still in 1428, when he summoned fifty Highland chiefs to a council at Inverness Castle, and there threw them into prison. In a mood of grim exultation he celebrated this unsavoury coup with an impromptu Latin couplet:

> *Ad turrim fortem ducamus caute cohortem,*
> *Per Christi sortem meruerunt hi quia mortem*

which may roughly be translated as

> *To a castle strong let us lure the throng,*
> *For by Christ's wrong they deserve not to live long.*

But despite his methods and his sentiments he executed only three of them.

It is possibly illustrative of his satisfaction with what he had achieved in the Lowlands that James extended his attention to the problem of the Highlands. In legislation of 1425 it had been admitted that rules applying to the compensation payable to victims of violent crimes could not be made applicable in the Highlands, because 'Hieland men commonly reft and slew ilk ane utheris' (i.e. Highland men commonly robbed and slew one another). James intended to put a stop to all this by making an example of the chief offenders and giving a stern warning to the rest.

The young Alexander, Lord of the Isles, the son of that Lord who had been defeated at Harlaw, was given a caution, or in Drummond's words 'lovely advice at the council table', and permitted to depart. However, he showed himself unamenable to advice, and early the following year, in a fierce spirit of defiance, he gathered an army and burnt Inverness, cauterizing perhaps the shame of his imprisonment. The Lord of the Isles was capable of making trouble on a large scale, for his army numbered ten thousand men. James did not underestimate him, and the swiftness and effectiveness of his retaliation shows clearly enough the support that he enjoyed. He in turn mustered his resources, marched into Lochaber and on 23 June 1429 he inflicted upon the Lord of the Isles a total defeat.

On 28 August, the feast of St Augustine, the Lord of the Isles came to Holyrood Abbey where James and his Queen were at Mass, and entered the Abbey church as a penitent, dressed only in his shirt and carrying a naked sword. Before the High Altar he knelt and offered his sword to the King. No doubt he came by prearrangement, for otherwise it is scarcely likely that he would have been permitted to enter the church. Doubtless by prearrangement also, the Queen interceded for his life. On such occasions it was customary for a medieval Queen to assume Our Lady's role of intercessor for sinners. It was a ritual of religious symbolism, designed to reveal in a King a Christ-like quality of mercy; it was not a proof that the Queen in question possessed a compassionate nature. Queen Joan played her part, the life of the Lord of the Isles was spared and his rebellion was punished with a short spell of imprisonment in Tantallon Castle.

The defeat of the Lord of the Isles did not end the turbulence of the Highlands, for in 1431 his kinsman Donald Balloch organized a new rising on his behalf. The Earl of Mar, the victor of Harlaw, this time commanded the royal forces, and was defeated by Donald at the battle of Inverlochy. Once more the King prepared to go to war himself, but Donald fled to Ireland, and after his departure the northwest was tranquil for the rest of the reign.

James realized, however, that law and order in the Highlands could not effectively be obtained by occasional military expeditions, but could be maintained efficiently only by constant attention. For this reason he made the centre of his authority, almost it could be said his capital, at Perth, where he was well placed to exert his authority equally over both Highlands and Lowlands. The fairly good relations with England, which resulted partly from his marriage and partly from the problems which faced the Regency Council of Henry VI, gave James an opportunity to concentrate upon the internal problems of his kingdom which had been denied to his recent predecessors and was to be denied to most of his successors also.

Despite the interruption of such crises as the two Highland rebellions, James continued his work of legislation, and initiated both legal and parliamentary reforms.

In his legislation James's underlying concerns were that his laws should be universal and efficacious. The Parliament of 1426 enacted that the King's laws should be universally applied, and that none of his subjects should be able to claim particular laws or privileges. During the reign of Robert II particular privileges had pertained to the earldom of Fife, and the Douglases still claimed their privileges within their lordship of Galloway. James was determined to impose a homogeneous body of law throughout the kingdom. To this end the same Parliament enacted that the laws should be registered, and that the Sheriffs should proclaim them in all the 'notable places' within their sheriffdoms, so that 'no one might have cause to pretend or alledge' ignorance of the law.

However, it was one thing to make such enactments, another to enforce them. James set about creating the means to ensure that 'full law and justice' should be available throughout the kingdom 'to poor as to rich, without fraud or favour'. In 1426 a new court was set up to deal with the innumerable 'causes and complaints' which hitherto had been brought before the King in Council, or before Parliament. The new court was to consist of the Chancellor and 'certain discreet persons of the Three Estates' who were to be appointed by the King. It was to hold its sessions three times a year wherever the King should direct, and its judgements were to be final.

The King had a double motive for founding the new court, which came in the next reign to be called 'The Session'. In the first place he was motivated by a desire to provide good justice for his subjects, and, as Professor Croft Dickinson observed, 'in medieval times the "good King" was the King who ensured "good justice" '. (For this purpose also James made the excellent provision that a 'poor man's advocate' should be available to 'any poor creature' who could not pay for one.) In the second place he was concerned to relieve the Council and Parliament from the time-consuming business of hearing causes and complaints, which interfered with the routine of government.

In his parliamentary reforms James sought to enlarge the scope of Parliament as a representative assembly, and to increase its efficiency. The Parliament of 1426 enacted that all tenants-in-chief of the King, prelates, earls, barons and freeholders were to attend future Parliaments and General Councils in person, an act which may show that the King was concerned to make the Parliament as representative of the 'Community of the Realm' as possible, by including the smaller barons and freeholders as well as the great feudatories.

Apparently these lesser men were the very ones who showed

reluctance to attend Parliament, rather than regarding it as a privilege to do so; for in 1428 a new act exempted them from personal attendance, upon condition that each sheriffdom elected two or more 'wise men' to represent the rest. When these representatives came to Parliament they were to elect their own 'common speaker of the parliament'. At the same time a distinction was made between those who were permitted to avail themselves of the convenience of being represented, and those who were bound to attend in person. Prelates, earls and some of the greater barons were to be summoned personally by special 'precept'. From this enactment arose a new class of peers, lesser than the earls and greater than the rest of the barons, who were at first referred to as 'Lords of Parliament', later merely as 'Lords'. Their titles soon became hereditary, possibly simply as a result of the repetition of the 'precepts' into the next generation.

It has been suggested that James I's parliamentary reforms may have been made with the intention of creating a bicameral Parliament like that of England. During his English captivity James had not neglected to observe the workings of the government. He may well have wished to import something of what he observed into his own kingdom. The Scottish Parliament, however, remained a unicameral assembly throughout the whole course of its existence. Possibly such an assembly was sufficient in scope for a nation numerically very much smaller than England; possibly it was better suited to the more egalitarian spirit of Scotland. The Scots' view of their own Parliament was perhaps best expressed by a fictitious character, Sir Walter Scott's Andrew Fairservice, in well-known words: 'In puir auld Scotland's Parliament they a' sate thegither, cheek by choul, and than they didna need to hae the same blethers twice ower again.'

The explanation of the reluctance of the lesser barons and freeholders to come to Parliament may have been simply that it was too expensive for them. Indeed, the cost of attending Parliament, especially when it was held at a place distant from their own homes, would have strained the resources of all but the greatest magnates. To reduce this strain as much as possible by accelerating the work of Parliament, the King devised the expedient of preparing the business in hand before Parliament met, and presenting it in readiness to receive assent.

In 1424, having decided upon the first requirements for the re-ordering of his country, James himself presented to Parliament the 'articles', or bills, which he had prepared. In 1426 he appointed a committee to prepare the parliamentary business. From this beginning there developed the 'Committee of the Articles' or 'Lords of the Articles'. Initially brought into being for the convenience of the members of Parliament, this committee ultimately became a constitutional device which enabled the last King of an independent Scotland to retain complete control over Parliament at a period when the English Parliament was progressing towards greater and greater freedom of action. After the Union of Crowns the Committee of the Articles likewise enabled the dominating faction in Scotland to control the Parliament throughout the last century of its existence.

While James I worked to secure peace, the rule of law and the smooth working of the government, he attempted at the same time to maintain friendly relations with the neighbouring powers. He was well aware that only a long period of peace could make possible the regeneration of his country that he intended.

As long as Scotland was an independent nation the dominant consideration in foreign politics was the triangular relationship of Scotland, France and England. For the most part, Scotland had to ally herself with the one power against the other, and, so long as the Kings of England persisted in their claim to overlordship of Scotland, the Kings of Scots were driven to ally themselves with France, frequently to the benefit of the French, and almost as frequently to their own detriment. More Scots, and more prominent Scots, died in the service of France than Frenchmen in the service of Scotland.

James I was fortunate in being able, for the greater part of his reign, to maintain peaceful relations with both his neighbours. At first, as a result of his marriage, and of the friendship of the powerful Beauforts, his relationship with England was closer; besides which, the terms of the Treaty of London inevitably made for cooler relations between Scotland and France than had existed during the Albany governorship.

In 1427 James sent emissaries to England offering to convert the existing truce into a perpetual peace, and even offering to undertake the necessary diplomacy in person. His embassy, however, coincided with a quarrel between the Regent Gloucester and Queen Joan's uncle Cardinal Beaufort. War in France and internecine quarrels left the English government little time to re-open the question of Anglo-Scottish relations which seemed to be adequately regulated by the

Treaty of London. The opportunity passed over by England was seized upon by France.

In the same year Charles VII, the uncrowned King of France, whose fortunes were at their lowest ebb before the saving appearance of St Joan of Arc, seized the advantage which England neglected and sent an embassy to appeal for the renewal of the Franco-Scottish alliance. His ambassadors were the Archbishop of Rheims, Alain Chartier, Chancellor of Bayeux, more famous to posterity as a poet, and Sir John Stewart of Darnley, Sieur d'Aubigny, a distinguished soldier and the founder of a famous Franco-Scottish family. Their proposal was a marriage between Charles VII's son the Dauphin Louis and James's eldest daughter Margaret, with whom was requested not a monetary dowry but a force of six thousand soldiers. The offer was attractive: it would be prestigious for a daughter of Scotland to be Queen of France; besides which, a suitable dowry would have strained severely the finances of the Crown, whereas fighting men were a commodity of which Scotland was never short. In addition to these considerations, history might well have made James doubt the future goodwill of England towards his country, if England should secure her territories in France, or even conquer it. There was no knowing whereth Henry VI might not grow up to emulate Edward I or Edward III. James's offer of perpetual peace had been declined; six thousand men might prevent a future War of Independence. James accepted the French proposal and betrothed his daughter to the Dauphin. He signed the treaty at Perth, and the King of France ratified it at Chinon in November 1428.

In France the fortunes of war had fluctuated wildly, but at the time of the Franco-Scottish treaty Charles VII's situation was desperate. The fate of Orleans, besieged by the English, was likely to be decisive. In the event, it was not the Scottish reinforcements which saved the King, but the miraculous relief of Orleans and the ensuing series of victories won under the inspiration of St Joan. Much of the hard fighting which was done under her leadership, however, was done by the Scots.

The justification of James's foreign policy lies in the events in France. If Orleans had fallen and Charles VII had been defeated, almost certainly war between England and Scotland would have followed. What would have happened if James, having failed to make a permanent peace with England, had refused the offers of France can only be added to the long list of unanswered questions of history. In the event, he proved to have made the right choice. After the relief of Orleans he was able to renew his truce with England until 1431; and in November 1431, before its expiry, it was extended to 1436.

In his relations with the Papacy James was as much concerned to protect the interests of Scotland as he was in his relations with the temporal powers. As previously mentioned, he was intensely orthodox, but his attitude to the Church was intelligent as well as devout. He was by no means uncritical of the Church's shortcomings, and he was forceful in demanding necessary reforms in the lives of both the secular clergy and the members of religious orders. He imported the strict Franciscan Observantines to be an example to laxer brethren, and in 1429 he established a Carthusian monastery at Perth. His second Parliament passed an act against heresy, though only one heretic was burnt during his reign. The unfortunate man who suffered at St Andrews in 1433 was a Hussite missionary from Bohemia, named Paul Crawar, or perhaps Kravar. For his devoutness, orthodoxy and practical zeal the Papacy could have found no fault with James I; trouble arose, in Scotland as elsewhere, from ecclesiastical politics.

James, it will be remembered, had given his obedience while he was still a captive in England to Martin v, the Pope elected by the Council of Constance. He, together with other rulers who had given their support to the Council, expected and hoped that in future Popes would be subject to General Councils of the Church, an outcome which could be expected to facilitate political dealings between secular governments and the Papacy. For example, a less autocratic Papacy would inevitably allow Kings a freer hand in making appointments to benefices, which was highly desirable since bishops and greater abbots were expected to be ministers of state. Both to increase his capacity to secure the appointments he desired and to prevent the export of currency, James legislated against ecclesiastics' going to Rome to solicit or purchase appointments from the Pope. Martin v, although appointed by a General Council, determinedly resisted the Conciliar Movement and defended papal autocracy. Inevitably he clashed with the King of Scots, who was equally determined to defend and to extend his own authority over the Church in Scotland. Martin v's successor, Eugenius IV, sent a conciliatory envoy who re-established good relations between

Scotland and the Papacy at the beginning of 1437, the year of James's death.

The preceding year witnessed the marriage of James's daughter Margaret to the Dauphin Louis. Margaret, who was twelve in the year of her marriage, was the eldest of a numerous family. Queen Joan had borne her husband two sons and six daughters. The sons, born in 1430, were twins named Alexander and James; Alexander died in infancy, James survived to succeed as James II.

Margaret, from whom her parents parted reluctantly, and with a touching display of public grief, departed to an unhappy marriage which ended eight years later with her death at the age of twenty, before her husband became Louis XI of France. With her departure began the last period of her father's reign, a short, troubled time which brought the reign inexorably to its violent conclusion.

The Anglo-Scottish truce, which was approaching its expiry, was violated by an English attempt to repeat past history. A fleet was sent out to intercept the ships which were carrying Margaret and her entourage to France. It was no piratical enterprise, but an act of national aggression which England could not disown. Though Margaret arrived safely in French waters, and sailed up the Loire to her marriage at Tours in May 1436, James, perhaps enraged as much by his own memories as by the attempted seizure of his daughter, determined upon reprisals. He laid a hasty and ineffective siege to Berwick. An English invasion followed, but the invading force was defeated by a Scots army under the Earl of Angus, at Piperden in Berwickshire. Foiled before Berwick, James turned his attention to Roxburgh, a Scottish fortress which had changed hands many times, and which was then in English possession. At Roxburgh he was equally unsuccessful, for Queen Joan came to his camp, and for reasons which have never been divulged persuaded him to abandon the siege. A probable explanation is that she brought news or rumours of conspiracy, a matter which demanded his attention more urgently than the question of the possession of Roxburgh.

Trouble was indeed stirring, but James did not discover the origin of it. Possibly he expected to find it in the Highlands and did not look for it where it was most dangerous – in his own household. At the centre of the conspiracy was Sir Robert Graham of Kincardine, who had nursed his enmity in secrecy almost throughout the reign, and allied with him were Walter Stewart, Earl of Athol, the King's uncle, and his grandson, Sir Robert Stewart, Master of Athol, who held office as Chamberlain.

James had shown favour to the Master of Athol, and possibly had tacitly admitted his place in the succession by granting to his grandfather the earldom of Strathearn, taken from Malise Graham. Since Strathearn was a male fief, it was correct that the earldom should pass not to Euphemia, daughter of David, Earl of Strathearn, but to David's younger brother Walter. The succession also, according to the provisions of Robert II, should pass to Walter and his descendants if the established royal line should fail. The King had one surviving son, Prince James; if he should die young the old Earl of Athol was the heir. Athol had had two sons; one had been slain at Inverlochy, and the other, who had been sent as a hostage to England, had died there. The Master of Athol, the son of the hostage, stood after his grandfather in the succession. Athol and his grandson might have been content with that position, but for Sir Robert Graham.

Graham had two grudges against the King, his own imprisonment, and what he conceived to be the wrongs of his nephew Malise Graham. For the sake of these wrongs Sir Robert Graham nourished his long hatred, and planned vengeance. Possibly his hatred, feeding upon itself in secrecy, in the end came to loom larger in his mind than the wrongs that inspired it; for when he became the mastermind of the final conspiracy against the King, he induced Athol to conspire in his own interests and those of his grandson.

'Hate works queerly,' commented Agnes Mure Mackenzie. 'Graham put him [Malise] aside now to gain his ends, unless he intended to double-cross Athol later.' He may well have intended to do so. In the meantime he revived in Athol's mind the old doubts of the legitimacy of the children of Elizabeth Mure, and convinced him that he, the only surviving son of Euphemia of Ross, was in truth the rightful King. Athol may have been loyal to the King hitherto; or he may have made apparent loyalty minister to ambition when he sat in judgement upon Murdoch and his sons. For his actions at the beginning of the reign he may be given the benefit of the doubt; not so for his actions at the end of it. In 1436 Sir Robert Graham spoke eloquently, and ambition loudly. If Athol wavered he gave way to temptation when a 'spaewife' or seeress told him that within a year he would wear a crown.

It may be questioned whether she was genuinely prophetic, or suborned by Graham to add the final persuasion.

In the autumn of 1436 James I attended his last Parliament, after which he held his Christmas Court in the Dominican priory at Perth. To the conspirators it must have seemed that he was delivering himself like a lamb to the slaughter, for the priory itself was not defensible, and it stood outside the walls of the town. When the Christmas season was over the King remained at the priory to receive the Bishop of Urbino, the Legate who came to reconcile him to the Pope.

On the night of 20 February 1437, the festive season past and the reconciliation made, the King spent a quiet evening in his chamber, playing chess with a young courtier who was nicknamed 'The King of Love'. Recently James had heard a prophecy that in this year a King should die in Scotland. Laughingly he quoted it to the young man, saying that both of them had need to beware. It was said that when James came to the shore of the Forth on his way to Perth a seeress had warned him that if he crossed the water he would never return. Among so many prophecies a man must either become utterly subservient to superstition or contemptuous of it. James, it seems, was the latter.

Late at night his courtiers left him. He was disrobed standing before the fire, and he put on a dressing-gown. The Queen was with him, and some of her ladies remained, talking awhile, until the King and Queen chose to retire for the night.

Into the quietness and tranquillity of the priory the Master of Athol admitted the conspirators: Sir Robert Graham and his son, Sir John and Thomas Hall and Christopher and Thomas Chambers, burgesses of Perth to whom the King was in debt. Walter Stratoun, a servant of the King, met the armed men outside the King's chamber, recognized their purpose, shouted 'Treason!', and was slain.

The scuffle outside gave the King a moment's warning. With quick thinking he seized the tongs from the fireplace and, aided by the Queen and her ladies, tore up floorboards to break a way through into the vault beneath the chamber, the only hiding place. It is frequently re-counted, though the tale does not occur in the earliest accounts of these events, that one of the Queen's ladies, Katherine Douglas, went to bar the door, and finding the great bar gone, removed in readiness from beneath the concealing curtain, thrust her arm through the slots which should have held the bar, and opposed her strength to that of the nine men who sought to force the door. She gave a brief respite and sustained a cruel injury.

The King was no longer the athletic young man who had come home to his kingdom thirteen years before; of recent years he had been described as 'oppressed by his excessive corpulence'. No doubt it was with difficulty that he forced his way into his hiding place. The murderers followed like a pack of hounds to the kill, and the Queen was wounded as she struggled vainly to hold them off.

In the darkness of the vault under the floor the King, unarmed and encumbered by his gown, fought for his life with his bare hands. But the end was not in doubt. He was left dead 'with twenty-eight wounds, most towards the heart'. One of the murderers was killed by Patrick Dunbar of Cockburn who came, too late, to the King's aid. The rest escaped from the priory that night but all were captured within the month.

For Athol and his grandson and Sir Robert Graham the murder achieved nothing. Graham had persuaded the rest that public rejoicing would follow the King's death, as the death of a tyrant, and that the country would rise to set Athol upon the throne as the rightful King. It did not do so, for Prince James lived, and none wished to see him superseded by Athol. The public mind held no memories of Elizabeth Mure and Euphemia of Ross; the King was the King and his son his lawful successor. Neither did the people of Scotland consider that the dead King had been a tyrant. The strength of his rule and the severity with which he had punished evil-doers had been blessings to those who had lived in times when the country had been 'a den of thieves'. When Sir Robert Graham went to his death in Edinburgh the populace showed its mood, shouting

> *Sir Robert Graham*
> *That slew our king*
> *God give him shame!*

Death was the only reward of all the conspirators, and probably it was the Queen's determination to avenge the horror of that night at Perth which condemned Graham and Athol to three days of torture. At the last the prophecy concerning Athol was fulfilled. He was crowned indeed, but 'crowned with a diadem of burning iron'.

So ended, with savage murder and yet more savage retribution, the reign of a King who had not only striven to impose law and order but also had sought to bring his people to 'a mild and sweet condition of life and manners'. To this end he had given his patronage to the University of St Andrews, and had advanced men of learning in the Church. He had invited craftsmen from England and Flanders to take up residence in Scotland, and to give instruction in their crafts; for, since the death of Alexander III, the condition of the country had been too disturbed to permit the practise and development of traditions of craftsmanship. Throughout the reign James had encouraged the practise of crafts and endeavoured to spread the civilizing influence of the arts. He had introduced into the cathedrals and churches of his country 'organs, being not much known before his reign'.

James I was buried in the Church of the Charterhouse of Perth. His heart was taken on pilgrimage to the Holy Land, and brought back to Scotland about the year 1443 by a knight of St John of Jerusalem. Perth, which he had favoured as his capital, may have been judged too insecure a place for the new King to reside in readiness for his coronation, which by tradition should have taken place nearby at Scone. Perth was too near the disorderly Highlands where Sir Robert Graham had won himself a strong following, and where trouble could be expected to break out as soon as the discipline of the King was no longer to be feared.

The new reign was to begin with a break in a long tradition: the coronation of the new King in the Abbey of Holyrood.

4
James II,
1437–1460

. . . le roy Scotiste
Qui demy face ot, ce dit on
Vermeille comme une amatiste
Depuis le front jusqu'au menton
(*Ballade des Seigneurs de Temps Jadis*, François Villon)

King James II's contemporaries nicknamed him 'James of the Fiery Face', and as that name implies the most obvious thing about him was his disfigurement. Half his face, in the words of François Villon's *Ballade*, was the colour of an amethyst from the forehead to the chin. It seems that Villon was not availing himself of poetic licence, for a contemporary drawing of James II as a young man, done by a German knight named Jorg von Ehingen who visited his court, provides visual evidence both of the aptness of the nickname and the truth of the description.

Besides depicting the King's birth-marked face with complete honesty, Ehingen produced a convincing drawing of a vigorous-looking young man, plainly but fashionably clad in doublet and hose and long, narrow shoes with 'piked' toes; his hair close-cropped in the rather unbecoming style which was then in fashion, his head covered by a broad-brimmed, low-crowned hat. To pose for his picture he assumed a confident stance, his feet well apart, his hands resting on the hilt of his dagger. His appearance matches the descriptions of his character as a man of action and a King who set little value upon ceremonial.

In 1437, however, the young man whose ability, dedication and strength of character made him at least the equal of his father, as a man and as a King, still belonged to the future. On 25 March, the day of his coronation, he was merely a wretchedly disfigured child of six, who must have seemed to all present a pathetic replacement for the King who had been murdered the previous month. Twelve years were to pass before he was able to assert his authority and begin to build upon what was left of his father's achievement.

The minority of James II was a period of disorder, but not of anarchy. The executions of Athol and his grandson obviated a succession crisis. The child King was crowned without interference from any rival claimant. The only possible disputant for the throne, Malise Graham, remained in England, an unregarded hostage. The man who might now claim to be heir presumptive, Archibald, fifth Earl of Douglas, whose mother was a daughter of Robert III, far from being regarded as a threat to the King, was appointed Guardian of the Realm.

The Guardian was a lethargic member of a notably energetic and ambitious family. The 'Black' Douglases, Earls of Douglas (so-called to differentiate them from a rival branch of the family, the 'Red' Douglases, Earls of Angus) were to provide James II with his greatest problem in internal politics; not because they possessed aspirations to supplant the royal line, but because a consistently pursued policy of territorial aggrandizement and the creation of a centralized bloc of family estates suggested the possibility of pursuing a policy of independence and even of separatism, like that of the Dukes of Brittany and Burgundy in relation to the Crown of France.

The rise of the Douglases, like that of the Stewarts in earlier centuries, had been gradual, and had been connected with good service to the Crown. The first Earl of Douglas was a nephew of 'the Good' Sir James Douglas, the faithful supporter of Robert the Bruce. The second Earl was the hero of Otterburn. Upon his death the earldom was inherited by a base-born son of 'the Good' Sir James, Archibald 'the Grim'. The fourth Earl added to the renown of the Douglases by fighting against the English in France, where he was rewarded for his services with the Dukedom of Touraine. To Shakespeare he was

> . . . *renowned Douglas, whose high deeds,*
> *Whose hot incursions and great name in arms*
> *Holds from all soldiers chief majority*
> *And military title capital*
> *Through all the kingdoms that acknowledge Christ.*

This despite the fact that his military ill-luck won him the nickname of 'the Tyneman', which means 'the Loser'. He was the Earl who signed the band with the old Duke of Albany in 1409, and showed his contempt for the authority of Murdoch by pillaging the customs. He was killed in France at the Battle of Verneuil in 1424.

The Douglas family had intrigued for James I's release during his English captivity, and had supported him throughout his reign. The fifth Earl, apart from one brief spell of imprisonment, had enjoyed the favour of James I. His good record, his kinship with the Royal House and the prestige of his family, made him appear to be an excellent choice as Guardian of the Realm during the minority of James II. Unfortunately his supine character and his policy of arrogant isolationism created a situation which tempted the ambitions of lesser men.

Though the King was crowned, the realm provided with a Guardian and James I's Chancellor, Bishop Cameron of Glasgow, continued in office, the government had certain inherent weaknesses which invited the possibility of coups d'état. Besides the character and attitude of the Earl of Douglas, there was the ambiguous position of the Queen Dowager. Queen Joan was properly allowed the custody of her son, and after the coronation she resided with him in Edinburgh Castle, of which the Governor was Sir William Crichton, who had been a trusted servant of James I. Undoubtedly Queen Joan expected to have a voice in the governing of the country, and possibly she expected an equal share of authority with Douglas and Cameron. She appears to have felt that Crichton, whose appointment made him the protector of her son and herself, interfered unwarrantably with her freedom of action. She decided to remove her son to Stirling.

The traditional story is that the Queen announced to Crichton her intention of making a pilgrimage to the White Kirk of Our Lady of Lothian, and that she smuggled the King out of Edinburgh in a clothing coffer and took him secretly to Stirling. Some historians have dismissed this dramatic tale as mere fiction, which perhaps it is; but the existence of the story suggests that Crichton was unwilling to relinquish possession of the King, and that the Queen may have had to use some kind of subterfuge to remove him from Edinburgh Castle.

The sequel illustrates what power was conferred upon a man of relatively meagre importance by the mere fact of possessing the King's person. When the Queen arrived at Stirling with her son the castle was occupied by Sir Alexander Livingstone of Callendar. He, like Crichton, had enjoyed the confidence of James I, but he was not officially the Governor of the castle. However, he quickly acquired that position, and having become by this means the protector of the King's person while he remained at Stirling, Livingstone, like Crichton, showed a marked disinclination to allow the King to depart again.

Livingstone at first attempted to secure himself by seeking the support of the Earl of Douglas against Crichton; and when Douglas refused, Crichton sought to persuade him to make a band against Livingstone, with equal lack of success. The rivals, fearing the neutrality of Douglas and the enmity of each other, thereupon decided to make common cause and to share the spoils of power; though, as future events were to show, each was privately resolved to oust the other at the first opportunity. In the meantime, Livingstone became the Guardian of the King, while Crichton displaced Bishop Cameron as Chancellor. The Guardian of the Realm looked on, not as a disinterested arbitrator but as a somewhat uninterested spectator. In the spring of 1439 he died. His supineness is not explicable as the consequence of long ill-health; for he died suddenly, the victim of an epidemic of the plague.

Immediately after the death of the Earl of Douglas, Queen Joan remarried. It is usually said that, feeling herself to be a helpless victim of the power struggle which raged around her, she married to acquire a protector. No doubt this is true; but possibly, besides seeking a protector, Queen Joan sought a partner in a bid to regain power. Her new husband was Sir James Stewart, known as 'the Black Knight of Lorne', younger son of Sir John Stewart of Invermeath, a man of no great distinction. Drummond suggests that he 'married the Queen Dowager, not so much out of love to her person as dowry, as of ambition, by her means intending to reach the government of the state, and get into his custody the person of the King'.

If so, the Black Knight of Lorne underestimated Sir Alexander Livingstone. On 3 August Livingstone forcibly entered the Queen's apartments in Stirling Castle and arrested her together with her husband and her brother-in-law. The Queen was 'warded' in reasonable comfort, but the two men were imprisoned in the castle dungeons in irons. On 31 August Livingstone produced the Queen before an assembly of representatives of the Three Estates, and extorted from her a formal pardon for his own act, and an agreement that he should have the custody of the King. Queen Joan may have been obliged to submit to these humiliations as the price of her husband's deliverance. The Queen and both men were freed, once Livingstone had secured the King and vindicated himself. Queen Joan never recovered political power, but she lived for six more years and bore the Black Knight of Lorne three sons: John, who became Earl of Athol; James, who became Earl of Buchan; and Andrew, who became Bishop of Moray.

The nine-year-old King, who was no longer permitted to see his mother, except in the presence of other people, remained in the custody of Livingstone. It was scarcely surprising that the following year he willingly submitted to a 'rescue' by Sir William Crichton. But though he was ambushed when hunting in the Park of Stirling, and carried off to Edinburgh, Crichton returned him to Livingstone again when the latter threatened civil war as the price of the King's rescue. Although Livingstone managed to gain the advantage by this means, in actuality he had no more wish than Crichton to put his ambitions to the test of a full-scale war. Both men feared the greater power of the House of Douglas, which now had a more ambitious head than the erstwhile Guardian of the Realm.

The Guardian's elder son, William, sixth Earl of Douglas and third Duke of Touraine, was sixteen when he succeeded his father. His youthful inexperience was matched by his arrogance and over-confidence. In territorial terms the young Earl was the greatest magnate in the realm. He possessed the old lordship of Galloway, which included the earldom of Wigtown and the area which is now the county of Kirkcudbright. He possessed Annandale, Ettrick Forest, Jedburgh, Lauderdale, Eskdale and Teviotdale, estates which covered a vast area and stretched across the Border; all this besides his dukedom in France. If the young Earl was pardonably proud of his territorial greatness, pride of blood might have made him greater still in his own eyes. He was descended from both the marriages of Robert ii; from the first through his father, and from the second through his mother, who was the sister of Malise Graham. It is scarcely surprising that he should have regarded his earldom as a Scottish equivalent of Brittany, and himself as a magnate who might at will ally himself to Scotland or secede from it.

He was too young to realize that there is no greatness which is not vulnerable, too ingenuous to realize that he was an easy prey to envious and unscrupulous enemies. Crichton and Livingstone feared what he might become, not what he was, and circumstantial evidence suggests that they found an ally in his great-uncle, James 'the Gross', the brother of his grandfather the fourth Earl.

In November 1440 the Earl of Douglas and his younger brother David were entertained as the guests of the King in Edinburgh Castle. They had come to the city with a great following – Douglas, it was said, rode throughout his lands at the head of a thousand horsemen – but in Edinburgh his followers were lodged about the city, and in the castle he had to trust himself to his host.

The young King received the Earl and his brother with delight and admiration, and his pleasure in their visit must have made the manner of its ending all the more horribly memorable. At the conclusion of a great dinner both the youths were seized, upon Crichton's orders, swiftly tried for treason in the King's presence, and executed at once in the courtyard of the castle. The King pleaded in vain for their lives, but his entreaties were brutally ignored.

The often-repeated story that as the last course of the feast a black bull's head was set before the victims, symbolizing that they were doomed to die, is probably a fictitious addition. The first historian to recount the story is Hector Boece, and he may well have derived it from a ballad, in which it had been included to heighten the drama of the terrible event. The art of the ballad-maker is frequently shown in the re-shaping, sharpening or colouring of real events, without altering beyond recognition the basic facts of the story. It may be from a ballad of the 'Black Dinner' that a well-known verse derives, lamenting the young Earl's fate:

> *Edinburgh Castle, Toune and Towre,*
> *God grant thou sinke for sinne,*
> *And that even for the black dinoir*
> *Earl Douglas gat therein.*

The heir to the earldom was James the Gross, and the outcome strongly suggests that he was a consenting party to his great-nephews' death. Their trial and execution had taken place in the most inexcusable circumstances, at the instance of both Crichton and Livingstone, for though Crichton was responsible as the Governor of Edinburgh Castle, he had taken very good care to include Livingstone as his partner in the deed. If James the Gross had not consented to what was done he would have inherited, besides the earldom, an obligatory blood-feud against Crichton and Livingstone. However, he showed them no enmity. He accepted the manner in which he came by his inheritance, and settled down to enjoy it peaceably. It may well be that his 'four stane of talch [tallow] and mair' disposed him to lethargy. There is no knowing whether the weight of his ill-doing oppressed him as much as the weight of his flesh.

The ambitious rivals who had sought to break the power of the Douglases gained what they desired for the time being. Though James the Gross inherited the earldom, the lordship of Galloway was inherited by the late Earl's sister, while Annandale as a male fief reverted to the Crown, and the Dukedom of Touraine to the Crown of France.

James the Gross died in 1443 and was succeeded by his son William, who was eighteen. In character, William, eighth Earl of Douglas, somewhat resembled his luckless kinsman and namesake; but though he was equally arrogant and magnificent, he was both cleverer and more fortunate. His policy was to divide Crichton and Livingstone and to reunite the Douglas estates. His first purpose was achieved by encouraging the ambitions of the Livingstone family at the expense of Crichton, his second by marrying the 'Fair Maid of Galloway', the sister and heiress of the victims of the Black Dinner. (At the same time her widowed mother was married to a Livingstone.) Though he lacked Annandale and Touraine he had greatly recouped the fortunes of his family. They were further enhanced by the advancement of his brothers: his younger twin, James, became Bishop of Aberdeen; the next brother, Archibald, became Earl of Moray in right of his wife; the next, Hugh, became Earl of Ormond; and John, the youngest, inherited the lordship of Balveny, the original inheritance of their father.

While the Douglases took the greater spoils, the Livingstones were awarded the lesser ones. Sir Alexander Livingstone became Justiciar, and his son Sir James, Chamberlain; Robert Livingstone of Linlithgow became Comptroller, and John Livingstone Master of the Mint. Robert Livingstone of Callander became Keeper of Dumbarton

Castle, another John Livingstone Keeper of Doune Castle, and two more members of the family were made keepers of the castles of Stirling and Methven. Sir William Crichton managed to retain control of Edinburgh Castle, but he lost the Chancellorship, which went to James Kennedy, Bishop of St Andrews. This was a mistake from the Douglas viewpoint.

Bishop Kennedy was the King's uncle, the son of Mary, daughter of Robert III, by her second husband, Sir James Kennedy of Dunure. At this time St Andrews was not the primatial see of Scotland. There was parity between the Scottish bishops, and the Church in Scotland was under the direct protection of the Papacy, a situation which had come into being to protect the Scottish dioceses from the pretensions of the English archdiocese of York. In the course of time, however, the Bishop of St Andrews had come to be regarded unofficially as the premier Bishop of Scotland. Kennedy was able to derive from his position the spiritual authority of the Primacy, and to bring to it the moral authority of a character of singular purity and force.

Kennedy was above the unscrupulous rivalry of Crichton and Livingstone, and he was not in the least intimidated by the ambitions of the Earl of Douglas. If Douglas pursued his own aggrandizement at the expense of the integrity of the kingdom, Kennedy looked to the future and dedicated his efforts to strengthening the position of the King. Indeed, for James II the rise of Bishop Kennedy was the most fortunate event of the later years of his minority.

The Earl of Douglas, seeking to extend his influence over the country while the opportunity provided by the minority remained to him, made a band with the Earl of Crawford, the greatest magnate in the north-east of Scotland. Crawford, who had a personal grudge against Kennedy, made a raid on the Bishop's lands in Fife. Kennedy retaliated by excommunicating him. In the middle of the fifteenth century excommunication was still a spiritual weapon of great efficacy; it possessed a power of terror which it was to lose through overuse during the ensuing century. Crawford endeavoured to maintain an attitude of detached contempt, but exactly a year after the laying on of the excommunication he was killed in an affray. So great was the superstitious horror of the event that none dared give him burial until Kennedy had raised the excommunication and given orders for his interment. This event greatly increased the Bishop's authority.

Nonetheless, Kennedy did not rely upon spiritual weapons to combat the combined influence of Douglas and his allies. A practical politician as well as an uncompromising churchman, he was prepared to make use of whomsoever he found available to serve his purposes. The man most obviously available was Sir William Crichton, to whom Kennedy restored the Chancellorship. Throughout the minority Crichton had shown himself to be both self-seeking and unscrupulous, and at the Black Dinner he had been guilty of a double murder which even the formality of a treason trial had not been able to disguise as justified execution. And yet, the power of the Douglases was a threat to the authority of the Crown, and in a savagely unscrupulous fashion Crichton may have been attempting to serve the King's best interests as well as his own. Though Kennedy could not have approved of Crichton's methods, he may have discerned and approved a basic intention in him to serve the King. Crichton had been a loyal servant of James I, and under the influence of Kennedy he was to be a loyal servant of James II. Possibly the best explanation of his character is that he was a man who needed a masterful guiding hand, whether it were that of King or prelate.

Kennedy and Crichton managed to hold the balance of power against the Douglases and Livingstones for the remainder of the minority. The King appears to have had a personal liking for Douglas, but he did not extend it uncritically to all Douglas's allies and partisans. In historical perspective it appears obvious that the King's majority would bring about great changes; to the participants in the events of the time it may not have appeared obvious at all.

Some indication that the power struggles which afflicted Scotland during that minority of James II were relatively superficial in their effect upon the country is reflected in the fact that during the minority Scotland's national prestige did not fall from that high level to which James I had raised it. A series of advantageous marriages arranged for the daughters of James I strengthened Scotland's commercial and political relationships with the European powers.

In 1442 the Princess Isabella was married to Francis, Duke of Brittany. Since the Duke followed a pro-French policy the marriage provided a secondary support for the Franco-Scottish alliance. Commercial relations with the Low Countries were stimulated by the marriage in 1444 of the Princess Mary to Wolfaert van Borselen, Lord of Campveere, in Zeeland, the nephew of Philip 'the Good', Duke of Burgundy. In the same year James I's eldest daughter, the Dauphine Margaret, died in France, and Charles VII suggested that his son should marry her sister, the Princess Eleanor. James II consented, and the necessary papal dispensation was sought, and refused. In 1449 Eleanor married Sigismund, Archduke of Austria, who had originally been betrothed to a French Princess, and upon her death had requested Charles VII to negotiate a Scottish match for him. James I's youngest daughter, the Princess Annabella, was brought up at the court of Savoy, and betrothed to the Duke's son Louis, Count of Geneva. This betrothal was broken at the request of Charles VII, who was on bad terms with Savoy at the time, and Annabella returned to Scotland in 1455. She and the remaining daughter of James I, the Princess Joan, who was dumb, were both married in their own country.

In the meantime, Scotland's system of international marriage alliances, which can be seen almost entirely as an extension of the Franco-Scottish alliance, had been completed by the marriage of the King himself.

By 1448 the personality of the King, who was eighteen years old, was beginning to be of political importance, and he took some part in the negotiation of his marriage. Initially he expressed to Charles VII his desire to marry a kinswoman of the Royal House of France. Charles at the time wished to draw Burgundy into the Franco-Scottish alliance, with a view to isolating England. Therefore he suggested that James should marry the Duke of Burgundy's niece, Marie of Gueldres. There is some evidence that Scottish envoys had already visited Marie's father the Duke of Gueldres; doubtless they had spoken approvingly of his daughter, for James accepted the French King's suggestion.

On 18 June 1449 the fleet bringing Marie of Gueldres to Scotland sailed into the Forth; she disembarked at Leith, escorted by Wolfaert van Borselen. Philip the Good had provided his niece with a dowry of 60,000 crowns, and the marriage brought Scotland commercial agreements with Burgundy, Holland, Brabant, Zeeland and Flanders. In addition to these advantages Marie herself was civilized, devout and intelligent, and is said to have been beautiful. On 3 July she was married to James II in the Abbey of Holyrood, and crowned Queen of Scots.

The marriage marked the end of the King's minority, though his position as master in his own kingdom was for a time disputed by the Earl of Douglas. In his struggle to impose his authority the King had the assistance of an able and determined consort. Furthermore, Marie contributed to the strengthening of her husband's position by being notably successful in her dynastic duty. She bore the King three sons: James, born in 1451, who reigned as James III; Alexander, Duke of Albany, and John, Earl of Mar. There were two daughters of the marriage, Mary and Margaret, and a fourth son, David, who died in infancy.

At the time of the King's marriage the prestige of the Douglas family was very high. In 1447 the truce with England, well-kept since the beginning of the reign, expired, and the following spring there was an outbreak of Border warfare. In May the English burnt Dunbar, and the Scots replied by burning Alnwick; in July the English burnt Dumfries, and the Scots burnt Warkworth. The Earl of Douglas was the hero of the Scottish exploits, and his brother Hugh, Earl of Ormond was the victor in a more serious engagement in October, when he defeated an English invasion at the Battle of the Sark, near Lochmaben. The loyalty and energy of the Douglases was in the best tradition of their family, and there is no reason to suppose that the King felt anything but satisfaction and gratitude.

Towards the end of 1449, after some abortive negotiation, a new truce for an indefinite period was signed with England. Henry VI, now shorn of almost all his French possessions, and unable to control internecine power struggles, could not afford to be at enmity with Scotland. The truce gave both sovereigns the opportunity to concentrate upon internal affairs, though with very different results: Henry VI, saintly, scholarly and incompetent, was to be the helpless victim of other men's ambitions, and to lose his throne and life in the Wars of the Roses; James II was to overcome the forces of disorder which threatened to plunge Scotland into similar turmoil, and for the rest of his short reign to provide his subjects with the benefits of strong government.

At the outset of his personal rule it appears that James II hoped to enjoy the loyal service of the Earl of Douglas. He laid the blame for the disorders of his minority upon the Livingstone family; and indeed the power and office which had accrued to the Livingstones during the 1440s must inevitably have made them a target for the King's resentment and other men's enmity. It is probable that they acquired a new and powerful enemy in Marie of Gueldres, for upon her marriage the Queen was granted the castle of Methven and the customs of Linlithgow, and both residence and revenue were in the hands of the Livingstones. Doubtless the Queen stimulated the King's resentment, for less than six months after the marriage the Livingstones fell from power.

Sir Alexander Livingstone had been one of the commissioners who negotiated the truce with England. But hard upon that success he was arrested and imprisoned in Blackness Castle. His sons and kinsmen followed him, and, in the words of the contemporary Auchinleck Chronicler 'all officeris that war put in be thaim war clerlie put out of all officis, and all put doun that thai put up. And this was a gret ferlie [marvel]'. Only two members of the family were executed; but significantly they were those who had been responsible for withholding Methven Castle and the customs of Linlithgow from the Queen.

The Earl of Douglas, who had used the Livingstones when it suited his own purposes, made no move to save them even though they were linked to his family by marriage. Indeed, he benefited by their fall, by accepting from the King a grant of some of the Livingstones' forfeited lands.

Douglas, who like many members of his family possessed charm as well as a forceful personality, had no doubt done all that he could to win and to hold the King's favour. So far he had done so successfully and without surrendering any of his ambitions. James, however, was not blinded by his liking for the Earl; he was aware of the need both to hold his loyalty and to keep his power within bounds.

In 1450 Pope Nicholas v proclaimed a Jubilee Year, the purpose of which was to celebrate the end of the Papal Schism. Ambassadors who came to felicitate the Pope, and pilgrims who came to claim the plenary indulgence offered them during that year, converged upon Rome. The Scottish embassy was headed by the Earl of Douglas, whose appointment as ambassador was both a signal honour and a means of removing his influence from internal politics while the King established his authority in Scotland.

Douglas took the opportunity provided by his embassy to visit the courts of England, Burgundy and France. In England he established a potentially treasonable connection with Richard, Duke of York, the father of the future Edward IV; in Burgundy he received nothing more than a sumptuous and friendly reception from the tactful Philip the Good; in France he sought and failed to obtain the restoration to his family of the dukedom of Touraine. He took with him his brothers Moray and Ormond, and visited his brother the Bishop of Aberdeen who was at that time resident in Paris. John Douglas of Balveny was left at home to look after the family interests.

James II took advantage of Douglas's absence to establish his authority with a year of vigorous activity. The first Parliament held under the King's personal rule passed legislation which recalled that of James I in its intentions, for it was designed to re-establish the rule of law throughout the country, to enhance the authority of the King's officers, and to protect the defenceless mass of the population from 'spulzeouris' (spoilers) and 'masterful beggaris'. There was legislation against usury, against the import of poison, and against the export of gold. The establishment of 'The Session' was re-enacted. A new law was passed 'for the safety and favour of the poor people that labour the ground', which declared that upon the sale of land all extant leases should remain in force for the term originally negotiated, which provided the least-privileged members of society with a safeguard against sudden eviction.

1450 also saw the foundation by Bishop Kennedy of the College of St Salvator in the University of St Andrews, and the foundation of the University of Glasgow by Bishop Turnbull. James II somewhat tardily granted his charter to the new University in 1453.

In the meantime James's attention was taken up by many violent matters; first of all by troubles in the Douglas territories which were in the care of Belveny. The youngest of the Douglas brothers may have lacked the authority to keep order among the tenants and 'dependers' of the Earl; or he may have been unwise enough to encourage them to flout the King's efforts to impose the rule of law. At all events, the disturbances warranted royal intervention, and James quelled them by seizing and destroying a number of Douglas strongholds, and by executing those of the Earl's dependers who refused to take an oath of fealty to himself. At this point John, Lord of the Isles and Earl of Ross, the son of Alexander, Lord of the Isles who had rebelled against James I, followed his father's example, and in support of the Douglases sacked Inverness. James quelled this rebellion also without difficulty.

On his return from Rome the Earl of Douglas found the King in a very much stronger position than he had been the previous year, and himself in a situation commensurably less favourable. The King allowed him to see a glimpse of royal displeasure, and then received him fully into favour once more at the request of Marie of Gueldres, who was given the part of speaking in his defence before Parliament. The Earl was doubtless intended to learn the lesson that he was the King's subject, and that favour was dependent upon good behaviour. He did not learn it.

Gradually the King discovered the means by which the Earl was building up his power: intrigues with the Yorkists in England, and a band with the Lord of the Isles and with Alexander Lindsay, the new Earl of Crawford, who was known as 'the Tiger Earl'. James summoned Douglas to Stirling Castle, and the Earl betrayed an uneasy conscience by refusing to come without a safe conduct, which was granted him.

On 22 February 1452 Douglas supped with the King, who afterwards took him aside into a little room, and there revealed his knowledge of the Earl's treasonable dealings. He requested the Earl to reaffirm loyalty and good faith by repudiating his band with the Earl of Crawford and the Lord of the Isles. The Earl refused. The King sought to persuade him and the Earl remained obdurate. No doubt the King was doubly angry because he liked Douglas and for reasons of friendship as well as policy he was giving him a chance to redeem himself. But Douglas refused to see reason. Tempers ran high, abuse was exchanged and the King, enraged at the Earl's refusal to obey him, drew his dagger and struck him in the throat. Those who had heard the quarrel from the next room rushed to his aid and, headed by the Captain of the Guard who was armed with a pole-axe, finished off the Earl of Douglas with many blows. It is said that, after the murder, the body was thrown from the window into the Privy Garden of the castle, and was subsequently given burial there.

The only thing that can be said in extenuation of the King's act is that it was a crime of passion, unpremeditated and regretted. It was doubly to be regretted, both as a crime which would burden his conscience and discolour his reputation, and as an act of violence which would breed yet greater violence.

Indeed, the immediate consequence of the King's crime was nothing less than a nationwide conflagration. In a literal blaze of violence the Bishop of Aberdeen, plucked from his ecclesiastical career to inherit his dead brother's earldom, rode into Stirling at the head of several hundred men and burnt the town. In May the Earl of Crawford led a rebellion in the north, and was defeated near Brechin by the first Earl of Huntly who commanded the royal forces. Crawford's comment, as he fled from the field, was that he would gladly have spent seven years in hell to have gained such a victory. James himself, with an army of thirty thousand men, marched in pursuit of the new Earl of Douglas, who recognized the inevitability of defeat and surrendered to the King near Dumfries.

Parliament had already exonerated the King from the murder, on the grounds that the late Earl's traitorous refusal to repudiate the band had justified his death; and that he was, in the tactful words of the Parliamentary judgement, 'guilty of his own death by refusing the King's gentle persuasion'.

Accordingly, James, ninth Earl of Douglas, was obliged to give the King formal forgiveness for the murder of his brother. The King showed clearly enough his remorse for the murder by the generosity with which he treated the new Earl. He granted him the earldom of Wigtown, which had been annexed to the Crown at the time of James's campaign against Douglas of Balveny; he gave him permission to obtain a dispensation to marry his brother's widow 'the Fair Maid of Galloway'; he offered him an opportunity to repay generosity with loyalty by appointing him to head an embassy to England.

Douglas went to England, and took further advantage of the King's astonishing clemency to petition for the return of the long-exiled Malise Graham. (Incidentally, if it had been the policy of the Douglases to supplant the established royal line, they would have left Malise Graham where he was; obviously, his redemption was a good action towards a kinsman who might at the same time have some nuisance value in Scotland.) James, still seeking to quiet his conscience with acts of generosity, agreed. But, not surprisingly, the Earl of Douglas was not won by any clemency or generosity; whatever reparation the King offered, he nursed his enmity, though for a time he concealed it.

Donald Balloch of the Isles, a troublemaker from the previous reign, burnt Inverkip, but the rest of Douglas's allies made their peace with the King. The 'Tiger Earl' of Crawford presented himself as a penitent, and was pardoned at the intercession of Huntly who had defeated him the previous year; and the Lord of the Isles was likewise received into the King's peace.

The reconciliations were followed by a short period of uneasy calm; then came the last resurgence of the Douglas problem and its violent conclusion.

The last phase of the struggle between James II and the Douglas family coincided with the outbreak of the Wars of the Roses in England. This was not fortuitous, for the treasonable connection between the Douglases and the Yorkists was well established. However, although the regal aspirations of the Duke of York may have inspired rebellious and ambitious thoughts in the Earl of Douglas, there was more difference between these two overmighty subjects than there was similarity. York aspired at first to be the heir of Henry VI; later he progressed to attempting to supplant him. The Douglas family, in the persons of its various earls, did not aim quite so high. In the words of a recent Scottish historian, Mrs Rosalind Mitchison: 'The Douglases were descended from both of Robert II's marriages: if they had tried for the crown they would have been a real menace. Instead they aimed alternately at general political domination, for which they would ally with other houses, or at effective separation.'

James II fought both aspects of their ambition for most of his reign. The latter aspect showed its most overt, though by no means its most dangerous, manifestation early in the next reign. (The participation of the last Earl of Douglas in a treasonable agreement to partition the kingdom will be recounted in the next chapter.)

Besides the difference of aims between the disaffected nobles of England and those of Scotland, there was also a decisive difference between the political conditions of the two countries. In England there was a weak King, not indeed mad but subject to periodic mental breakdowns; a disputed succession in which the Yorkist claim to the throne was plausibly better than that of the established House of Lancaster; and a nobility which divided its allegiance between the rival Houses. In Scotland there was a strong King who enjoyed the support of the majority of the nobility, clergy and commons, and who was opposed by a single family – though admittedly a very great one – and its allies. The situation in England led to thirty years' fighting for the Crown; the situation in Scotland to a violent conflict which was swiftly concluded.

The year 1455 was a fateful one for both countries. In England it witnessed the first Battle of St Albans which inaugurated the Wars of the Roses; in Scotland it witnessed the Battle of Arkinholm, in which the Earl of Douglas and his brothers were utterly defeated.

The victor of Arkinholm was Douglas's inimical kinsman the fourth Earl of Angus, who commanded the royal forces. Two of Douglas's brothers gave their lives for his cause: Moray was slain in the battle, Ormond was wounded and captured, and subsequently executed. The Earl himself, with his youngest brother Balveny, escaped. Douglas fled first to the Isles, where he made a last attempt to stir up trouble; thence he fled to England. He offered his allegiance to the English Crown, and received at the instance of the Duke of York a pension of £500, 'until he is restored to his heritage, taken from him by him who calls himself King of Scots'. The implication of these words is that Douglas had recognized the ancient English claim to overlordship of Scotland, which was brought out and refurbished like an old weapon every time there was the slightest sign of trouble between the two countries.

The power of the Douglases was broken not only by a heavy defeat, but also and more decisively by the capture of their two greatest strongholds, Abercorn in West Lothian and Threave in Kirkcudbrightshire. The fall of these castles meant that the Douglases no longer possessed centres of resistance to which they could summon their forces, and from which they could offer the King defiance.

The manner of their capture was in itself a lesson to any nobleman who might contemplate defying the power of the Crown. Both castles were reduced by the royal artillery. At Abercorn the defenders were overawed by 'a gret gun, the quhilk a Frenchmen schot richt wele'. At Threave they surrendered before the terror and the efficacy of a 'great bombard', which according to tradition was Mons Meg – 'that massive piece of ordnance . . . which is still to be seen in Edinburgh Castle and for which', in Professor Gordon Donaldson's words, 'generations of Scots had an almost superstitious veneration'.

Gunnery was the latest development of military science, and James

 II recognized its potential, and added to the royal artillery with great enthusiasm.

The Kings of Scots had possessed artillery of a sort since the previous century. A small gun, but clearly a wonder in its time, had been obtained in 1384, in the reign of Robert II. Its purchase is recorded in the Exchequer Rolls: 'pro uno instrumento dicto gun, £4'. James I, in the last year of his reign when he went to war with England, spent £590 on the manufacture of guns. He was preparing efficiently for those unsuccessful enterprises, the sieges of Berwick and Roxburgh. James II, besides inheriting his father's artillery, acquired guns from the Low Countries when he married Marie of Gueldres. These were the prestige weapons of the age, and it is probable that Mons Meg was one of them; the name of the great gun suggests the place of its origin.

Besides being prestigious and effective (Mons Meg had a range of two miles) artillery was enormously expensive. The best guns came from abroad, as did the best gunners and all gunpowder (and to fire Mons Meg once required 105 lbs of gunpowder). Only the Crown could afford expensive foreign ordnance and all that went with it; this gave the King a new power to overawe the disaffected and to defeat the rebellious.

However, it is significant of the King's good relations with his nobility that in 1456 Parliament enacted that in time of war certain of the lords should be called upon to provide 'cartis of weir' (carts of war), each one to have mounted upon it two cannon of two chambers apiece, and that they were to be manned by trained gunners. The King may have possessed the ultimate deterrent to rebels in his great foreign guns; but certainly, had he not been on excellent terms with his lords, and confident of so continuing, the King would never have permitted, let alone requested them to provide themselves with guns, of any sort.

This is a very eloquent illustration of the fact that the reign of James II should not be described, as it very frequently has been, as a period of conflict between the Crown and 'the nobility'. There was conflict indeed, but as previously stated it was conflict between the Crown and a section of the nobility: the Douglas family and the families which at one time and another were allied with it – the Livingstones, Crawford and his kindred the Lindsays and the Lord of the Isles and his kin. The ninth Earl of Douglas made an ally of the first Lord Hamilton, but Hamilton went over to the King in 1455.

For the rest, there is plenty of evidence of good relations between the Crown and the nobility, and of a deliberate policy on the part of the King to build up a loyal nobility, and to take it into partnership with the Crown in the governing of the country.

During the reigns of James I and James II most of the early medieval earldoms, with their vast territories, had become vested in the Crown, either by reversion or by annexation. The patrimony of the Crown was greatly increased by the acquisition of the earldoms of Carrick, Fife, Lennox, Mar, Strathearn, Moray and Buchan. Moray, however, was bestowed upon Crichton's son, and Buchan upon the King's half-brother James, the second son of his mother by the Black Knight of Lorne.

James II created new semi-honorific earldoms, which possessed no such great territorial endowments, but which bound the recipients of honour in bonds of obligation to the Crown. The earldom of Huntly dated from the King's minority, but it was the policy of James's majority to increase the power of the Gordons of Huntly at the expense of that of the Lindsays of Crawford. Furthermore, he married his sister the Princess Annabella to the second Earl of Huntly. The earldom of Athol was revived for the benefit of John, the eldest of his three half-brothers. The earldom of Morton was bestowed upon a loyal Douglas, Sir James Douglas of Dalkeith, to whom the King married his dumb sister, the Princess Joan. Hay of Errol, the Constable of Scotland, was created Earl of Errol in 1452, a year in which James II required the support of all the loyalists he could muster; and from his reign also date the earldoms of Argyll, Marischal and Rothes. The confidence which the King placed in his loyalist earls is illustrated by the part that Huntly and Angus played in the overthrow of the Earl of Douglas.

That event was followed by a period of tranquillity. The King was enabled to give his full attention to the problems of government, and he did so with a vigour which recalled the rule of his father. The dedication with which he sought the public good, his determination to impose the rule of law, his desire to give his subjects security and prosperity, made him a worthy successor of James I. The popularity with which he was rewarded is the best proof of his success.

To secure the success he had achieved, to strengthen the Crown and the country and to better the lives of his people are the discernible purposes of the legislation of the last five years of James II's reign. The Parliament which met in August 1455 passed an act which defined the inalienable patrimony of the Crown: 'Forasmuch as the poverty of the Crown is oft-times the cause of the poverty of the realm and many other inconveniences . . .' In future the Crown was to possess inalienably the lordship of Galloway, and Ettrick Forest; the castle of Edinburgh and the existing Crown domains in Lothian; Stirling Castle and the surrounding royal domain; the castle of Dumbarton; the castle of Falkland and the earldom of Fife; the earldom of Strathearn; the castle and lordship of Inverness and of Urquhart, and Redcastle in the Black Isle. The strategic arrangement of the castles and lands of the Crown obviated the future development of such separatist aspirations as the Earls of Douglas had shown. At the same time the act ensured that the patrimony of the Crown was and would remain far greater than that of the greatest among the nobility. By this act James II did all he could to ensure that the ascendancy of the Crown achieved in his reign would be maintained for his descendants.

The Parliament which passed this act also passed legislation designed to enhance the power of the Crown as the fount of justice. The powers of the Wardens of the Marches were to be reduced (the Earls of Douglas had held this office); in future Wardens were not to be empowered to try cases of treason. No 'regalities' were to be granted in future without the consent of Parliament. A regality has been described as 'a system of legal administration reproducing in miniature that of the King'; a 'Lord of Regality' (Bishop Kennedy, for example, was one) would have competence to try all cases except those involving treason. In addition to limiting legal powers which might be open to abuse, the King created by Act of Parliament a debt court, which could operate in any burgh, in which twelve men appointed by the Privy Council should have power to deal with all litigation involving the sum of £5 or under.

The Parliament which met in the autumn of the following year, 1456, gave its attention to the defence of the country, and elaborated upon the defence acts of the previous reign. As under the previous acts, all men were to possess armour and weapons according to their means. All able-bodied men between the ages of sixteen and sixty were to be prepared to march to the Border in defence of their country; but no poor man who was not adequately armed would be compelled to cross it. This Parliament passed the legislation previously referred to concerning 'cartis of weir'. Peaceful matters were also dealt with. New currency was ordered and foreign exchange rates were regulated. Humane legislation was passed concerning outbreaks of plague: plague-stricken persons who possessed the means to support themselves were not, as previously, to be evicted from their homes and towns by force, but were permitted to remain isolated in their houses.

The Parliament of 1458 likewise elaborated upon the legislation of the previous reign. An act was passed to enforce the practice of archery, though indeed the development of artillery was rapidly rendering archery militarily obsolete. However, all men were commanded to practise it, and at each practice to shoot at least six times (three had been obligatory in the previous reign). Those who absented themselves, or who persisted in playing golf or football instead, were to be fined, and the fines were to be used to provide drinks for law-abiding archers. No doubt this was a popular piece of legislation with the archers; but somehow it did not wean the mass of the Scots away from their national pastimes of football and golf.

Again as in the previous reign, acts were passed for the improvement of agriculture, the protection of game and the destruction of predators.

The increase of prosperity was witnessed by the passing of sumptuary laws, as had also occurred in the reign of James I. Commoners were not to be permitted to wear silk, scarlet or marten fur, unless they held municipal office. Agricultural workers were to wear grey or white on working days, though they were to be allowed to wear red, green or blue on holy days. (The legislation of the previous reign had forbidden the wearing of excessive quantities of pearls. Since they were found in great abundance in many rivers of Scotland, possibly the intention of the sumptuary law was to reserve the bulk of them for the export trade.) Upon the subject of sumptuary laws in general, Agnes Mure Mackenzie observed:

'. . . historians treat them by tradition, as a joke or as a foolish reactionary measure . . . but in fact they had probably a more subtle reason. . . . The Middle Ages, with their intensely systematic outlook, had a very sharp sense of social distinctions and their outward marks . . . a man whose position in society is clearly defined is not self-conscious about it.'

In other words, sumptuary laws were intended to discourage invidious class consciousness and the resultant social unrest.

The Parliament of 1458 gave James II a remarkable testimonial: 'God of His grace has sent our Sovereign Lord such progress and prosperity that all his rebels and breakers of his justice are removed out of his realm, and no masterful party remaining that may cause any breaking in his realm. . . .' Parliament entreated the King to continue his good work, 'that God may be empleased of him, and all his lieges may pray for him to God and give thanks to Him that sends them such a Prince to be their governor and defender'. No doubt he would have continued, had not the troubled condition of England led Scotland into war once again, and brought the King to his early death.

The Earl of Douglas was indirectly the cause of the new troubles, for after his flight to England James wrote to Henry VI protesting at the reception which had been given to the rebel. Henry VI had always been disposed towards peaceful relations with Scotland, and it was unfortunate that the protest reached England during one of the King's breakdowns, and was dealt with by the bellicose Duke of York who was acting as Protector.

His reply was insolent in the extreme. It ignored James's protest and renewed the English claim to overlordship of Scotland in undiplomatic and indeed insulting language.

James was naturally enraged, and he replied with actions not words, by leading a force across the Border in the autumn of 1456, and raiding Northumberland. This may well be criticized as an overviolent retort to objectionable words, but James showed that his enmity was towards the Duke of York not towards the King of England, for as soon as King Henry recovered and York was displaced from his protectorship, James at once offered a truce. In July 1457 a new truce, to last for two years, was concluded.

In the summer of 1459 sporadic Border warfare was resumed, in which the Earl of Douglas is said to have participated. James went to war in earnest the following year, ostensibly as the ally of Henry VI against the Yorkists, but also with the hope of recovering the Scottish possessions which remained in English hands. In July 1460 Henry VI was captured at the Battle of Northampton, and carried a prisoner to London. His Queen, Margaret of Anjou, and his son Prince Edward made their way to Scotland, seeking help and refuge.

Upon receiving news of the Battle of Northampton, James, who had gathered an army which included a contingent brought by the Lord of the Isles, advanced to Roxburgh and laid siege of the castle, which was held by a Yorkist governor, Lord Falconberg. There, on 3 August, he met his death; a death which was the direct result of his enthusiasm for gunnery.

'This Prince,' wrote the sixteenth-century chronicler, Lindsay of Pitscottie, 'mair curieous nor became him or the maiestie of ane King, did stand neir hand by the gunneris quhen the artaillezerie was dischargeand,' and one of the guns, which had probably been overcharged with gunpowder, burst with the force of the explosion and instantaneously killed him.

It was a wasteful and utterly unnecessary end for a vigorous King who was in the prime of life, able, popular and ill-spared since he left an heir who was still a small child. He was greatly lamented, not only because of his qualities and achievements, but also because great numbers of his subjects looked back to the disordered period of his minority, and realized that with another child-King on the throne troubled times were all too likely to return.

Besides being mourned by his subjects, James II received the praise of posterity. In the sixteenth century, George Buchanan, whose praise is worth quoting because he was always a stern critic of Kings, wrote:

'He showed such valour against his enemies, and such clemency to those that submitted themselves, that all Estates were much afflicted for his loss. And his death was the more lamented because it was sudden, and that in the flower of his youth too; after he had escaped so many dangers, and when the expectation of his virtues was at the highest.'

But without taking expectations into consideration there is much to praise. Perhaps T. F. Henderson, writing at the beginning of this century, wrote the best brief summary of his virtues and achievements:

'He owed much to his father's achievement and example; but he had perils to meet which during his father's reign remained undeveloped, and meeting them with consummate courage and decision, he dealt with them in a manner that was completely effective.'

Grief for the King could not be permitted to interfere with either war or government. As soon as Marie of Gueldres received the news of her husband's death she went at once to Roxburgh, taking with her their eldest son. She urged the commanders of the army not to abandon the siege, but to make the King's death the occasion of a victory, not of an ignominious repulse. They responded to her appeal, and Roxburgh was regained for Scotland. The King's body, meanwhile, was carried back to Edinburgh, and given burial in Holyrood Abbey, where he had been both crowned and married.

On 10 August the nine-year-old James III was escorted from Roxburgh to the nearby Abbey of Kelso for his coronation. It was solemnized with as much splendour as the circumstances allowed, and the tragedy of the occasion was a little alleviated by the victory at Roxburgh, which seemed to provide a good augury for the new reign.

5
James III,
1460–1488

At morn a King with sceptour, suord and croun,
At evin ane deid deformit carioun
(*The Testament of the Papyngo*, Sir David Lindsay of the
Mount)

King James III did not resemble his father in either character or
appearance. He was peace-loving and of a gentle nature, devout and
civilized and a patron of the arts, in all of which he took after his
mother, Marie of Gueldres. It is a tempting supposition that he may
have resembled her in appearance also. Marie of Gueldres was said
to have been beautiful, and certainly her son deserved that description.
The chronicler Ferrerius described him as outstanding among the
princes of his time both for his beauty and his elegance.

In leaving his image to posterity a King who is a patron of the arts
possesses an advantage over those who are unconcerned with such
matters. We owe our knowledge of James II's appearance to the fact
that he permitted a German knight to draw him; the survival of his
image is the result of someone else's interest. But James III commissioned from Hugo van der Goes a great altarpiece for the Collegiate
Church of the Holy Trinity in Edinburgh, which Marie of Gueldres
had founded. On one of the two surviving wings of the altarpiece there
is a fine portrait of him; on the other, the portrait of his Queen,
Margaret of Denmark.

James III is shown kneeling at a *prie-dieu*, crowned, and robed in
crimson and gold brocade, and wearing a royal mantle with a cape of
ermine. He is a dark-complexioned, foreign-looking young man, with
long black hair, fine aquiline features, and delicately arched brows.
His expression is tranquil, it suggests that he possessed an inner serenity,

despite the fact that he led a turbulent life and endured many tribulations.

At the beginning of his reign, however, it appeared that most of the tribulations usually attendant upon a royal minority might be avoided. Marie of Gueldres had more vigour and political intelligence than Queen Joan Beaufort had shown at the beginning of the previous reign; and Bishop Kennedy was a churchman of greater moral authority and political experience than the greatest churchman of the beginning of James II's minority, Bishop Cameron of Glasgow. Furthermore, there was no great family, liket he House of Douglas, awaiting an opportunity to assume supreme power. The Crown, it seemed, was well endowed with supporters, and without rivals.

Whether or not Marie of Gueldres was accorded the title of Regent appears uncertain; but she assumed the headship of state and ruled with the aid of a Regency Council.

The first political problem which Queen Marie had to face after the coronation of her son was the perennial problem of Scotland's relationship with England, and in particular the effect upon that relationship of the warfare between York and Lancaster. James II, it will be remembered, had maintained friendly relations with Henry VI, and had shown himself inimical to the Duke of York who had given a favourable reception to the rebel Earl of Douglas.

Late in 1460 Queen Marie received the Lancastrian fugitives, Margaret of Anjou and her son Prince Edward. They were entertained at the Collegiate of Lincluden, near Dumfries, where Margaret of Anjou suggested a marriage between her son and Queen Marie's elder daughter, the Princess Mary. At this time the Lancastrian position was too precarious to make the proposal attractive to the Scots; Queen Marie refused the hand of her daughter, but she provided Margaret with a supply of Scotland's ever-plentiful commodity, fighting men.

At the end of the year Margaret marched south with an army of 'Scots, Welsh, and other strangers and northernmen', and on the last day of December she defeated the Duke of York at the Battle of Wakefield. After the battle he was decapitated, and his head was set up in ignominy above one of the gates of York. The Yorkist claim was inherited by his son, Edward, Earl of March, soon to become King Edward IV. In the meantime Margaret marched on to win the second

Battle of St Albans; but she failed to occupy London, which was entered instead by the Earl of March, who had himself proclaimed King on 4 March 1461, in the face of two Lancastrian victories. He then pursued the Lancastrians northwards and routed them on Palm Sunday at the Battle of Towton. Margaret, this time accompanied by King Henry as well as their son, fled once more to Scotland.

Again Marie of Gueldres gave the fugitives a gracious reception, but this time she drove a harder bargain with them. In return for Scottish help the hard-pressed Lancastrians were obliged to surrender Berwick, a diplomatic victory which enhanced the prestige of Queen Marie and her council, especially since it followed the recovery of Roxburgh, which had so fortunately inaugurated the reign.

The supplanter of the unhappy Henry VI possessed political acumen as well as military skill. Edward IV may have been a libertine and a lover of ease, but neither pleasure nor laziness ever blunted his intelligence. In the course of a fairly long reign he was to be a dangerous neighbour to the King of Scots, and he began as he was to go on. He held a useful pawn in the Earl of Douglas, who had long ago allied himself to the House of York. Richard of York had retained him as a convenient trouble-maker; Edward IV now found a larger use for him.

Into Edward's scheme was drawn the Lord of the Isles, tempted afresh by the conditions of a minority, and that hoary trouble-maker Donald Balloch, a rebel in the two preceding reigns. In 1462 Douglas, the Lord of the Isles and Donald Balloch signed with Edward IV a traitorous agreement which Andrew Lang rather absurdly dignified with the name of 'The Treaty of Westminster–Ardtornish' (Ardtornish Castle on the Sound of Mull was a stronghold of the Lord of the Isles), whereby the three Scottish signatories were to become the liegemen of the King of England, and, if with their help he should conquer Scotland, all the country north of the Forth was to be partitioned between them. Douglas was to be restored to his estates in southern Scotland, which he likewise was to hold of the English King.

Edward IV probably had no expectation that this agreement would be put into effect; but he knew that he could rely on the three traitors to cause enough trouble to deflect the Scottish government from assisting the House of Lancaster. That precise result was the limit of their achievement.

The Lord of the Isles, supported by Donald Balloch, established himself in regal state at Inverness, and Douglas with his brother John of Balveny led a border raid in which Balveny was captured, and subsequently executed. Douglas, the last survivor of five brothers, fled once more to England. He had a long career of treason before him still. The Lord of the Isles gave his submission to James III when the young King visited Inverness in 1464; but in the meantime the Treaty of Westminster–Ardtornish had had the effect which Edward IV desired.

'It is credible to the intelligence of Marie of Gueldres,' Professor Gordon Donaldson remarks, 'that she seems to have been one of the first to see that Douglas and the Lord of the Isles might be neutralized if Scotland came to terms with Edward IV and abandoned what now seemed to be the lost cause of Lancaster.' Indeed, that cause seemed to be altogether lost, since Margaret of Anjou had just been defeated, after invading northern England with a small force under the command of Pierre de Brézé, lent her by the French King Louis XI. A Scottish force commanded by the fourth Earl of Angus rescued Brézé, who was besieged in Alnwick, and Margaret fled back to France.

After that, Queen Marie, threatened by the English King's diplomacy as well as by the hostilities at Alnwick, which might well have caused a full-scale war on behalf of an ally already defeated, was justified in feeling that the wisest course was to make peace with the victorious Edward IV. Furthermore, her uncle Philip of Burgundy, who was allied to Edward, sent an ambassador to Scotland urging her to do so.

The Queen's change of policy was not supported by Bishop Kennedy, who remained faithful to the Lancastrian interest. He may have felt that since Margaret of Anjou still enjoyed the support of Louis XI the Lancastrian cause might not be as lost as it seemed, and that French help might yet re-establish Henry VI on his throne. Kennedy saw the restoration of Henry as highly desirable, since he had always been friendly disposed towards Scotland.

Queen Marie's policy won the support of a group of the younger lords, while the older ones adhered to the traditional Lancastrian policy and supported Kennedy.

One of the young noblemen who adhered to Queen Marie's party was Adam Hepburn, Master of Hailes. Scandal named him the

Queen's lover, and her credit suffered as Queen Joan's credit had suffered when she became the wife of the Black Knight of Lorne. It appears that the intelligent Marie of Gueldres had learnt a lesson from the past, since she avoided Queen Joan's mistake of making a *mésalliance*; and it seems unlikely that having done so she would have been fool enough to commit the greater error of forming an even less acceptable association. However, she was evidently indiscreet in the favour which she showed to Hepburn of Hailes, and the resultant calumny damaged her good name. As Queen Marie's influence waned that of Bishop Kennedy increased, and by the end of 1462 he had replaced her as head of state. But there remains the possibility that ill-health rather than scandal may have been the chief cause of the Queen's political eclipse, for she died in December 1463, at the age of thirty.

It may have been some satisfaction to her in the last months of her life that Bishop Kennedy was obliged to change his policy and come to terms with Edward IV as she had wished to do the previous year. Margaret of Anjou, indomitable and ill-fated, had made yet another invasion and had been defeated at Hexham. Louis XI accordingly made a truce with Edward IV. Kennedy followed his example. Indeed, he concluded that the Lancastrian defeat had been final, and he attempted to negotiate a perpetual peace. Perpetuity proved impossible to guarantee; but a truce was made, to last until 1479.

Kennedy gave the kingdom two years of stability, at the end of which almost five years had passed since the death of James II. It appeared that the minority of James III might pass in a mercifully uneventful manner. But Bishop Kennedy died on 10 May 1465, shortly before the King's fourteenth birthday, which was 10 July. At the age of fourteen a King was considered to be 'of perfect age', and to have attained a nominal majority. After Kennedy's death no regent was appointed. The young King ruled alone, and his inexperience invited a coup d'état.

The aspirant for power was Lord Boyd of Kilmarnock, whose brother Sir Alexander Boyd was the King's military tutor, and the Keeper of Edinburgh Castle. The Boyds conspired with others who were eager to share the spoils of power: the late Bishop's brother, Lord Kennedy, who was Keeper of Stirling Castle, his half-brother, Patrick Graham, Bishop of Brechin and others who served to make a strong party, but who played a less prominent part in the events that followed.

In July 1466 the King was at Linlithgow, where he was presiding over the Exchequer audit. No doubt he was all too willing to be lured away from this dreary task by the suggestion of a hunting party. He went, in the company of the Boyds, and was forcibly carried off to Edinburgh Castle, where he remained, treated with all respect, but in effect a prisoner. In October Parliament met in Edinburgh and the King was induced, either by persuasion or duress, to make a speech declaring that he had accompanied Lord Boyd to Edinburgh of his own free will.

Lord Boyd then caused himself to be appointed the King's guardian, although James was supposed to be old enough not to need one, and the following year he made himself Chamberlain. Once he had effectively established himself as head of state, he endeavoured to consolidate the position of his family by marrying his son Sir Thomas Boyd to the elder of the King's two sisters, the Princess Mary. Thomas Boyd was created Earl of Arran, and appointed Sheriff of Arran and Wigtown and Steward of Kirkcudbright. The King was said to have 'a great hatred' for him, possibly because he considered him an unworthy husband for his sister, possibly because the marriage and the earldom illustrated his own powerlessness in the hands of the Boyds.

Lord Boyd had pursued his ambition in a sufficiently unscrupulous fashion, but once he had attained it he proved to be a man of considerable political intelligence. He negotiated for the King a highly advantageous marriage, with Margaret of Denmark, the daughter of Christian I, King of Denmark, Norway and Sweden.

By the terms of the agreement reached in 1468 King Christian was to provide his daughter with a dowry of 60,000 Rhenish florins. However, meeting some difficulty in raising the promised sum, Christian announced that he would pay 10,000 florins and would pledge the lands and rights of the Norwegian Crown in Orkney as security for the remaining 50,000. But in 1469, when the time came for him to part with his daughter and her dowry, Christian found himself unable to raise even 10,000 florins. Therefore he sent the King of Scots 2,000 and pledged his lands and rights in Shetland in addition to those in Orkney.

King Christian never redeemed his pledge, and James III was subsequently able to annex Orkney and Shetland to the Crown of Scots. In 1471 James further strengthened his position in the Northern Isles by inducing the Scottish Earl of Orkney, who had held his earldom of the Norwegian Crown, to exchange his lands there for equivalent lands in Fife. Thus the Scottish Crown acquired its northernmost holding of Crown lands, and the boundaries of the kingdom reached their fullest extent.

In the meantime the marriage of James to Margaret of Denmark had taken place in the Abbey of Holyrood, on 13 July 1469, three days after the King's eighteenth birthday. His bride was only thirteen years old.

Queen Margaret's portrait by van der Goes, on the opposite wing of the altarpiece to that of the King, shows the Queen likewise at her devotions. She is shown kneeling at her *prie-dieu*, clad richly and elegantly in a dress with a jewelled bodice and a skirt of dark blue velvet bordered with ermine. Her hair is completely concealed by a heart-shaped head-dress embroidered with pearls and surmounted by a delicate coronet which follows the contours of the head-dress. Her face, which has no claim to beauty of features, has a singular beauty of expression; it suggests the 'charm of spirit' and the 'kindness and gentleness of character' attributed to her by Ferrerius. The same chronicler gives her further praise:

> 'To the King her husband she showed herself so obedient that it would, to my mind, be difficult to find in any nation a marriage which was happier and more free from trouble. . . . Her piety towards the powers above and to the religion of Our Lord Jesus Christ was so great as to leave far behind that of virgins dedicated to God and cloistered in nunneries.'

James III showed his opinion of her worth when, the year after her death, he petitioned the Pope for her canonization.

As in the instance of his father, the King's marriage marked the conclusion of the minority and the beginning of his personal rule. Inevitably, it also marked the eclipse of the Boyds. The ease with which Lord Boyd had achieved his coup d'état in 1466 was principally due to the fact that there was no overshadowing power like that of the House of Douglas in the previous reign. His tenure of power was not troubled by any such internecine struggles as had attended the uneasy ascendancy of Livingstone. But his overthrow was as swift and easy as his rise had been, when the King was ready to bring it about, and for the corresponding reason that while he had lacked powerful rivals he had also lacked powerful friends.

In the very month of the King's marriage, the Boyds fell. Thomas Boyd, Earl of Arran, who had been sent to Denmark to escort the King's bride to Scotland, immediately upon his arrival at Leith was warned of his impending doom by his wife the Princess Mary. As soon as Margaret of Denmark had disembarked, Arran and his wife sailed back to Denmark in the same ship. Lord Boyd, who was on an embassy to England, also received a warning, and escaped abroad. In November 1469 Parliament declared the Boyds guilty of treason by their abduction of the King, and forfeit in life, lands and goods. The only member of the family to lose his life, however, was Sir Alexander Boyd, who was beheaded.

It is possible that the King, once freed from the resented ascendancy of the Boyds, may have experienced remorse for this execution. Certainly he showed thereafter extreme reluctance to impose the death penalty; indeed, his contemporaries considered that his too frequent exercise of the prerogative of mercy was an encouragement to violent crime.

A satirist suggested that the King granted pardons in return for payment:

> *Bot of a thing al gude men mervalis mair :*
> *Quhen grete consale, with thine awn consent,*
> *Has ordanit strate justice na man to spair,*
> *Within schort tym thou changis thine entent,*
> *Sendand a contrar lettir incontinent,*
> *Chargeand that of that mater mair be nocht ;*
> *Therat the warld murmuris that thou art bocht.*

But this is the only suggestion that the King used pardons as a source of gain; the usual complaint is that he was too merciful by temperament.

However, in the early years of his reign the royal authority seems to have been exercised effectively enough; for almost a decade the King prospered and the country with him.

In 1473 the succession was secured by the birth of a prince, who subsequently reigned as James IV. Margaret of Denmark bore her husband two more sons: a second James, born in 1476 (probably at the time of his birth the heir was ill and not expected to live, which would account for his being given the royal name), and John who was born in 1479.

During the 1470s the King managed to turn the political problems that arose to his own advantage. A problem which was protracted for more than half the decade was that of Patrick Graham and the bishopric of St Andrews. Graham, the Bishop of Brechin who had been a party to the Boyds' coup d'état, had succeeded Kennedy his half-brother as Bishop of St Andrews. Probably by reason of his involvement in the coup, he was not popular with the King. He was an intensely ambitious man, and, as later events were to prove, unhappily infected with *folie de grandeur*.

James, suspicious of his ambitions, forbade him to go to Rome for his consecration as Bishop of St Andrews, but in 1471, in disobedience to the King's commands, he went. The Archbishop of York was at that time pressing his claim to authority over the Scottish bishoprics, and Graham took the opportunity of persuading Pope Sixtus IV to create St Andrews an archbishopric and himself Primate of Scotland.

He returned in 1473 to find that his action, which had self-evident political advantages, had aroused a great deal of resentment among the Scottish bishops, who, as previously mentioned, had hitherto enjoyed parity with one another, and were reluctant to submit to the authority of a primate. He found, furthermore, that his independent action had increasingly antagonized the King.

Patrick Graham had made powerful enemies, though it took them some time to bring him down. Probably the most astute and dangerous of them was William Scheves, the King's friend and the royal physician, a cultivated but none too scrupulous man, a priest, a bibliophile and an astronomer, and, in the way of medieval astronomers, also an astrologer. Scheves may have been behind the levelling of a charge of heresy against Graham, which resulted in the latter's excommunication by the University of St Andrews. A papal commission was then appointed to investigate the alleged heresy, and give judgement. Perhaps the strain of such a deluge of troubles was too much for the unfortunate Archbishop; his *folie de grandeur* gained a complete hold upon him, and he played into the hands of the commission by declaring that he was not merely Primate of Scotland but Pope of Rome. The result was that in 1476 the commission found him not heretical but mad. In consequence he was deposed from his arch-bishopric and confined in the Augustinian priory on St Serf's Island in Lochleven for the remainder of his life. The King reaped the advantage of the privilege which Graham had initially obtained from the Pope: he secured the appointment of his own nominee to the archbishopric – William Scheves.

James also managed to turn the affairs of England to Scotland's advantage, temporarily at least.

In 1469 Edward IV, who seemed to have ensured his retaining the throne he had won, by defeating Margaret of Anjou at Hexham and capturing Henry VI, was faced with a sudden reverse of fortune. Edward's traitorous brother the Duke of Clarence conspired with Warwick, the great 'Kingmaker' who aspired to be the power behind Edward's throne and was alienated by the King's ability and independence. Clarence and Warwick slipped over to France, made common cause with Margaret of Anjou, and led an invasion of England, to oust Edward and reinstate Henry VI. Briefly they were successful: 1470 saw Edward a fugitive and Henry temporarily restored. But Fortune, as usual, favoured the House of York. Edward returned to defeat Warwick at Barnet and Margaret at Tewkesbury. Margaret's son, Prince Edward, was murdered after the battle, and Henry VI, once more a prisoner in the Tower, was likewise done to death.

These violent events were accompanied by Border disturbances, which suggested the need for a review of the Anglo-Scottish truce. Discussions took place in 1471, which resulted in a new truce for fifteen months only. In 1473 the late Bishop Kennedy's magnificent ship, the *St Salvator*, was wrecked on the English coast near Bamburgh. On board was the Abbot of St Colm, who was rescued and then held prisoner for ransom, in contravention of the truce which was still in force.

Anglo-Scottish relations were strained by this incident; but Edward IV was in a conciliatory mood because he was contemplating war with France and had no wish to see James III drawn into hostilities against him as the ally of Louis XI. The situation was delicate, as Louis had recently attempted to involve James in his war with the young Duke of Burgundy, Philip's son Charles the Rash. When this potential embroilment came to nothing, Edward made haste to secure his northern frontier with something more binding than a short-term truce. James was equally willing to take advantage of the occasion, and accordingly in 1474 a truce for forty-five years was negotiated, and the infant Prince James was betrothed to Edward's four-year-old daughter, the Princess Cecilia.

In the event, Edward did not go to war with France. He led an invasion indeed, but permitted himself to be bought off by Louis XI, with whom he signed the Treaty of Picquigny in 1475. The Anglo-Scottish truce, however, remained unbroken, and James III turned his attention from the Border to another perennial trouble-spot, the northwest of his kingdom.

In 1464, as previously mentioned, the Lord of the Isles had offered his submission to James III at Inverness. But in the ensuing decade, while James had been involved in other matters – the rise and fall of the Boyds, his marriage, the negotiations over Orkney and Shetland and the exigencies of foreign politics – the Lord of the Isles had once again assumed a degree of independence which threatened the integrity of the kingdom. It was obvious that the time had come to deal with him.

He was summoned to appear before Parliament, and when he disobeyed the summons the Earls of Athol, Crawford, Huntly and Argyll were commanded to visit his domains with fire and sword. He thereupon submitted to the King, and resigned to him the earldom of Ross. James received his submission in a conciliatory spirit. Though the earldom of Ross was annexed to the Crown, the Lord of the Isles was confirmed in the possession of the rest of his lands and created a Lord of Parliament. The King's generosity reconciled him to the Crown, but unhappily it did not end the turmoils of the northwest, for, from the later 1470s and for the rest of the reign, the area was in perpetual tumult caused by the ambitions of Angus, the base-born son of the Lord of the Isles, who sought to supplant his father, and to assert as great an independence as ever he had possessed.

This problem, however, was not one to which the King was able to give the attention it demanded, for the late 1470s saw the beginning of the troubles which were to beset him for the rest of the reign. Before giving some account of those troubles it is worth observing that since the beginning of his personal rule James III had shown himself to be neither so supine nor so incompetent a ruler as he is sometimes represented as having been. Indeed, the first nine years of his rule sufficiently justify Ferrerius's statement that 'among the princes of his age he was active and lively in every way'.

James's troubles began when his next brother, Alexander, Duke of Albany, reached maturity and experienced the temptations of ambition. It would be an over-simplification to say that those troubles were wholly caused by the traitorous activities of Albany, though Albany was an extremely dangerous man, a far greater threat in the context of Scottish politics than the contemporary figure in the English political scene whose career most nearly paralleled his own, Edward IV's brother Clarence. The basis of James's problem was his own personality, which as time passed increasingly caused him to be compared to his own detriment with both his brothers, Albany and Mar.

From the viewpoint of his contemporaries – at least those whose opinions mattered, the magnates of Scotland – James III was not a readily comprehensible character. He shared none of their enthusiasms; he showed a contemptuous lack of interest in the accomplishments which they considered important. Though he appears to have enjoyed an occasional hunting expedition he was a poorish horseman. He was wholly unmilitary, 'and desyrit never to heir of weiris [wars] nor the fame thairof'; and indeed, he disdained the knightly skills at which a medieval King was expected to show prowess. He may have had a mild interest in swordsmanship since he had a favourite who was a swordsman, and another who was said to have attracted his interest initially by displaying expertise in a swordfight. But that was the limit of his concern with such matters.

The King's pleasures were entirely connected with the arts. Lindsay of Pitscottie censoriously observed, 'He delyttit mair in singing and playing wpoun instrumentis nor [than] he did in defence of the bordouris or the ministratioun of iustice.' If this was not strictly true it was at any rate the impression created by the amount of time that the King devoted to music. It is noticeable that whereas music and literature were considered 'honeste solaces' for the athletic James I, in James III they were regarded as time-wasting addictions. Music, especially that of the harp, the lute and the organ, and the choral music provided by the choir of the Chapel Royal, seems to have been his greatest pleasure. Poets also enjoyed his patronage, and it was an age in which fine poetry was written by poets who disciplined their inspiration with exquisite craftsmanship. The greatest poet of the period was Robert Henrysoun. He was not, like William Dunbar in the next reign, exclusively a court poet, but his finest poem *The Testament of Cresseid* was written for a court audience. The sombre opening exemplifies its mood and style:

> *Ane doolie sessoun to ane cairfull dyte*
> *Suld correspond, and be equivalent.*
> *Richt sa it wes quhen I began to wryte*
> *This tragedie, the wedder richt fervent,*
> *Quhen Aries, in middis of the Lent,*
> *Schouris of haill can fra the north discend,*
> *That scantlie fra the cauld I micht defend. . . .*
>
> *I mend the fyre and beikit me about,*
> *Than tuik ane drink my spreitis to comfort*
> *And armit me weill fra the cauld thairout.*
> *To cut the winter nicht and mak it schort*
> *I tuik ane quair, and left all uther sport,*
> *Writtin be worthie Chaucer glorious*
> *Of fair Cresseid, and worthie Troylus. . . .*

Besides appreciating contemporary literature, and collecting classical manuscripts, the King was interested in painting, and the survival of part of the van der Goes altarpiece testifies to his awareness of the merits of the Flemish School.

His greatest interest, however, was in architecture, and the extravagance of his building schemes may have been the basis of the charges of avarice which were made against him. If, in order to finance his schemes, he was as Pitscottie said 'wondrous covettous', he was also a lavish spender of the proceeds of his covetousness. The Great Hall of Stirling Castle, which is now in process of restoration, was the work of his favourite, the architect Robert Cochrane, who may also have built the Chapel Royal of Stirling, which was demolished and replaced in the reign of James vi. He is likewise credited with the building of the Great Hall of Falkland, which was burnt down in 1654.

The King did not neglect the minor arts either. He possessed a magnificent collection of jewels, of which only an inventory survives.

It is impossible not to regret the disappearance of such an example of the fifteenth-century jeweller's art as his chain of gold swans set with rubies and diamonds and white enamelled swans set with pearls. His artistic preoccupation extended to the design of the coinage, and the beautiful silver groats issued in the later years of his reign, which show an unusual three-quarter-face representation of the King's head, are reputed to bear the first renaissance coin-portrait outside Italy.

Unfortunately for the King patronage of the arts did not win him the respect of his magnates who, as one modern writer puts it, 'identified aesthetic taste with effeminacy'. Some historians have done the same. One who judiciously avoids side-taking writes:

> 'The character of James III has been the subject of more dispute among historians than those of other Scottish monarchs. Between those who would paint him in the gaudy and sinister colours of an Edward II, and those who regard him as the wronged victim of a wild age, one may well hesitate.'

But the 'gaudy and sinister colours' referred to, those of politically ill-judged homosexual attachments, may well be the right colours in which to depict him.

Insulated from the majority of his nobles by antipathy of interests, the King gathered about himself a coterie of favourites, some of whom shared his artistic predilections, some of whom apparently did not. Ferrerius and Pitscottie have recorded their names.

Those who could claim distinction in the arts were Robert Cochrane, the architect, he whom the King was first said to have seen not engaged about his profession but embroiled in a fight; and William Rogers, an English musician whom Ferrerius described as 'musicus rarissimus', adding that in 1529 there were many musicians in Scotland who boasted of having been his pupils. Two other favourites were James Hommyl, the King's tailor, and Leonard, his bootmaker, of whom Professor Donaldson remarks, in apology for the King's favour to them, 'it was a time when men of substance spent vast sums on their personal adornment, and James may have shown his good taste in his clothing as in other things'. The favourites who were not connected with the arts were Torphichen the swordsman, one Preston who was grudgingly admitted to be a gentleman, and John Ramsay of Balmain, who was a youth of good family.

Since the favourites were for the most part men of obscure origins to whom the King's favour brought wealth and influence, inevitably they were unpopular. But the extreme detestation with which these men, who were not admitted to political office, were regarded by an influential group among the nobility is not easily explicable except upon the hypothesis that the King's relations, or suspected relations, with some of them aroused disgust.

George Buchanan, writing in the late sixteenth century, certainly missed no opportunities for innuendo in referring to the King's favourites, and concluded by describing him in the later years of his life surrendering to the ascendancy of Ramsay, and 'drowned in voluptuousness'. However, Buchanan also accused the King of other immoralities, including incestuous relations with the younger of his sisters, the Princess Margaret, an accusation which does not occur in any earlier history. Buchanan, though a great scholar, was also an unscrupulous scandal-monger, and he may have exaggerated the King's immorality to give greater point to his moralizings on the subject of the King's downfall.

It is a commonplace of Scottish history that the nobility looked askance at James III; but it is always an over-simplification to refer to 'the nobility' *en bloc*. Many of the magnates, whether or not they found the King a sympathetic or praiseworthy character, were unswervingly loyal to him throughout the reign; but many were alienated, partly by disapprobation of his character, partly by the fact that James, making no concessions to their prejudices, relied in his dealings with them upon authority unalloyed by tact. It was the King's misfortune that those whom he alienated the Duke of Albany made haste to cultivate.

Both the King's brothers were aggressively normal young men. The Duke of Albany, says Pitscottie, 'lowit nothing so weill as abill men and goode horse and maid gret cost and expenssis thairon; for he was wondrous liberall in all thingis pertening to his honour'. In other words, he spent money on what were considered to be the right things. He was admired, according to the same chronicler 'for his singular wisdom and manheid'; manhood one may grant him, though wisdom is hard to discern. He had 'a werie awfull continance quhen he plessit to schew himself unto onfriendis' (unfriends, i.e. enemies).

The Earl of Mar was 'fair and pleasant faceit' and he too, in contrast to the King, had all the proper interests and accomplishments: 'He wssit [used] mekill huntting and halking with wther gentill men pastyme or archorie and wther knychtlie games, as the intertening of great horse and meiris quhairby thair ofspring might florisch.'

Hunting, hawking, archery and horse-breeding may have absorbed the energies of the Earl of Mar, not so those of the Duke of Albany. James had doubtless hoped to satisfy Albany's ambitions and make use of his abilities by employing him as Warden of the Marches; but some time in 1478 Albany was arrested, accused of abusing his powers as Warden and of treasonable intercourse with England and was imprisoned in Edinburgh Castle. Mar was likewise arrested, and imprisoned at Craigmillar. There was some talk of his having attempted to compass the King's destruction by magic, though this was probably nothing but sensational gossip. Dilettante black magic has always had its adherents, and in the late fifteenth century it was particularly fashionable. If magic had attracted the Earl of Mar, inevitably gossip would have said that he had been arrested for practising it against his brother. The most likely reason for his arrest is perhaps that he had become too closely identified with Albany in sympathy to allow James ease of mind.

Unhappily, the Earl of Mar died in prison, to the great injury of the King's reputation. The official explanation of his death was unlikely enough to be both absolutely true and at the same time unconvincing. It was announced that he had been bled for a fever, had become delirious and torn off the bandages while he was unattended, and had bled to death before he was found. The announcement was made by William Elphinstone, Official of Lothian, an ecclesiastic who enjoyed the King's favour, and was regarded as an incorruptible person. Even his good name, however, did not serve to carry complete conviction in the matter. But, whatever the King's contemporaries suspected, most historians have been inclined to exonerate him from the death of Mar. The consensus of opinion is that it was accidental.

In the spring of 1479 the Duke of Albany escaped from Edinburgh Castle. The account of his escape given by Pitscottie is a grim and dramatic story, true in essence even if it had collected apocryphal details.

The Duke of Albany, it appeared, had friends in France, who sailed to Newhaven near Leith in a ship purporting to be that of a wine-merchant. They sent to Albany, in Edinburgh Castle, two barrels, one containing wine and the other a coil of rope and his instructions.

Albany invited the Captain of the Guard and the three men on duty to come and drink with him, and warned his attendant to 'drink no wyne that night bot keip him fresche ffor he knew not quot he wald have adoe'. The Captain and his men drank deeply. 'The fyre was hott and the wyne was stark [strong]'; wine and heat worked on the guests while Albany looked on with only a show of participation. When he judged that intoxication had levelled the odds, he sprang on the Captain and despatched him with his dagger, then did likewise to one of the men, while the other two were killed by his attendant.

The prisoners heaped the bodies on to the fire, 'and efterwart tuik out thair cordis and past to the wall heid at ane quyit place quhair the watches might have no sight of thame'. Albany sent his attendant down first, but the rope was short, and the young man fell and broke his thigh. Albany returned to his chamber, tore up the sheets of his bed and knotted them into an additional length of rope. He then went back to the wall, joined the makeshift rope to the existing length, and went over himself. He descended without mishap, picked up his injured attendant, and carried him to a safe hiding-place before walking to Newhaven where he boarded the French ship which sailed immediately. He was well out at sea by the time the holocaust in his bed-chamber revealed his escape, and the ruthless and savage manner in which it had been accomplished.

In France Albany was well received by Louis XI, who arranged a rich and aristocratic marriage for him, to Agnès de la Tour d'Auvergne, daughter of the Comte de Boulogne. Whatever ambitions had led Albany into treasonable courses before his imprisonment, after his escape all his ambitions were directed to one end, that of supplanting his brother on the throne of Scotland. Louis XI was not disposed to support this enterprise; but before long Albany found himself a more obliging ally in Edward IV.

In the meantime the King of Scots was experiencing a period of unpopularity, which made the activities of Albany all the more dangerous. Albany and Mar had both been popular, and the imprisonment of the one and the death of the other had adversely affected the King's public image.

In addition to this personal cause of the King's unpopularity, there was the larger cause of a protracted economic crisis. Depreciation of the currency had continued steadily since the reign of David II. Professor William Croft Dickinson wrote: 'Exact calculations are impossible, but roughly we may say that in 1393 a pound of silver was worth 528 pennies; in 1440 it was worth 768 pennies; in 1451 it was worth 1,152 pennies; and in 1483 . . . 1,680 pennies.'

Inevitably, at a period when the King was personally responsible for the government, such a problem as inflation, which has proved to be beyond the resources of a modern government to solve, and which was certainly beyond the power of one man and his advisers to solve, was blamed upon the King.

James did what he could to meet the demands of the situation. Despite the ever increasing number of pennies coined from the pound of silver there was a severe shortage of specie. Accordingly the King issued copper farthings which, it was declared, were intended 'for the eise and sustentatioun of the Kingis liegis and almous deid to be done to pur folk'; in other words, for the convenience of the people in small transactions, and for charity. The experiment was not a success. The people expected the coinage to be of gold and silver, and they viewed the small dark coins with the gravest suspicion, and in some areas refused to use them at all. They scornfully called the new coins 'black money' or 'Cochrane's plaks', because the King's favourite was blamed as the originator of the experiment.

Possibly Robert Cochrane may have fancied himself as an economic expert as well as an architect, but evidence is lacking. However, here again the economic situation and the personal causes of the King's unpopularity interacted with unfortunate consequences. Rightly or wrongly, Cochrane was blamed, and the King suffered for it.

James III might have been able to avail himself of the services of men of non-noble origins as successfully as Louis XI was able to do so, if the favour which he showed them had not been so blatant and so extravagant, and if the recipients of his favour had not flaunted it in a manner that was certain to be offensive. Cochrane, according to Buchanan, was 'a man endowed with great strength of body and equal audacity of mind', a combination of qualities which, though it might please the King, was unlikely to endear him to the mass of the nobility. His arrogance, and the resentment which it aroused, was increased when he received a grant of the lands which had belonged to the late

Earl of Mar, and possibly the title itself, though this is according to sixteenth-century chroniclers, and again contemporary evidence is lacking.

At any rate, the King's popularity was at an unenviably low ebb when Anglo-Scottish relations deteriorated once more in 1480.

When Louis xi refused to aid Albany's treasonable designs against his brother he sent an emissary to Scotland with instructions to attempt to arrange a reconciliation between Albany and the King, and to enlist Scottish help against England. The emissary, a Scottish doctor of the Sorbonne named John Ireland, was successful in winning the King's liking and respect (indeed, some years later he settled in Scotland and became the King's confessor), but his mission was unsuccessful as the King refused either to be reconciled with Albany or to break his truce with England. Rather, he strove to strengthen it by proposing a marriage between his sister Margaret and Anthony Woodville, Earl Rivers, the brother of Edward iv's Queen, Elizabeth Woodville.

Edward's attitude, however, had altered since 1474. Possibly influenced by Albany who hoped to benefit from bad relations between his brother and the English King, Edward responded to James's proposals with a series of impossible demands: that the King of Scots should acknowledge English overlordship; that Prince James, who was betrothed to the English Princess Cecilia, should be sent to England; that Berwick should be surrendered to the English, and the Earl of Douglas be restored to his estates.

James was naturally incensed, and, as was to be expected, he refused to consider the English demands. Furthermore, they caused him to reconsider his recent dealings with Louis xi, to whom he probably felt that it would be advisable to offer a gesture of friendship to requite his refusal to support Albany. Therefore, he sent an emissary to Edward requiring him to desist from aiding Burgundy against France, otherwise he himself would feel obliged to intervene on behalf of France. Edward refused with incivility, and hostilities followed.

The fifth Earl of Angus burnt Bamburgh, and an English fleet attacked the south-east coast of Scotland. It was repulsed by the Scottish sea captain Sir Andrew Wood, who was rewarded for his victory with the estate of Largo in Fife. A full-scale war threatened: Edward iv prepared to invade Scotland, and James made ready to march against him. War was averted by the intervention of a Papal Nuncio, who desired both Kings to abandon their enmity at a time when Christendom was threatened by the advance of the Infidels. This was not an empty form of words, for since the fall of Constantinople in 1453 the Turks had spread throughout eastern Europe and by this date constituted a very real threat to the west.

James, a reluctant warrior, was probably thankful to obey the Pope. But in March 1482 he caused Parliament to set on record that:

'Gif [if] sa be that the King of England will nocht apply him to the pece but continew in his weir, our Soverane Lord takis witnes of God that it is again[st] his will, and that he sal nocht be the causer nor occasion of effusion of Christen bluid, but in his richteous querel and defens; and sal, God willing, defend the realme in honour and fredome, as his nobill progenitouris has done in tymis bygane.'

No doubt he would have done so, to the best of his ability, if a substantial group of the nobility had not decided otherwise.

Edward IV showed himself less obedient to the Pope, for reasons which quickly emerged. It seems logical to see Albany's influence behind the insolent demands which Edward IV had made of the King of Scots, for Albany would have foreseen perfectly what his brother's reaction to them would be. He now offered to accede to most of those same demands in return for English assistance in supplanting his brother.

On 10 June 1482, at the Castle of Fotheringay, Albany, calling himself 'Alexander of Scotland, by the gift of the King of England', signed an agreement whereby he promised that if he were placed upon the throne of Scotland by English aid, he would acknowledge Edward as his overlord, terminate the alliance with France and make no other alliances without Edward's leave, and surrender to England Berwick, Lochmaben, Eskdale and Annandale. In addition, he agreed that if he could divorce his French Duches she would marry the Princess Cecilia himself, and that if he could not obtain a divorce he would marry his heir to an English bride. Upon these disgraceful terms he was provided with an English army commanded by Edward's brother, Richard, Duke of Gloucester (the future King Richard III). Together Albany and Gloucester marched north to lay siege to Berwick.

In July James mustered his army on the Burgh Muir of Edinburgh, and marched down Lauderdale to encounter the invaders and relieve Berwick. The disaffection which had been mounting ever since the arrest of the King's brothers may have been brought to a head by the King's appointing Cochrane his Master of the Artillery. The nobles who were automatically the King's general staff on a campaign may have been simply unwilling to accept Cochrane as one of themselves. Their displeasure would certainly have been aggravated by the fact that the King had somewhat unnecessarily brought with him not merely Cochrane but most of the detested favourites; this would have seemed an additional insult, on top of the injury of Cochrane's staff appointment.

What followed cannot have been premeditated. If it had been, probably the army would never have left Edinburgh at all. However, it marched as far as Lauder, and there encamped. A disgruntled gathering took place, which included the Earl of Angus, a man who was unpopular with the King as the son-in-law of Lord Boyd, and who has been described by a modern historian as 'a chronic and individualistic trouble-maker'; the Earl of Buchan, the King's uncle; the Earls of Huntly, Crawford and Lennox, and Lord Gray. The trend of their discussion was that the favourites were insufferable, and that something ought to be done. Lord Gray stirred up trouble by recounting the fable of the mice who agreed that it would be a good thing to bell the cat, and found that their only problem was to decide who was going to do it. Angus announced that he would do it, and thereby became known both to his contemporaries and posterity as 'Archibald Bell-the-Cat'.

The appearance of Cochrane at what he supposed to be a council of war brought matters to a climax. Pitscottie recounted, with some very good imaginary dialogue, the arrest of the unfortunate Cochrane, the insults heaped upon him by the disaffected lords, his spirited resistance, the sudden eruption of resentment against the favourites, the rush to the King's pavilion to seize the rest of them and the appalling culmination: the hanging of the favourites over the Bridge of Lauder, before the eyes of the King.

Of the favourites previously named there were two survivors. One was James Hommyl, the King's tailor, who had been fortunate in not being brought on the campaign; in after years he is recorded as receiving gifts from the King. The other was John Ramsay of Balmain, who, when the rest were seized, locked his arms around the King's neck and clung to him with such desperation that the lords hesitated to take him by force for fear of doing violence to the King's person. James pleaded for his life, which was reluctantly granted. After that the King was forced to witness the killing of the rest.

When all was over the army, under the command of Angus and his supporters, marched back to Edinburgh, with the King as a prisoner. He was entrusted to the care of his uncles Athol and Buchan, and confined in Edinburgh Castle.

Clearly, in these violent events there had been no forethought at all, and the perpetrators of them were faced with the problem of what to do next. Albany was before Berwick with an English army on Scottish soil. The rebel lords sympathized with what they conceived to be Albany's wrongs, but most of them upon reflection did not altogether approve his method of avenging them, and they would have approved even less had they known of his traitorous agreement at Fotheringay. In view of their subsequent behaviour, it seems probable that Angus and Gray knew of it, but not the rest.

The King's situation was by no means as desperate as it appeared, for with the favourites eliminated and the English over the frontier, few even of the King's harshest critics wished for a coup d'état. Albany may have expected to find the nobility of Scotland waiting to put him on his brother's throne, but he did not do so. He found instead the perpetrators of the Lauder Bridge massacre in a self-effacing mood, and Archbishop Scheves, the Bishop of Dunkeld, the Earl of Argyll and the Chancellor Lord Avondale empowered to treat with him on his brother's behalf. Public opinion also, it seemed, had undergone a change in the King's favour, and the burgesses of Edinburgh were demanding his release.

Albany accepted the realities of the situation, and decided to make the best of it for the time being. With secret assurances of his fidelity to the agreement of Fotheringay, Albany left Gloucester to reduce Berwick, accompanied the negotiators to Edinburgh and joined his voice to those of the citizens in demanding the release of the King.

James was unaware of the full extent of his brother's treason, though the very manner of Albany's return to Scotland cannot have led him to suppose that Albany was anything but treacherous. However, he was obliged to accept Albany as his deliverer, and then await further developments. The four intermediaries arranged that upon the release of the King, Albany should be restored to his estates and offices, and should take an oath of loyalty to his brother. On these terms a formal and insincere reconciliation was effected.

On 25 September the King emerged from the castle, where he had been a prisoner since the end of July. To illustrate his reconciliation with his brother he rode down to the Abbey of Holyrood with Albany sitting behind him on the same horse. They were greeted with public rejoicing, but it cannot be supposed that the King could find it in him to rejoice, with the Lauder Bridge massacre a recent memory, and the loss of Berwick to be laid to Albany's charge. However, he showed gratitude to the citizens, whose loyalty had been influential in forcing Albany's hand: he gave the Provost of Edinburgh the powers of a sheriff and the privilege of raising the citizens in arms under their own banner. Tradition says that this banner, the famous 'Blue Blanket', was embroidered by Margaret of Denmark and her ladies.

After the reconciliation came the last and most curious phase of the relationship between Albany and the King. At first James kept Albany perpetually at his side; he caused him to accompany him everywhere, eat at his table and share his bed. The impression created was that Albany was in the highest favour; the intention was probably to prevent his making mischief. But Albany remained a problem: whether he were more dangerous employed or unemployed would be difficult to judge. James may have decided to make a last attempt at winning his loyalty; 'to shame him by trusting him', as one historian put it. On 11 December Albany was appointed Lieutenant of the Kingdom, and entrusted with its defence. Short of giving him the throne, James could have done no more to fulfil his ambitions and to employ his ability and energy.

Inevitably, as it seems from the viewpoint of history, Albany betrayed the trust. He inaugurated the year 1483 by sending Angus and Gray to England, to reaffirm on his behalf the agreement of Fotheringay, and to promise Edward IV the allegiance of them all. Edward in turn agreed to support them, and to assist in restoring the Earl of Douglas to his inheritance.

Comings and goings between Scotland and England, however, were always liable to discovery, and within a matter of a few weeks

Albany's new treason was divulged to the King. On 19 March he was dismissed from his Lieutenancy of the Kingdom, and he and his supporters were forbidden to come within six miles of the King. It was an insufficient punishment, for Albany was disgraced but not disarmed. Perhaps the explanation of James's leniency to him may have been a sense of culpability for the death of Mar. Albany did not delay his trouble-making: he returned to England, and before he went admitted an English force to the Castle of Dunbar.

On 2 June Albany was declared a traitor, forfeit in life, lands and goods. But Fortune had already deserted Albany, for on 9 April his patron Edward iv had died. In the ensuing political turmoil in England the ambitions of Albany were of little consequence. The boy King Edward v was the victim of the power struggle between Richard of Gloucester and the Woodville faction, the kindred of the King's mother. Gloucester first became Protector, and then usurped his nephew's throne, and Edward v and his younger brother disappeared in circumstances which will probably remain for ever controversial.

Richard iii was never secure on his throne; his brief reign was a continuous struggle to maintain himself. He was not disposed to spare attention for Albany. However, Albany had still one friend in England: the long-exiled Earl of Douglas. Two years to the very month after he had besieged Berwick with an English army, Albany was reduced to joining Douglas in a desperate venture, backed only by five hundred men of their own followings.

In July 1484 Albany and Douglas invaded Scotland by the western route and attacked Lochmaben. It was the time of the annual fair and the town was crowded. The little force was routed, and though Albany escaped Douglas was taken prisoner. He was brought before the King, upon whom it is said that he turned his back. Douglas, who had lost one brother to the dagger of James ii, two to the executioner's axe and one on the battlefield, could not have been expected to love the Stewarts, even though the fault lay with the Douglases in the first place.

Despite the fact that Douglas was caught at last after a lifetime of treason, James showed his customary mercy. But his judgement had a certain fitness in it: he condemned the Earl to resume the career for which he had been designed, by ordering him to spend the rest of his life as an inmate of the Abbey of Lindores. The words with which

Douglas received his sentence, if true, are a sufficient comment on his character: 'A man who can do no better must be a monk.'

Albany fled first to England, and when he learnt that he had no more to hope from Richard III, he crossed to France. He met his end the following year 1485, when he was accidentally killed by a splinter of a lance as he sat spectator at a tournament. By his French Duchess he had one son, John, who later played an honourable part in Scottish politics, and made reparation for the treasons of his father.

After the defeat of Albany and Douglas at Lochmaben, James was no longer threatened by English support of Scottish traitors. In September 1484 a new truce was negotiated between Scotland and England, supported by a new marriage alliance. Richard III had declared the children of Edward VI to be bastards, so that the English bride now proposed for Prince James was Richard's niece, Anne de la Pole, daughter of Richard's sister and the Duke of Suffolk.

This arrangement, however, was short-lived. Richard III's eagerness for peace with Scotland was motivated by his own insecurity. His son, Edward of Middleham, died in 1484, and as a childless King as well as a usurper Richard was more vulnerable than ever. His overthrow by the Lancastrian claimant of indisputable illegitimacy, Henry Tudor, is one of the best-known events in English history. Indeed, his defeat and death at the Battle of Bosworth on 22 August 1485 is often invoked as an arbitrary point of demarcation between 'medieval' and 'modern' times. In Scotland the supplanting of one English usurper by another had no such significance; in fact, the effect that it had upon Anglo-Scottish relations was, for the time being, surprisingly slight.

Henry VII successfully established his dynasty which lasted for just over a century, intermarriage with which ultimately brought the Stewarts to the throne of England. At first, however, he wore his crown uneasily, and was eager to secure his northern frontier while he concentrated upon building up his authority at home. Accordingly, the truce signed with Richard III was followed by a new truce with Henry VII, and a new series of royal betrothals. Henry VII linked the Lancastrian and Yorkist claims to the English throne by marrying Elizabeth of York, eldest daughter of Edward IV and Elizabeth Woodville, who was now once again reinstated in legitimacy. He proposed that peace with Scotland should be guaranteed by the marriage of James III to Elizabeth Woodville, and of two of his sons to two of her daughters, which was agreed on 21 November 1487.

The King of Scots was enabled to contemplate this diplomatic marriage by the death of Margaret of Denmark, which had occurred in July 1486. Politically Queen Margaret had been self-effacing; domestically she had shown her husband exemplary devotion. In view of his addiction to his favourites she had perhaps had much to endure and he the best of reasons for regarding her as a candidate for sainthood. He lost no time in petitioning Pope Innocent VIII for her canonization.

James III was in high favour at the court of Rome. In 1486 Innocent VIII had sent to Scotland as Papal Legate the Bishop of Imola, who had brought James the Golden Rose, the symbolic gift yearly presented to the ruler whom the Pope deemed to be the most faithful son of the Church. Also, in response to James's appeal for papal support, the Legate brought a brief which threatened with excommunication any individual, layman or cleric, who disobeyed the King, and with interdict any city, burgh, university or college which defied royal authority. In support of the King's appeal and the Pope's commands, the Legate was unsparing in applying the sanctions of the Church to the unruly.

But Hector Boece has a story of how James was overcome with his habitual lenity in a manner that undermined the Legate's efforts and his own intentions. He was riding to the church of Restalrig near Edinburgh with the Bishop of Imola and William Elphinstone, now Bishop of Aberdeen and one of his most trusted advisers. They encountered a man who was being led to his execution, having been convicted of murder. The man broke free from his guards, flung himself down before the King, and prayed for pardon explaining that the murder had been an accidental killing. James asked the advice of the Papal Legate, who replied 'Fiat Justitia'. But James, who had been moved to compassion, turned to Bishop Elphinstone and said, 'Is this the mercy of Italian priests? You used to give me very different advice. Fiat Misericordia.' Elphinstone evidently shared the King's Christian views on forgiveness; but they were out of tune with contemporary views on the necessity of stern justice to discourage violent crime.

In 1487, in response to the King's request for the canonization of his late Queen, Innocent VIII empowered Archbishop Scheves,

Bishop Elphinstone, Robert Blacader, Bishop of Glasgow and the Abbot of Holyrood to conduct an inquiry into the virtues and miracles of Margaret of Denmark. Thus the process of her canonization was officially begun, but it was not continued beyond the end of the reign.

At the same time the Pope granted the King the privilege of having his nominations to bishoprics and greater benefices considered at Rome during a period of eight months after they should fall vacant; a valuable concession, which was of greater advantage to James III's successor than to himself, for little time was left him in which to avail himself of it.

After the King had extricated himself from his difficulties of 1482–3, it might well have appeared that his problems were over. Albany was defeated, and soon departed to his end in France. Upon the death of Louis XI in 1483 the French alliance was reaffirmed by a treaty with his successor Charles VIII. Peace was secured with England, James recovered Dunbar and during the last years of the reign he was driving a hard bargain with Henry VII for the restoration of Berwick. In the final stage of the negotiations it was agreed that Berwick should be declared neutral territory, pending a meeting between the two Kings which was to take place in January 1488, but which was deferred until July. The meeting never took place, for by July 1488 James III was dead. The position of Berwick remained anomalous. The town continued to be held by the English, though the county of Berwickshire was and is part of Scotland; and the technically neutral status of Berwick is still acknowledged by the fact that in certain official documents Berwick is listed individually after Wales among the territories of the United Kingdom.

The reign of James III concluded in violence. Although many reasons can be adduced to account for the final rebellion of the reign, most of them can be traced to the basic cause of the King's unpopularity. James was regarded as a negligent governor, lax above all in his attempts to assert the rule of law. The Parliaments of 1473, 1478, 1479, 1484, 1485 and 1487 urged him in outspoken terms to give more attention to this all-important matter. Beneficial legislation during his reign mostly took the form of the re-enactment of that which was regarded as good, necessary and possibly unenforced, from the two preceding reigns. On the other hand, James was by no means unsuccessful in foreign politics. Possibly the explanation is that he was interested in diplomacy but uninterested in the routine of government. If so it was a fault for which he paid dearly.

The King won sympathy in 1482 because of his imprisonment, and because Albany forfeited his popularity by bringing in the English army which took Berwick. But James apparently made no attempt to convert this change of feeling in his favour into lasting popularity. Despite the fact that his patronage of unacceptable favourites had played a great part in causing his earlier unpopularity, James did not court new popularity by making any concessions to public opinion in this matter. John Ramsay, the survivor of the Lauder Bridge massacre whose life James had purchased at the cost of his own humiliation, was created Earl of Bothwell and allowed far greater political influence than had been enjoyed by Cochrane and the rest. He was employed on embassies to England and appointed Captain of the King's guard. According to Ferrerius, at Ramsay's suggestion no-one except himself was permitted to carry arms in the King's presence. 'He was,' wrote Ferrerius, 'so great a favourite with the King that nearly all the affairs of the Scottish court were subject to his arbitration. Having been elevated but a short time before to the earldom of Bothwell by the King, he seemed to behave more extravagantly than the other nobles and great men.' The favour which James showed Ramsay after the murder of Cochrane in some respects parallels the favour which Edward II of England showed Hugh Despenser the younger after the killing of his first favourite Piers Gaveston; in both instances the consequences of committing the same mistake twice over were disastrous to the King.

As previously stated, James III did not alienate the Scottish nobility *en bloc*, but he alienated a sufficiently large number of individuals to permit a strong opposition party to come into being.

Paradoxically, the opposition to James III may have been rendered more dangerous by the strengthening of the King's position in his later years. In order to recoup that position he had been obliged to digest the insult to his sovereignty offered at Lauder Bridge and the slaughter of his favourites; but, as Drummond put it, 'notwithstanding all his protestations and outward demeanour . . . yet he meditated revenge,' and he was resolved 'that ere long he would be avenged upon all whom he either knew were accessary, or suspected to have been upon the plot of Lauder Bridge, or his committing to the Castle of

Edinburgh.' They, accordingly, concluded, 'that it was sometimes better to commit a fault unpardonable, than venture under the pardon'.

The actual occasion of the rebellion against James III is often said to have been his annexation of the revenues of Coldingham Priory to finance a double choir for the Chapel Royal of Stirling, so that a full choir could remain in residence and another accompany him to provide choral music wherever he went. This, however, is an over-simplification of the Coldingham question, and the simple statement suggests an arbitrary and ill-advised action on the part of the King, of which he was not guilty.

The priory of Coldingham was a cell of the Benedictine Abbey of Durham. The community of English monks survived the Wars of Independence, but its presence was unwelcome in Scotland as it provided a centre for espionage. Early in James III's reign there was an English prior, a Scottish aspiring-prior, who was a member of the Home family, and a rival Home aspirant who was resident in Rome. In 1472 James III proposed to convert the priory into a collegiate Chapel Royal with the 'Roman' Home as provost; a scheme which received papal approval. However, the Scottish-based Homes expelled the two remaining English monks and took possession of Coldingham. The Roman Home died in 1478. While James was embroiled in his troubles with Albany he had little time to think of Coldingham, but when he had extricated himself from those troubles he turned his attention to it again. Coldingham lacked a community and was in the hands of a recalcitrant family. James persuaded the obliging Innocent VIII to permit him to suppress the non-functioning priory altogether, and convert its revenues to enlarging the choir of Stirling. This not unreasonable solution to a protracted problem naturally enraged the Homes who had taken possession of Coldingham. They participated vigorously in the rebellion which led to the King's downfall, but, though the Coldingham problem played its part in the events which preceded the rebellion, it was probably a matter of timing not causation. There seems no reason to suppose that had there been no suppression of Coldingham there would have been no rebellion. Indeed, the rebellion took place when the King's heir was old enough to be of use to the opposition party, and not old enough to resist its purpose.

The opposition was headed by Angus, the ringleader of the Lauder

Bridge rebellion. It included Lords Gray, Home, Hailes and Lyle, the Bishop of Glasgow and the Earl of Argyll, who had succeeded Lord Avondale as Chancellor and had recently been displaced in favour of Bishop Elphinstone. The King's party was not unimpressive, for it included the Earls of Huntly, Errol and Athol, and the Earl of Crawford (to whom the King in the last months of the reign gave the title of Duke of Montrose), Archbishop Scheves and Bishop Elphinstone. It included also the new nobility with which the King was seeking to strengthen himself: his favourite Bothwell, Lord Kilmaurs, recently created Earl of Glencairn, and the newly ennobled Lords Ruthven, Drummond and Sempill.

At the beginning of 1488, the King, threatened with rebellion, went north to raise supporters, leaving Prince James at Stirling; and on 2 February the Keeper of Stirling Castle, doubtless by prearrangement, handed the Prince over to the rebels. In May the forces of the King and the rebels met near Blackness, where there was an indecisive skirmish followed by a 'Pacification'. The Prince remained in the hands of the rebels, and the King agreed to the formation of a new council, which was in effect a Council of Regency. No doubt, with the Prince out of his control he felt himself forced to submit to unreasonable conditions, and no doubt he was marking time and had no intention of abiding by an agreement made under duress.

After the Pacification of Blackness the King attempted to return to Stirling Castle, but was refused entry by the traitorous Keeper, Sir James Shaw of Sauchie. This incident proved the insincerity of the Pacification and led to the resumption of hostilities.

On 11 June 1488 the King and the rebels met in battle within sight of the castle, not far from the scene of Robert the Bruce's victory of Bannockburn. Contemporaries called the place 'the Field by Stirling', and posterity named the engagement the Battle of Sauchieburn. It was a tragic engagement, for both the protagonists were unwilling to play their parts. James III, though forced to defend his sovereign rights, was at the best of times a reluctant soldier; his son, an unconsenting rebel, was perhaps more reluctant still.

The most circumstantial account of the battle and its aftermath is given by Pitscottie, whose great-uncle David, second Lord Lindsay, fought for the King.

Pitscottie tells how Lord Lindsay gave the King a great grey

The Great Seal
of Robert, Duke
of Albany, who
governed
Scotland during
the English
captivity of James I.

This much-damaged
portrait by an unknown
artist may be
the ruins of a
good likeness
of James I, the
poet and law-giver who
established the greatness
of the Royal House of
Stewart.

Jacob von gots
gewalten kiing
von Schottland

A contemporary drawing of James II by Jorg von Ehingen, a visitor to the
court of Scotland. Clearly depicted is the disfigurement which gave rise to
James II's nickname 'James of the Fiery Face'.

Silver groat of James III, issued 1485–8. This beautiful coin is reputed to bear the first renaissance coin portrait produced outside Italy.

Head of James III, detail from the altarpiece by Hugo van der Goes.

Left Margaret of Denmark, the saintly consort of James III, depicted at her devotions, attended by St Canute, patron of Denmark. The opposite wing of the altarpiece, from which the detail portrait of James III is taken, shows the King at his devotions, attended by St Andrew, patron of Scotland, and accompanied by a boy who may be either one of the King's brothers or his eldest son, later James IV.

William Elphinstone, Bishop of Aberdeen, founder of Aberdeen University, and Chancellor of Scotland under James III and James IV.

Requiem for James III. Illumination from the *Book of Hours* of James IV.

Left James IV at his devotions, attended by his patron, St James the Great. Illumination from the *Book of Hours* of James IV.

Right Portrait of James IV.

Portrait of his Queen, Margaret Tudor (detail). Both these pictures are seventeenth-century copies of contemporary portraits.

James v and his second Queen, Marie de Guise.

Left Gold 'Bonnet Piece' of James v. The coin is so called because it shows the King wearing a bonnet, or hat, with a crown of ornament, instead of the Crown of Scots, as was more customary in representing the King on the coinage.

Opposite James v. Sixteenth-century portrait by an unknown artist.

Marie de Guise in later life, as Queen-Regent of Scotland.

Left Medallion of Mary, Queen of Scots and her first husband, as 'King and Queen of Scots, Dauphin and Dauphiness of France'.

Opposite Henry Stuart, Lord Darnley, second husband of Mary, Queen of Scots, with his younger brother, Lord Charles Stuart.

Miniature of Mary,
Queen of Scots, by
François Clouet.

Memento Mori panel
of Mary, Queen of Scots.
This picture is painted
on a ridged board.
Viewed from facing left,
it shows a portrait of
Mary, Queen of Scots,
and from the right a
picture of a skull. If
viewed from centre front
it presents an image of
a decomposing head.

Mary, Queen of Scots and James VI, 1583, by an unknown artist. Mary and her son never met after her flight to England. This picture may have been painted from existing likenesses of mother and son to stimulate enthusiasm for 'the Association', a scheme for Mary's restoration to the throne of Scotland as joint sovereign with her son, which was canvassed by her Catholic allies between 1582 and 1585.

James VI as a child, by Arnold van Bronkhorst.

James Douglas, fourth Earl of Morton, the fourth and last of James VI's Regents, executed in 1581. Portrait by Arnold van Bronkhorst.

Esmé Stuart, first Duke of Lennox, cousin and favourite of James VI, who was responsible for the downfall and execution of Morton.

Two coins of James VI·
1575. The child-King
in armour, represented
as the Champion of the
Reformation, bearing a
sword and an olive
branch, symbolizing his
readiness to defend
Protestantism by arms
or disputation.

The 'Hat Piece' of 1592,
an informal image of the
King echoing in style the
James V 'Bonnet Piece'.

Portrait of James VI
the age of twenty-ni
in 1595. The theme
the elaborate jewel i
King's hat, represen
a capital A, is the in
of his wife, Anne of
Denmark.

Miniature of Anne
Denmark, consort o
James VI.

charger, telling him that in pursuit or in flight the horse would serve
him equally well. It may not have been a very appropriate gift for an
indifferent horseman, but the King 'thankit him greatlie', and chose
to ride it into battle.

The King, it appears from Pitscottie's narrative, was responsible for
the ordering of his own battle. His army outnumbered that of his son,
but it is obvious that the Prince had better generals. The fortunes of
war turned against the King and it was for flight not pursuit that he
used Lord Lindsay's horse.

In his flight from the field the King was thrown from his horse and
injured. He was rescued by the miller of Bannockburn and his wife,
who carried him into the mill and gave him attention in ignorance of
his identity. He desired them to bring him a priest, and they asked his
name, presumably so that they might tell the priest who required him.
James replied, 'I was your King, this day at morn.' Then, says Pitscottie, 'the myllaris wyfe clappit hir handis and ran fourtht and cryit
for ane priest to the King.' She found a man who said he was a priest,
and brought him back with her to the mill. The man, whose identity
has never been discovered, knelt to the King and asked him whether he
were mortally hurt or not. The King replied that though he might
recover he desired absolution; probably he doubted the safety of his
hiding place and the mercy of his enemies. If so, he was right to doubt,
for they had found him already. The unknown man gave the King no
absolution, but drew his dagger and 'gif him four or fyve straikis ewin
to the hart'.

Pitscottie declared that some believed the King's murderer to have
been a servant of Lord Gray. Buchanan wrote, 'There were three that
pursued him very close in his flight, i.e. Patrick Gray, the head of his
family, Stirline Ker [Stirling of Keir] and a priest named Borthwick:
it is not well known which of them gave him his death's wound.' The
priest may indeed have been the assassin, but it was a mystery that was
never solved.

Some days after the battle the King's body was found in or near the
mill. It was taken to the Abbey of Cambuskenneth, and buried with
great solemnity beside the body of Margaret of Denmark, before the
high altar.

On the whole, historians have judged James III severely, accepting
the opinion of his opponents. Yet, despite his personal and political

failings and despite the unhappy conclusion of his reign, he was not altogether an unsuccessful King. During a personal rule of nineteen years he had shown a remarkable talent for political survival, in which he compares creditably with contemporary English monarchs: he had witnessed the end of the reign of Henry vi, the reign of Edward iv, the brief episode of Edward v, the reign of Richard iii, and the early years of Henry vii. No wonder Henry's official historian Polydore Vergil thought he was an old King, even though he was only thirty-six when he died!

Nor was survival his only achievement. He successfully defended the sovereign status of his kingdom against the treasons of Albany and the ambitions of Edward iv. By the acquisition of Orkney and Shetland he left the kingdom larger than he found it, and that by diplomacy and not imperialism. Furthermore, by his patronage of the arts he left to posterity some more enduring monuments than the ephemeral successes of many Kings whose reputations stand higher than his.

6

James IV,

1488–1513

He had a wonderful force of intellect,
an incredible knowledge of all things,
an invincible magnanimity, the sublimity
of a royal heart, the largest charity,
the most profuse liberality

(Erasmus, of James IV)

James IV was fifteen years old when the murder of his father made him King of Scots. He was too young to have had any control over the actions of the rebels who secured possession of his person, yet he was old enough to feel culpable for the events which had given him his kingship. Before the Battle of Sauchieburn he had issued orders that his father's life should be preserved; but the first Parliament of his reign had the task of announcing to foreign governments that upon the 'unhappy field' by Stirling 'James, King of Scotland, quhom God assolze [pardon], faider to oure Soverane Lord, happinit to be slane'.

For that happening James IV experienced a sense of guilt from which it appears he felt that no-one had the power to absolve him, for he vowed that he would refuse absolution, even were it offered by the Pope. He chose, as the means of coming to terms with his burden of guilt, the self-imposed penance of wearing around his waist an iron chain, to which he added extra links as the years passed. In several likenesses of the King the penitential chain is depicted.

There are many likenesses of James IV, most of which probably derive from a common source. Whether the auburn-haired boy clad in scarlet and ermine, kneeling behind James III in the van der Goes altarpiece, is Prince James or one of the King's brothers is a matter of controversy. Among the indisputably authentic portraits of the adult

James IV there is no outstanding work of art; but the surviving pictures show a vigorous and intelligent-looking man with long, dark auburn hair. He was, according to the Spanish ambassador, Pedro de Ayala, 'as handsome in complexion and shape as a man can be'. All his portraits show him as clean-shaven, but he was bearded when Ayala saw him in the middle 1490s. 'He never cuts his hair or beard,' the Spaniard wrote, 'it becomes him very well.'

Ayala found much to admire in James IV:

'He speaks the following foreign languages: Latin, very well, French, German, Flemish, Italian and Spanish. . . . His own Scottish language is as different from English as Aragonese is from Castilian. The King speaks, besides, the language of the savages who live in some parts of Scotland and of the Islands.'

That a foreign visitor should write thus of the Highlanders and the Gaelic language vividly illustrates how profound a dichotomy had developed between Highlanders and Lowlanders by the end of the fifteenth century.

Of the King's character Ayala wrote:

'He fears God and observes all the precepts of the Church. . . . Rarely, even in joking, a word escapes him that is not the truth. . . . His deeds are as good as his words. For that reason, and because he is a very humane Prince, he is much loved. . . . James possesses great virtues and few faults worth mentioning.'

Ayala's criticism of one of those few faults is frequently quoted:

'He is courageous, even more than a King should be . . . I have seen him often undertake most dangerous things. On such occasions he does not take the least care of himself. He is not a good captain because he begins to fight before he has given his orders.'

Less frequently quoted is James's reply:

'He said to me that his subjects serve him with their persons and their goods, in just and unjust quarrels, exactly as he likes, and that therefore he does not think it right to begin any warlike undertaking without himself being the first in danger.'

Ready to participate in the dangers and the pleasures of his people, easy of access, generous in handing out alms, rewards and compensations, James IV was the very antithesis of the remote figure of his father. For his kingly qualities he was respected and for his spontaneity and informal warmth he was beloved. Despite the unhappy beginning of his reign it did not take him long to win the love and respect of his people.

On 26 June 1488 James IV was crowned at Scone. The exigencies of the political situation at the outset of the two preceding reigns had demanded that James II should be crowned at Holyrood and James III at Kelso. The reversion to the ancient tradition in the instance of James IV suggests that the young King and his counsellors were anxious to stress that though the reign had been inaugurated by coup d'état and murder it carried no taint of usurpation. The King's penance illustrated his sorrow and repentance for the manner in which he had entered his inheritance; his coronation at Scone illustrated the continuity of his reign with those of his dynastic predecessors and of the earlier Kings of Scots.

A public illustration of continuity with the past was followed by an inaugural policy of moderation designed to win the support of any influential men who were ill-pleased with the outcome of the Battle of Sauchieburn, or ill-disposed to give their loyalty to the new regime.

The first Parliament of the reign enacted that the heirs of those who had been slain at Sauchieburn fighting for James III should inherit the estates of their fathers, just as if their fathers had died 'at the faith and peace of our Sovereign Lord the King', as effective a way as possible of ensuring that bygones should be bygones. The Earls of Buchan and Crawford and Sir Andrew Wood made their peace with the new regime. John Ramsay, Earl of Bothwell, was deprived of his title, which was later conferred upon Lord Hailes. He suffered no other penalty for having been the favourite and the loyal servant of James III; but desire to avenge the murder of his King, and what he conceived to be his own wrongs, led him into a career of treason which did him little credit but which is wholly understandable. He died, an unreconciled subject, in the last year of the reign.

Though the victors treated the vanquished with moderation, at the same time they did not scruple to take advantage of their victory. Lord Home assumed the office of Great Chamberlain, and also became Warden of the East March, Baillie of Ettrick Forest, Keeper of the castles of Stirling and Newark, Steward of the Earldom of Mar and guardian of one of the King's brothers. Lord Hailes, besides becoming

Earl of Bothwell, was appointed Master of the Household, Warden of the West and Middle Marches, Keeper of Edinburgh Castle, and guardian of the second of the princes. Other members of the Hepburn family became Keeper of the Privy Seal, and Clerk of the Rolls, the Register and the Council. Angus became the official guardian of the King, but James matured rapidly and soon showed that he had little need of tutelage, least of all the tutelage of a man who could claim only the dubious qualification of being an experienced troublemaker.

In 1489 three powerful and intransigent lords, to whom the new regime had not made itself acceptable, led a rebellion. The Earl of Lennox and Lord Lyle rebelled in the west. Lord Forbes supported them in the north by raising an army which marched under the banner of a bloodstained shirt, which Forbes declared to be that of the murdered King. However, the rebellions did not command general support; the new King was beginning to be popular, and the rebels could not offer an alternative government. The rebellions were speedily crushed, and the castles of the rebel lords reduced by the royal artillery. After their defeat the three principal offenders were forfeited, as an illustration of the danger of defying the royal authority. But James IV was more concerned to win universal support than merely to crush disaffection. Clemency followed severity. Lennox, Lyle and Forbes were presently restored to their titles and estates, and a general pardon was extended to those who had fought for them. Thereafter James IV's authority was established and accepted.

There remained one influential malcontent, the late King's friend Archbishop Scheves. James IV advanced his principal ecclesiastical supporter, Bishop Blacader of Glasgow, at Scheves's expense, by raising the see of Glasgow to the dignity of an archbishopric, though it was some time before the King could persuade the Pope to issue the necessary bull in support of his Act of Parliament. During 1489, 1490 and 1491 he wrote several times requesting the Pope's support, without result; probably Scheves was exerting his influence at Rome to oppose the King. However, in January 1492 the Pope finally acceded to James's request, and issued a bull separating the dioceses of Dunblane, Dunkeld, Galloway and Lismore from the province of St Andrews and subjecting them to the authority of Glasgow. The creation of a second archbishopric in Scotland had the unhappy effect of causing the same kind of unedifying strife between Glasgow and St Andrews as existed in England between York and Canterbury. The Archbishop of St Andrews remained primate of Scotland as Canterbury was primate of England; Glasgow, like York, constantly strove to secure an equal authority. Scheves, though he retained his primacy, played little part in public affairs; he remained neither acceptable to nor desirous of participating in the government of James IV.

During the early years of James IV's reign relations between Scotland and England were uneasy. Henry VII may have expected to encounter an inimical attitude on the part of the new Scottish government which had violently overthrown that of his late ally James III; and he was probably aware that James III's determined efforts to secure a lasting peace with England had not enjoyed universal support in his own country. Anglo-Scottish suspicion increased, and incidents at sea led to a dangerous mood of hostility between the two kingdoms.

In 1489 Sir Andrew Wood, with two ships, the *Yellow Carvel* and the *Flower*, captured five English vessels, which were privateering in Scottish waters. Henry VII gave a London merchant named Stephen Bull unofficial permission to attempt reprisals. Bull, with three ships, lay in wait near the Isle of May for Sir Andrew Wood, who was escorting a convoy of trading vessels to Flanders. On Wood's return to the Forth a great sea fight took place, and once again the Scots were victorious. Stephen Bull was captured and brought before James IV, who illustrated that a magnanimous King could respect a brave enemy, by giving him a present and sending him back to Henry VII. That generous gesture, in a tradition which the world has lost, gives the measure of James IV.

Henry VII was probably more irritated by the Scots' successes than impressed by the magnanimity of James. However, Henry had no wish for a full-scale war with Scotland. He was not belligerent by nature, neither was he sufficiently secure on his throne to risk embroilment in a major conflict. Unofficially sanctioned privateering and intrigues with Scots traitors were the limits of his anti-Scottish activity.

In April 1491 Henry entered into an agreement with John Ramsay, the Earl of Buchan, and Sir Thomas Tod of Sereshaw, that they should kidnap and hand over to him James IV and his next brother the Duke of Ross, 'or at the leste the said King of Scotland'. They received £266 13s 4d on loan, which was to be repaid if their plot miscarried, as indeed it did. Henry probably expected it to do so, for he also negotiated with the Earl of Angus, who promised that he would exert his influence to prevent James IV's making war with England. A mutilated document also reveals that Angus promised, upon certain conditions, to hand over the great Border castle of Hermitage in Liddesdale to Henry VII; possibly a condition may have been that he should do so if he failed to prevent the King from going to war.

James discovered Angus's new treason, and quenched this latest attempt to make trouble before it could take effect. Angus was warded in his own castle of Tantallon, and Hermitage Castle was given into the keeping of the new Earl of Bothwell. However, Angus's imprisonment was mild and brief, and he received other possessions in the west to compensate him for the loss of Hermitage. Once again, a politic blend of firmness and clemency paid off, for thereafter Angus remained loyal to James IV for the rest of the reign.

Henry VII had received clear evidence that James was moderate in dealing with international incidents, and that his authority was firmly established in Scotland; probably he decided that a truce with a strong neighbouring sovereign would be more advantageous to England than a state of unofficial hostility. In 1491 a truce was signed between the two countries, to last for five years.

The truce with England allowed James to turn his attention to the problems of the northwest. As narrated in the previous chapter, though the Lord of the Isles had been reconciled with the Crown, and had been reaffirmed in his title and estates as a Lord of Parliament, the northwest had been kept in turmoil during the later years of James III by Angus, the bastard son of the Lord of the Isles, who had striven to supplant his father, and to assert the ancient independence of the Lordship.

This Angus was murdered in 1490 by an Irish harper named Diarmaid O'Cairbre. The Dean of Knoydart wrote a Gaelic lament for Angus, and the following translation of part of it serves to illustrate the difference between the Gaelic poetry and the Scottish Court poetry of the period, and at the same time to provide a glimpse of the profound difference between the Highland and Lowland cultures:

> *Thou head of Diarmaid O'Cairbre,*
> *though great enough are thy spoils*
> *and thy pride, not too great I deem*

the amount of thy distress though
thou hangest from a stake.
I pity not thy shaggy mane, nor
that it is tossed by the wind of
the glens however rough; I pity
thee not that a withy is in thy
jaws, thou head of Diarmaid
O'Cairbre . . .
By thee was destroyed the King of
Islay, a man who dealt wine and
silver; whose locks were fresh and
crisp, thou head of Diarmaid
O'Cairbre . . .
Dear to me was his noble palm,
ungrudging of gold and silver;
who joyed in feast and hunting,
thou head of Diarmaid O'Cairbre . . .

The murder of this 'King of Islay', however, did not solve the problem of the northwest. A new aspirant to set up an independent Lordship appeared, in Alexander of Lochalsh, the nephew of the old Lord of the Isles. In 1491 Alexander captured Inverness, but was defeated by the Mackenzies of Kintail, who opposed him on behalf of the King. In 1493 the Lordship of the Isles was declared forfeit to the Crown. Though Alexander remained in rebellion, the old Lord of the Isles became the recipient of royal charity. He was welcomed at court and granted a pension; finally he retired to live his last days in Paisley Abbey, where he died in 1498.

Between 1493 and 1498 James IV paid several visits to the Isles. He attempted to enforce submission and to win support by displaying the strength of the royal authority, and by encouraging the men of the Isles, who had hitherto regarded themselves rather as subjects of the Lord of the Isles than of the King of Scots, to transfer their loyalty from the forfeited Lordship to the Crown.

James achieved some successes and experienced some setbacks. In 1494 he visited the Isles with a fleet under the command of Sir Andrew Wood, and left a garrison in the Castle of Dunaverty in Kintyre. But as soon as he sailed the castle was stormed by John

Macdonald of Islay, and the newly appointed Keeper was hanged before the eyes of the King. The winds and the seas, and the fact that the royal fleet had by this time divided, prevented the King from returning to deal with the rebel. However, the MacIan Macdonalds of Ardnamurchan, who had given their loyalty to the King, captured Dunaverty and sent John of Islay and his four sons to Edinburgh, to be tried and executed.

In 1497 Alexander of Lochalsh invaded the mainland a second time, and was again defeated, and subsequently slain, by the MacIans of Ardnamurchan. The following year the King, who had other matters to attend to besides the northwest, appointed the Earl of Argyll Lord Lieutenant of the Isles. He also appointed the Earl of Huntly Keeper of the Castle of Inverness, with similar powers as his Lieutenant in the north. Both earls endeavoured to do the King good service by imposing order in their respective areas of authority, but they expected their efforts to be rewarded by the advancement of themselves and their families. An unhappy consequence of the increased power of the Campbells of Argyll and the Gordons of Huntly has been commented upon by Professor Donaldson:

'A lieutenant with private ends to serve was not even necessarily interested in the preservation of order, for it was disorder which gave him the opportunities of aggrandizement: it was not by keeping the peace that he could earn his reward, but by putting down breakers of the peace, which is not quite the same thing.'

James, however, probably saw the problem of the Isles and the northwestern Highlands as a problem of integration, which could be solved by his lieutenants through the imposition of authority – an aspect of the problem to which he could not give his constant presence – and by himself through the winning of personal support from the Highlanders and Islesmen – an aspect of the problem to which he gave as much attention as he could.

The beginning of the sixteenth century saw a fresh outbreak of trouble when Donald Dubh, the son of that Angus who had been murdered in 1490, led a new rebellion and in 1503 burnt Inverness. Huntly quelled the rebellion, and James resolutely persisted in his efforts to regain and to hold the loyalty of his most recalcitrant subjects. Estimates of his achievement vary immensely, from T.F.Henderson's statement that 'the outstanding domestic achievement of James IV was the completion of the country's internal unification', to Professor Donaldson's statement that 'his achievement was less than is often supposed, and resulted in no permanent changes in the life of the Highlanders or in their relations with the central government.'

Certainly the achievement of James IV, remarkable though it appeared by the end of his reign, was temporary and did not even outlast his lifetime. Perhaps the fairest comment is that his achievement echoed that of Robert the Bruce. By his personal magnetism, aided by his knowledge of the Gaelic language, he won the loyalty of the Highlanders and Islanders; but his attempt to integrate the Highlands and the Isles into his kingdom ended at Flodden, and the perennial problem which they provided was revived in the reign of his son.

James worked upon the problems of the northwest in the interstices of the even more formidable problems of international politics. In the middle 1490s Anglo-Scottish relations were complicated by the arrival in Scotland of Perkin Warbeck, the pretender to the English throne who enjoyed the support of Margaret, Duchess of Burgundy, the sister of Edward IV and widow of Charles the Rash. James IV has been much criticized for espousing the cause of Warbeck, chiefly upon the grounds that he was foolish to be taken in by the claims of a Fleming of obscure origin, and more foolish still to go to war with England on his account. This, however, is twentieth-century reasoning. Warbeck claimed that he was Richard, Duke of York, the younger brother of Edward V. Edward and Richard, the 'Princes in the Tower', had disappeared at the beginning of the reign of Richard III, in mysterious circumstances. Though there is strong evidence that they were murdered in the Tower of London, even now that evidence is not absolutely conclusive, and towards the end of the fifteenth century, though their murder was rumoured their true fate was a complete mystery. Warbeck's claim to be Richard of York was quite plausible at the time, and was greatly strengthened by the support of Margaret of Burgundy, the real Richard's aunt. Warbeck was, furthermore, a handsome and attractive young man whose manners and appearance accorded well with his claim to Yorkist blood; indeed, a contemporary drawing of him gives him a strong resemblance to some likenesses of Edward IV. Whatever his ancestry, he was not an obvious imposter.

James had several sound political reasons for supporting 'Richard of

York'. In the first place, though a truce had been in force between Scotland and England since 1491, James had little reason to think that Henry VII was genuinely well-disposed towards him, or that Henry's diplomacy was honest. Henry had plotted with Ramsay to kidnap James and his brother the Duke of Ross, and had also indulged in treasonable intrigues with the Earl of Angus. Furthermore, in Agnes Mure Mackenzie's words, 'Henry, efficient but grasping and without charm, was not much loved by the country that he ruled: if Scottish arms should help the restoration of a young, attractive and legitimate King, there was every reason to anticipate that the venture would make for Anglo-Scottish friendship.' Warbeck was not the legitimate claimant; but the point is that in the fifteenth century it seemed likely that he was. And James IV 'must act on what he knew in 1495'.

Aside from the respective merits and demerits of Henry VII and 'Richard of York' as Kings of England, from the Scottish viewpoint there was the question of Berwick. The restoration of Berwick to Scotland had been under discussion at the time of James III's death. During the uncertain period at the beginning of the reign of James IV, before the King's authority was firmly established, the question of Berwick was allowed to lapse. Berwick remained in the hands of Henry VII; but 'Richard of York' promised to cede it to Scotland in return for Scottish help in securing his throne. This promise was perhaps decisive in inducing James IV to support the pretender.

In 1494 Margaret of Burgundy requested James IV to receive her nephew 'the Prince of England'. James agreed, though the visit did not take place until the following year. In November 1495 Warbeck arrived, and was magnificently received at Stirling. James, with characteristic generosity, made him an allowance of £1,200 a year, and permitted him to marry Lady Katherine Gordon, the daughter of the Earl of Huntly.

A new dimension was added to Anglo-Scottish relations by the intervention of Spain. Ferdinand and Isabella, joint sovereigns of the united kingdoms of Aragon and Castile, had consented to the marriage of their daughter Katherine to Prince Arthur, the elder son of Henry VII. They had no wish to see the inheritance of their prospective son-in-law threatened by a Yorkist pretender, legitimate or otherwise; they took it upon themselves to make peace between Scotland and

England, and to this end sent their ambassador, Pedro de Ayala, whose admiring comments upon James iv have already been quoted.

James received the flattering offer of the hand of a Spanish princess; but it did not take him long to discover that the three daughters of the Spanish sovereigns were already betrothed in England, France and the Holy Roman Empire. This is not to say that Ferdinand and Isabella could not have offered a bride of adequately noble birth; but James felt that he had been the victim of deception, and his resolve to go to war with Henry was strengthened.

War was declared in September 1496. The pretender was proclaimed Richard iv, and James invaded northern England with a small army, inviting 'King Richard's' subjects to rally to his support. Their response was negligible. Henry vii might not be personally popular, but evidently the benefits of his government were appreciated, and his subjects, to whom the repetitious invasions of Margaret of Anjou were a not too distant memory, had no wish to be embroiled in a renewal of the Wars of the Roses.

Then there was trouble between James and Warbeck. James decided to recoup the expenses of the campaign with plunder; Warbeck, resolutely playing the part of Richard iv, declared that he did not wish to shed the blood of his own subjects. The invading army withdrew.

Hostilities were renewed in the spring of 1497, but there was little serious fighting, for by this time James was disillusioned with the political possibilities of the pretender, and Henry was eager to make peace and especially to persuade James to surrender to him the person of Warbeck. This James refused to do, partly from motives of honour, partly because Warbeck was the husband of his kinswoman, Huntly's daughter. Warbeck himself had notions of propriety: he offered to disembarrass James of his presence by voluntarily leaving Scotland. James gratefully saw to it that his departure was not an ignominious flight. On 6 July Warbeck and his wife sailed from Ayr in a ship commanded by one of James's most distinguished captains, Robert Barton. Warbeck's eventful career was not yet at an end. He made one more attempt to win the English throne by invading Cornwall. But, faced with certain defeat at the hands of a stronger force, he abandoned his army and took sanctuary at Beaulieu. He surrendered upon the promise of pardon, confessed himself an imposter and was imprisoned in the Tower of

London. Induced to plot afresh possibly by *agents provocateurs*, he was executed in 1499.

The departure of Warbeck from Scotland paved the way for peace between Scotland and England. In September 1497 a truce was negotiated, largely by the good offices of Pedro de Ayala. Originally it was for seven years only, but in December further efforts by the Spanish ambassador led to its extension for the lifetimes of James IV and Henry VII and for one year beyond the death of the survivor, and to the additional agreement that they should submit any allegations of breaches of the truce to Spanish arbitration.

The following year Henry VII proposed that the King of Scots should marry his eldest daughter, the Princess Margaret. Henry had initially made this suggestion in 1495 in the hope of detaching James from the cause of Warbeck, but at the time James had turned a deaf ear. In 1499 he was still reluctant, but Henry persisted, and in 1500 went so far as to obtain from the Pope a provisional dispensation permitting the marriage. A dispensation was necessary because James IV and Margaret Tudor were within the 'forbidden degrees' of kinship. James's great-grandmother was Queen Joan Beaufort, wife of James I, and Margaret's paternal grandmother was Margaret Beaufort, Countess of Richmond.

James had a variety of reasons for being reluctant to commit himself to the English marriage. When Henry first began his persistent proposals that James should marry his daughter, James had a personal reason for hesitating: he was deeply in love with his mistress, Margaret Drummond.

As a young, unmarried King, James would not have been expected to live celibate. He was fortunate, as one of his twentieth-century biographers has observed, in living at a time 'in which the amours of a King were regarded as the proper revelation of royal virility'. His first mistress had been Marion Boyd, who in 1493 had borne him a son who was named Alexander Stewart. James was a conscientious father, and he gave his son an excellent education. In 1505, Alexander, who was destined for the Church, was sent to Padua to study under Erasmus, in whom he inspired affectionate admiration. Towards the end of the reign he was appointed Archbishop of St Andrews. Marion Boyd also bore the King a daughter named Catherine. Later, James had an affair with Janet Kennedy, an ambitious young woman whose previous lover had been the Earl of Angus. She bore the King a son, James Stewart, who was later created Earl of Moray. With Margaret Drummond the King's involvement was much more serious. There is a tradition in the Drummond family that the King and Margaret were secretly married, which, if true, would entirely explain James's un-enthusiastic response to Henry's offer of his daughter. Certainly James could have chosen his Queen from one of the noble families of Scotland; Robert II and Robert III had both done so. But far greater political advantages could be gained by a foreign marriage alliance. James might well have hesitated between personal and political considerations. The problem, however, whether it was the greater one of a secret contract, or the lesser one of a difficult decision, was solved in a tragic fashion.

In 1500 Margaret Drummond and her sisters Euphemia and Sibylla died of poisoning, immediately after they had breakfasted, in their father's castle. Who had administered the poison was never dis-covered. Suspicion fell on the Kennedy family, probably for obvious reasons. But whether the Kennedys had any part in the triple death or not, it was inevitable that the possibility of James IV's marriage to Margaret Drummond would have aroused violent envy and enmity. David II's second Queen, Margaret Logie, had been born a Drum-mond, and the Drummonds had given Scotland a second Queen in Annabella, the consort of Robert III. Many families might have felt that the influence of the Drummonds would grow too great if their line provided a third Queen of Scots. It seemed that Margaret Drummond had died the victim of family jealousy. There remains the possibility that she and her sisters died accidentally of food poisoning; murder was assumed because in the sixteenth century the danger of contamination was not understood.

James was grief-stricken at Margaret Drummond's death. She was buried with her sisters in the cathedral of Dunblane, and Masses were said for the repose of her soul, at the King's expense, until the end of his life.

Her death, tragic though it was, removed any personal impediment to the King's marriage with the daughter of Henry VII. There were still, however, certain political objections. Henry was desirous not only to make peace with Scotland, but also to link Scotland, England and Spain in alliance against France. The power of France had grown steadily under Louis XI and Charles VIII and it continued to grow under Louis XII. It was viewed with alarm by the neighbouring powers. England inevitably feared the increasing might of her old enemy; Spain was threatened when Charles VIII inaugurated an expansionist phase by invading Italy in 1494. Both France and Spain cast covetous eyes upon parts of Italy, and backed their covetousness with specious claims. The influence of the Italian wars overshadowed Anglo-Scottish relations for the rest of James IV's reign.

James did not wish to be drawn fully into Henry VII's political schemes. He accepted the advantages of converting his truce with England into a 'perpetual peace', and of cementing the peace with a marriage alliance; but he declined to lay Scotland open to the possibility of English domination by submitting to Henry's request that he should formally repudiate the alliance between Scotland and France. It had now endured for so long, and had been so frequently renewed, that it may fittingly be referred to by its traditional name of the 'auld alliance'.

In October 1501 James at last accepted Henry's offer of the hand of his daughter. While the King of Scots had shown himself a most reluctant bridegroom, the prospect of a Scottish marriage for the English Princess had been greeted unenthusiastically by the councillors of Henry VII. When Henry announced the betrothal to his Privy Councillors, one of them offered the objection that since Margaret was third in succession to the English Crown, should she marry the King of Scots and then be predeceased by her brothers, the Princes Arthur and Henry, then England would fall to the Crown of Scots. Henry's answer, as reported by the sixteenth-century Scottish historian Bishop Lesley, was

> 'Supposing, which God forbid, that all my male progeny should become extinct, and the kingdom devolve by law to Margaret's heirs, will England be damaged thereby? For since it ever happens that the less becomes subservient to the greater, the accession will be that of Scotland to England, just as formerly happened to Normandy, which devolved on our ancestors in the same manner, and was happily added to our kingdom by hereditary right, as a rivulet to a fountain.'

After the Union of Crowns Henry VII's words were considered to have been prophetic.

Once James had agreed to the marriage, the terms of peace were negotiated on his behalf by the Earl of Bothwell, the Archbishop of Glasgow and Andrew Forman, Protonotary Apostolic. The two Kings bound themselves to a '. . . good, real, sincere, true, honourable and firm peace, friendship, league and confederation, by land, sea, rivers and in all places . . . always to endure for all future times in perpetuity', as though seeking by the sheer weight of synonyms to carry greater conviction. The treaty was made under papal confirmation, which laid automatic excommunication upon whichever party should break the peace. Henry VII signed the double treaty of marriage and perpetual peace at Richmond on 24 January 1502, and James IV ratified it, at the high altar of Glasgow Cathedral, on 22 February. It was agreed that Margaret should go to Scotland the following year, when she would have reached the age of thirteen. James would then be thirty. In the meantime the marriage was celebrated by proxy.

Early in 1503 Margaret Tudor's mother, Elizabeth of York, died shortly after her ninth confinement. Her passing cast a shadow upon the royal family of England. Henry VII lapsed into sombre grief. He became an isolated man, and his judicious parsimony grew into the unendearing miserliness for which he has become proverbial. Margaret, oppressed by family mourning, seems to have departed almost with alacrity to meet an unknown husband and become Queen of an unknown country.

On 2 July 1503 Margaret left Richmond Palace, escorted by her father and his court, and progressed in state to Collyweston in Northamptonshire, a manor which belonged to the King's mother, the Countess of Richmond. There she took leave of her father and grandmother, and began her slow and stately journey to Scotland.

The pageantry of Margaret's northward progress, and the ceremonial with which her marriage to James IV was celebrated, were described in detail by John Young, Somerset Herald, who attended upon her throughout. The details of the journey have been summed up by Margaret's most recent biographer, who observes that the child-Queen 'descended from her litter, mounted her palfrey, stood to receive addresses, kissed holy relics, heard Mass, feasted, danced and conversed, with changeless aplomb and unbroken serenity'. She reached the Castle of Dalkeith, just south of Edinburgh, on 3 August.

That same evening Margaret received an informal but probably expected visit from the King of Scots. That an impatient bridegroom should brush aside formality, and hasten unannounced to meet his betrothed, was a convention of the period which James would have been expected to observe. Reluctant as he was, he observed it perfectly. The following day Margaret progressed to Newbattle, a little nearer Edinburgh, and the King paid her a second informal visit. James found her playing cards with her ladies. When he entered the room, Somerset Herald reported:

'The Queen, rising, advanced to receive him very gladly, of her good will kissing him. After that the King of Scots gave salute to all her ladies. He was dressed in a black velvet jacket, bordered with crimson velvet and edged with white fur. . . . After some words re-hearsed, the minstrels began to play a basse dance, which was danced by Queen Margaret and the Countess of Surrey [the Earl and Countess of Surrey had escorted Margaret to Scotland]. . . . Wine and bread were then served to the King, who took the bread and with it served his Queen. Likewise he took the cup, and served her first of all with wine.'

After this quasi-sacramental refreshment, James took leave of her. The manner of his departure greatly impressed Somerset Herald: 'James of Scotland did leap upon his horse without putting his foot in stirrup; and the said steed was a right fair courser; and forward the King spurred, let follow who might.'

The marriage took place on 8 August in the Abbey of Holyrood. According to the Herald's description, Margaret was dressed in a gown of white and gold damask, bordered with crimson velvet. She wore a crown which had been made for her in Scotland from eighty-three gold coins. Her red hair, which was loose, reached the ground. Of James the Herald wrote:

'He wore a robe of white damask figured with gold, a jacket with slashes of crimson satin, and the border of black velvet, a waistcoat of cloth of gold, and a pair of scarlet hose. His shirt was embroidered with gold thread, his bonnet black velvet, looped up with a rich balas-ruby, and his sword was girt about him.'

The nuptial Mass was concelebrated by the Archbishop of Glasgow and the Archbishop of York. The poet William Dunbar wrote an allegorical poem *The Thistle and the Rose* in honour of the occasion,

and an elegant lyric which was set to music and sung at the festivities
which followed the solemnization of the marriage:

> *Now fair, fairest of every fair,*
> *Princess most pleasant and preclare*
> *The lustiest¹ one alive that been*
> *Welcome to Scotland to be Queen.*

> *Young tender plant of pulchritude*
> *Descended of imperial blude,*
> *Fresh fragrant flower of fairheid schene²*
> *Welcome to Scotland to be Queen.*

> *Sweet lusty luesome³ lady clear*
> *Most mighty Kinges daughter dear,*
> *Born of a princess most serene,*
> *Welcome to Scotland to be Queen.*

The magnificence of the occasion was undoubted, and the Queen
received the praises which courtly convention demanded. But the
splendour of the outward show disguised some unpleasant truths. Upon
impressing the visitors from England, which was necessary for the
maintaining of his prestige, the King of Scots had spent vast sums
which he could ill afford; and he had spent them upon marrying a
Princess who possessed few qualities likely either to inspire his love or
to win his respect.

Despite the courtly praises of Dunbar, Margaret was not the 'fairest
of every fair'. She was small and plump, her features were unexceptional
and her expression sullen. At least in youth she possessed two good
attributes in her white complexion and her long red hair. Of her
character more than one historian has remarked that she possessed the
faults of the Tudors but lacked their brains. She was, indeed, acquisi-
tive, querulous and unremittingly egotistical. She was a skilled per-
former on the lute and the clavichord, and a mistress of etiquette, but in
other respects her education had been neglected. She had been brought
up to enjoy the privileges of royalty, but not to understand the responsibilities of regality. It may be said in extenuation, of her as of many
other people, that her upbringing was to blame for her faults of

¹ loveliest.   ² radiant beauty.   ³ lovesome.

character. As James IV possessed a strong personality, and the advantage of seventeen years' seniority, he kept her in order during his lifetime; after his death her intrigues troubled Anglo-Scottish relations for many years.

Margaret bore James IV six children, of whom the last was born after his death. Only one of them survived, the son who was born in 1512, and who the following year succeeded his father, and reigned as James V.

Shortly after her marriage Margaret wrote to her father, touchingly expressing her homesickness 'with a wish I were with your Grace, now and many times more', and less pleasantly complaining that 'this King [James IV]' did not pay enough attention to her wishes; though indeed his reception of her had lacked nothing in graciousness and kindness. He had shown much natural kindliness in inviting her to sit in his chair of state when the stool set for her at a banquet had proved too low, and in requesting the Countess of Surrey to trim his beard when Margaret had complained that it was too long. In after years Margaret admitted to her brother Henry VIII, 'our husband is ever the better the longer to us'.

During the fifteen years which had elapsed between his accession and his marriage, James IV had worked hard to improve the internal condition of Scotland; he had become, and for the rest of his reign was to remain, the guiding spirit of his country in a remarkable period of its development.

From very early in his reign James IV had realized the importance of imposing the rule of law throughout his kingdom, as the foundation upon which all other constructive work must be laid. 'The Session', the supreme court founded by James I and continued by James II, had ceased to function efficiently during the reign of James III, when judicial sessions of the King's Council had been held to hear civil causes. James IV, anxious to relieve his Council of the burden of much judicial work, revived the Session, which was directed to sit during specified terms in the year, in Edinburgh. The centralization of the supreme court in Edinburgh was influential in establishing Edinburgh as the capital of the kingdom. James III had indeed recognized it as 'principalior burgus regni nostri' – the principal burgh of our realm – but since Stirling had been his favoured place of residence Edinburgh had scarcely functioned as a capital.

Besides improving the administration of civil justice, James IV gave his attention to criminal justice, himself tirelessly presiding over the Justice Ayres – itinerant criminal courts – throughout the country, and especially upon the Borders.

Shortly after his marriage, James decided to test the effectiveness of his efforts to pacify his kingdom by riding alone from Stirling to Elgin. He did so in one day, with no other ill-effects than those of exhaustion. When he had recovered from his exertions he made a pilgrimage of thanksgiving, for the peaceful state in which he had found his kingdom, to the shrine of St Duthac at Tain.

James IV was concerned not merely to impose law and order throughout his realm, but also to improve the living conditions of his subjects. Much of the beneficial legislation of his reign was designed to encourage trade, local industries and agriculture. The economy of Scotland was still basically agricultural, and in the Highlands pastoral. Gunpowder and armaments, wines and luxury goods had still to be imported, in exchange for wool, rough woollen cloth, barrelled herring and salmon, marten furs, which were of high quality, and Scottish pearls, which were highly prized, though less so than those which came from the East. The fishing industry, which contributed both to home consumption and to exports, was encouraged by the enactment that coastal towns should build fishing vessels of twenty tons and raise their crews from the 'stark idill [strong and unemployed]' men of the towns. Improvement of agriculture, which Ayala observed was still very primitive, received encouragement through acts which ordered land-owners to establish orchards, hedges and plantations. 'Feuing' – i.e. leasing of lands for fixed money rents instead of agricultural or military service – was encouraged, and security of tenure ensured by the enactment that the 'feu' should hold good for the feuar's heirs. The intention of this legislation was that 'for the assured hope . . . of enjoying and holding a tenure in perpetuity' the tenants would be encouraged to construct better farm buildings, cultivate waste land, plant trees, breed fish in fresh water on their land or in 'stanks' (artificial ponds), build dove-cotes and establish 'orchards, plesaunces and warrens'.

Besides endeavouring to increase the prosperity of his people, James was aware of the importance of improving the quality of life through education. In 1494 he was associated with Bishop Elphinstone in founding the University of Aberdeen, Scotland's third university. James himself wrote to Pope Alexander VI requesting the necessary bull authorizing the foundation. He explained that the new university was particularly intended to provide for the needs of his Highland subjects 'considering that in the northern and north-eastern parts of his kingdom there are certain places separated from the rest of the kingdom by arms of the sea and very high mountains, in which dwell men rude and ignorant of letters'. Aberdeen would be very much more accessible for them than the existing foundation on the eastern side of Scotland at St Andrews; Glasgow was reasonably accessible for the men of the west and the Isles. The new university was founded in 1495, and was the first university in the British Isles to have a faculty of medicine.

The following year James initiated what has been claimed as the first compulsory education act. It required 'all barrons and freholdaris that are of substance' to send their eldest sons to school at the age of eight or nine, where they were to remain until they were 'competentlie foundit and have perfyte latyne'. From school they were to proceed to one of the universities, to spend three years upon the study of 'art and jure [law]'. In all probability this act was very incompletely enforced; but it illustrates James's preoccupation with the importance of the law. His intention was to create a competent administrative class for the future, and to ensure that those who possessed heritable jurisdictions would have sufficient knowledge of the law to preside over their local courts with efficiency and justice.

With such preoccupations James could not fail to discern the potential uses for education and communication of the greatest technical advance of the previous generation: the invention of the printing-press and movable type.

In 1507, under the auspices of the King, Walter Chepman and Andrew Myllar set up Scotland's first printing-press in Edinburgh. Chepman was a prosperous Edinburgh merchant, who presumably financed the enterprise. Myllar was a printer who had learnt his craft in France; books survive printed by him at Rouen in 1505 and 1506. Scotland was late in acquiring the printing-press, for Gutenberg had set up his press at Mainz in about 1454, and Caxton had established his at Westminster in 1470. However, no time was lost, for the King's licence permitting Chepman and Myllar to set up their 'prent' commanded them to print 'Mass-books, manuals, matin books and portuus-books [portable breviaries] after our own Scots use, and with legends of Scots saints, as are now gathered and eked by the reverend father in God, and our trusty councillor, William [Elphinstone], Bishop of Aberdeen'. They were also commanded to print the laws and Acts of Parliament. But these, it appears, were too complex for them, for the first Acts of Parliament which have survived in printed form are those of James v's Parliaments of 1535 and 1540. Chepman and Myllar printed much poetry, chiefly that of Chaucer and of the Scots poets Henrysoun and Dunbar. By 1510 they had produced the two-volume Aberdeen Breviary, which contained the 'propers' of the Scottish saints, the favoured project of Bishop Elphinstone.

The establishment of the printing-press was but one example of the intelligent patronage of the King. Unlike his father, James IV was not an isolated connoisseur, but a highly practical patron whose policy was to encourage a great diversity of arts, crafts and sciences. Dunbar wrote a poem in which many of them are enumerated:

> *Schir, ye have mony servitouris*
> *And officaris of dyvers curis,*
> *Kirkmen, courtmen and craftismen fyne,*
> *Doctouris in jure and medicyne.*
> *Divinouris, rethoris and philosophouris,*
> *Astrologis, artistis and oratouris,*
> *Men of armes and vailyeant knychtis,*
> *And mony uther gudlie wichtis:*
> *Musicianis, menstralis and mirrie singeris,*
> *Chevalouris, cawandaris and flingaris:*
> *Cunyouris, carvouris and carpentaris,*
> *Beildaris of barkis and ballingaris:*
> *Masounis lyand upoun the land*
> *And schipwrichtis hewand upone the strand:*
> *Glasing wrichtis, goldsmiths and lapidaris,*
> *Pryntouris, payntouris and potingaris.*

It is not always observed that Dunbar's purpose in listing all these professions was to point out that poets, especially himself, were disregarded. This was not strictly true, as Dunbar was the recipient of a pension which he eventually persuaded the King to raise to £80 a year, which was then a very respectable sum.

Among the sciences which particularly interested the King were dentistry and surgery. There is surviving evidence that he was even eager to try his own hand at them. He paid a man fourteen shillings to be permitted to extract one of his teeth, while another man received twenty-eight shillings 'to give the King leave to let him blood'. (James paid his experimental patient the same fee of twenty-eight shillings which he paid his own doctor when he required to be bled himself.)

James's interest in surgery and concern for its improvement led to the foundation of the College of Surgeons in 1506, and the surgeons felt sufficiently confident in the King's understanding of their require-ments to petition him to be allowed to dissect once yearly the corpse of an executed criminal, 'since every man aucht to knaw the nature and substance of everything that he workis, or ellis he is negligent'. In understanding the need for dissection to aid the study of anatomy James was in advance of his times, for anatomical study was generally suspect as being akin to necromancy.

James, however, had yet more *avant-garde* interests. One of his *protégés*, who received little sympathy from contemporaries, was a renaissance scientist named Damian, whose studies the King financed by securing his appointment as Abbot of Tungland. Damian was an alchemist, and it is usually said that the King was naïvely credulous in entertaining hopes of his discovering the secret of transmuting base metals into gold. Certainly much alchemical study was devoted to this end, which had obvious economic possibilities; medieval and renaissance heads of state did not disregard the possibility that alchemy might solve their financial problems. Since the alchemists' experiments did not lead to successful results in this field, they are frequently mocked as char-latans or at best as benighted pursuers of the impossible. The trans-mutation of metals, however, was merely one of their concerns. Their principal interests were the perfectibility of matter and of human nature; at least it may be said in their favour that the pursuit of per-fection through allied scientific and spiritual study is not an idea which deserves to be mocked.

Besides being an alchemist Damian was a pioneer of aviation. An attempt at flight from the battlements of Stirling Castle was satirized by William Dunbar:

> . . . *he* [Damian] *assailyeit*
> *To mak the quintessence, and failyeit;*
> *And quhen he saw that nocht availyeit,*
> *A fedrem on he tuke,*
> *And tuke in Turky for to fle;*
> *And quhen that he did mount on he*
> *All fowill ferleit quhat he sowld be*
> *That evir did on him luke.*
> *And evir the cuschettis at him tuggit,*
> *The rukis him rent, the ravynis him druggit,*
> *The hudit crawis his hair furth ruggit,*
> *The hevin he micht not bruke.*
> *He schewre his feddreme that was schene,*
> *And slippit out of it full clene,*
> *And in a myre up to the ene,*
> *Amang the glar did glyd.*

If Damian made a personal attempt at flight he was a brave man indeed, and if his notebooks had survived like those of Leonardo, we might have had a more impressive glimpse of his experiment than that which emerges from Dunbar's mockery. The future, at any rate, vindicated his aspirations, and proved that the King had not been a fool to take them seriously.

It is worth remarking that James IV's interests in surgery, alchemy and aviation may have amazed or amused some of his subjects, but in him esoteric interests were not deplored or despised as they had been in his father. The explanation is probably that because James IV was a more accessible personality and a more popular King public opinion permitted him his eccentricities. His popularity even allowed him to indulge in enthusiasms which necessitated heavy expenditure.

James IV, like his father, was a lover of architecture, and his reign witnessed much building. At Stirling, Falkland and Linlithgow he added to buildings which dated from the previous reign, and at Edinburgh he began a new royal residence, in readiness for his marriage. The Palace of Holyroodhouse, beside the Abbey founded by David I, was usable by 1503, but work continued on it throughout the reign, and also during that of James V.

James IV's most extravagant expenditure, however, was upon shipbuilding. He inherited a few ships from his father, and he inherited the services of Sir Andrew Wood. From these small beginnings he determined to make Scotland a maritime power. In the course of his reign he built a navy, and his greatest achievement was the construction of the *Great Michael*, which was launched in 1511. The *Great Michael*, the largest warship of the age, was 240 feet in length and her timbers were 10 feet thick. She carried a crew of 300 sailors, 120 gunners and a further complement of 1,000 fighting men, or marines in twentieth-century terms of reference. The building of the *Great Michael* was said to have consumed all the oaks of Fife, except those in the forest of Falkland, the King's hunting preserve. It was, in the opinion of a modern historian, 'a shocking example of megalomania, of an undeveloped country indulging in the latest thing in expensive armaments . . .'.

The King, however, had other reasons than self-aggrandizement for wishing to develop his navy. His greatest ambition in the later years of his reign was to combine the sovereigns of Europe in a crusade against the Turks. Ever since the fall of Constantinople the Turkish menace had been growing, and in his awareness of it James showed more political intelligence than other contemporary sovereigns. His anxiety was shown to have been justified in the decade after his death, when the city of Belgrade and the Island of Rhodes fell to the Turks. The defeat of the King of Hungary at Mohács in 1526 brought the threat to the threshold of Western Europe, and in 1529 the Turkish armies appeared before Vienna. Had James IV gained the attention of his fellow sovereigns at the beginning of the sixteenth century these Turkish successes might have been obviated by conjoint action; and had his fleet been welcomed in the Mediterranean, and supported by others, Turkish sea-power might also have been more successfully withstood. As it was, the Turks were not decisively defeated at sea until the Spanish victory of Lepanto in 1571.

At the opening of the sixteenth century the voice of James IV was already that of one crying in the wilderness, and by the end of the first decade any hope of uniting the sovereigns of Europe upon any common purpose had disappeared. Louis XII of France, the Emperor Maximilian and the young Henry VIII of England, who succeeded in 1509, were all capable of paying lip-service to the idea of a crusade, but none of them was prepared to abandon his personal ambitions in favour of the good of Christendom. Indeed, the very concept of Christendom was fast becoming an anachronism.

James IV may not have had any illusions concerning the political ambitions of his fellow sovereigns; but initially he hoped that they might be united against the Infidel by the influence of the Pope. Unhappily Pope Julius II had interests as secular as those of any temporal sovereign. He was misguidedly resolved to consolidate the estates of the Church in central Italy into a principality which, he intended, should be capable of asserting its influence upon the powers of Europe by secular means as well as by spiritual authority. In Italy, which during the early decades of the sixteenth century was the cockpit of Europe, the struggle took place which eventually led Scotland into a new war with England, a war which brought the reign of James IV to its disastrous conclusion.

In 1508 Julius II united Louis XII and the Emperor in the League of Cambrai against Venice. His aim was to reduce the power of the great maritime republic, and to absorb certain Venetian territories into the states of the Church. If England and France should go to war, Julius looked to James IV to intervene against England. James had no wish to become embroiled with England, since he was bound by the treaty of perpetual peace, signed under papal confirmation, a fact which at this stage Julius II chose conveniently to forget. In the hope of winning James's unconditional support, Julius gave flattering encouragement to James's project for a crusade. He sent him a purple and gold cap of maintenance and a sword which he had blessed (subsequently it became the Scottish Sword of State), and he gave him the title of 'Protector of the Christian Religion'. James was not led astray by these compliments, and events showed that he was right to take a slightly cynical view of papal blandishments, for by the end of 1508 England had joined the League of Cambrai.

The Venetians were defeated, but the victorious French proved to be beyond papal control. The French conquered northern Italy, which was entirely outside the scope of Julius's original intentions. Furthermore, he tardily realized that the destruction of Venetian sea-power encouraged the encroachment of the Turks in the Mediterranean. If he lacked the vision to see the need for a crusade, at least he had a limited awareness of the Turkish threat. Therefore, in a complete reversal of his previous policy he allied himself with Venice against the

French. Louis XII appealed to the French clergy to summon a General Council of the Church, to condemn the secular activities of the Pope. Julius did not scruple to employ spiritual as well as secular weapons against his political enemies; he denounced the King of France as schismatic, and in 1511 formed the 'Holy League', in which Spain, Venice, England and a little later the Emperor Maximilian were allied against France.

James IV had watched these developments at first with disapprobation and then with alarm. As previously mentioned, he had not repudiated the 'auld alliance' with France when he bound himself to England by treaty and by marriage; but until the very end of the reign of Henry VII it had remained possible for him to retain this dual alliance without political embarrassment. The machinations of Julius II began to create trouble; the accession of Henry VIII led to it irrevocably.

Henry VIII, eighteen years old at his accession, inherited a prosperous kingdom, thanks to his father's talent for saving money. He could afford warfare, he was bellicose by nature, and he was eager to win military glory. The formation of the Holy League seemed to offer him an excellent opportunity to do so.

As this dangerous situation developed, Anglo-Scottish relations deteriorated. From the outset of his reign Henry VIII seems to have been at pains to reveal to his brother-in-law that he considered him an inferior. Just before Henry's accession one of the Scottish Wardens of the Marches, Sir Robert Ker of Ferniherst, was murdered by an Englishman 'the bastard Heron'; Henry VIII protected the assassin, contrary to the terms of the perpetual peace, and James was naturally angered at his inability to obtain redress. Further trouble was caused by an incident at sea. Two Scottish ships, the *Lion* and the *Jenny Pirwin*, commanded by one of James's famous captains, Sir Andrew Barton, were involved in a sea-fight with two English ships. Sir Andrew Barton was killed, and the *Lion* was towed into the Thames as a prize. James took particular exception, as the English ships were not pirate vessels but were commanded by the Earl of Surrey and his son Sir Edward Howard, later appointed Admiral of England. James, in hot anger, wrote to Henry demanding that the *Lion* should be returned and Surrey and his son put on trial for breaking the peace. Henry replied that it was not customary to accuse a prince of breaking a treaty when he had only done justice to a pirate.

At the end of 1511 James wrote to the Pope declaring that Henry VIII was deliberately contravening the peace treaty, attacking the Scots 'by land and sea, slaying, capturing and imprisoning' them; he therefore suggested that any contravention of the treaty on his side should no longer incur spiritual penalties. However, as Henry VIII was a member of the Holy League and James was not, Julius II was not disposed to oblige him. Indeed, the following year, at Henry VIII's request, Julius II authorized the excommunication of James if Scotland should go to war with England. By that time the prospect of war had become imminent.

Louis XII, threatened by the Holy League, appealed to James for a formal renewal of the 'auld alliance', and James, doubting the possibility of maintaining friendly relations with Henry VIII, agreed, thus binding himself to assist Louis if Henry should invade France. Louis on his side promised to do all in his power to assist James's project for a crusade; whether he was prepared to do so with much seriousness may be doubted, but the sincerity of his promise was never put to the test.

James IV had a good reason for reverting to the traditional policy of alliance with France. If France should be dismembered or even heavily defeated by the adherents to the Holy League, and Scotland be left face to face with an inimical England, then James knew that he might look for a recurrence of the English claim to overlordship of Scotland, and of all the concomitant troubles which had bedevilled the fourteenth century.

Until the last James endeavoured to assist Louis XII by diplomacy and not by the sword. He exhorted Ferdinand of Spain to use his influence to reconcile Louis and the Pope. He reproached the Pope himself for making trouble between Christian Princes. 'What,' he wrote, 'can be worse than that a Holy Father and a Christian son should level their swords at each other's throats?'

Julius II died at the beginning of 1513 and was succeeded by Leo X. Briefly it seemed possible that without Julius's influence the mis-named Holy League might fall apart and the threat to France be averted. Spain and France indeed concluded a truce. But Julius II had been manipulating the ambitions of European sovereigns for his own purposes, and those ambitions were not altered by his death. Henry VIII was still desirous of glory, still hopeful of regaining some part of England's medieval empire in France. On 5 April 1513 he concluded the Treaty of Malines with the Emperor Maximilian, which bound both of them to attack France. Ferdinand of Spain then had second thoughts, and on 18 April he too entered the treaty. Their action committed James to war with England.

Pitscottie's story, that the Queen of France sent James a turquoise ring and requested him to invade England as her knight, may well be true; it would have been a gesture in accordance with the diplomatic manners of the time, but it would not have influenced the course of events, which was shaped by larger considerations.

At the end of June Henry VIII invaded France, and in his camp at Calais he was visited by James IV's principal herald, Lyon King of Arms, with an ultimatum. His angry reply fully justified James's declaration of war, and illustrated that James's reading of the international situation, including the threat to Scotland, had been correct:

> 'Thus say to thy master, that I am the very owner of Scotland and that he holdeth it of me by homage, and in so much as now contrary to his bounden duty he being my vassal doth rebel against me, with God's help I shall at my return expulse him from his realm, and so tell him.'

On 16 August Henry VIII defeated the French in a pointless but satisfyingly 'glorious' victory at Guinegate. One week later, on 22 August, James IV invaded England, and proceeded to reduce three English castles, Norham, Etal and Ford, which served the double purpose of safeguarding his line of retreat, and of drawing northward the army which had been left to defend England, which was commanded by the Earl of Surrey. In the meantime, James's fleet, headed by the *Great Michael*, under the command of the Earl of Arran, sailed to the assistance of the French King. Unhappily, the naval half of the enterprise was hopelessly mismanaged by Arran, and more unhappily still the best of James's gunners had sailed with him, thus reducing the efficiency of the Scottish artillery which encountered Surrey.

The battle took place on 9 September near Flodden Edge in Northumberland, which gave the battlefield its name. The two armies were probably fairly evenly matched in numbers, the King of Scots and the Earl of Surrey each commanding approximately 20,000 men. What cost the Scots the battle was the greater effectiveness of the English artillery, which inflicted heavy losses at the beginning of the battle, and the greater suitability of the English weapons to the conditions of the engagement. The Scots were armed with fifteen-foot wooden spears, the English with bills, which had an eight-foot shaft and a long axe-like blade terminating in a spike.

The Scottish spearmen, dislodged from a strong position on high ground by the English artillery-fire, charged downhill, irresistible as long as they kept moving. When their impetus was halted in the muddy ground where they encountered the English, they found their long spears useless against the bills of the enemy. The shafts of the spears were hacked through by the blades of the English bills, and spearmen who managed to draw their swords were still defenceless against the longer reach of their adversaries. The King himself charged with his spearmen, and died early in the battle. His fate bears out Ayala's comment: 'He is not a good captain, because he begins to fight before he has given his orders.' No doubt his primitive heroism cost him his life, and possibly the battle, both of which might have been saved by more prudent generalship. At least, had the King lived to withdraw his men in good order the magnitude of the slaughter might have been greatly lessened. However, James had long ago answered Ayala's criticism by explaining that he felt bound to repay the loyalty of his subjects by being himself the first in danger. For this costly heroism his subjects loved and admired him, and it likewise aroused the admiration of an English chronicler who exclaimed, 'O what a noble and triumphant courage was this, for a King to fight in a battle as a mean soldier!' By the sixteenth century Kings and generals for the most part had ceased to be warriors.

With the King died his illegitimate son Alexander, Archbishop of St Andrews. He was, according to his tutor Erasmus, so short-sighted that in order to read at all he had to hold a book almost touching the end of his nose. On the battlefield he must have been totally ineffective, his presence there a gesture of love and loyalty to his father. The brilliant young scholar and founder of a new college in the University of St Andrews came to a tragically inappropriate end.

With the King and his son died two bishops, three abbots, one dean, nine earls, fourteen lords, three Highland chiefs and members of almost every prominent family in the kingdom. The number of the nameless dead has been variously estimated. The English claimed that they had slain ten thousand Scots, which would have amounted to half the army. Probably the Scottish losses were not so high, especially among the Borderers, those very 'Flowers of the Forest' whom the romanticism of later generations especially lamented. However, the death of the King, and of so many of his leading subjects, gave Flodden the appearance and the reputation of an unparalleled national disaster.

The fact that the body of James IV was neither seen nor given burial in Scotland may have contributed to the myth that he had survived the battle and would return. Myths of survival and impending return are curious phenomena, which have been inspired by popular heroes as diverse as King Arthur and Lawrence of Arabia. Reluctance to accept the death of a hero may offer a partial explanation of a survival myth; a myth of impending return may, in the case of a popular ruler whose reign has provided 'Golden Age' benefits, owe its origin principally to wishful thinking. The most prosaic version of the myth of James IV was that, having survived the battle, he had gone on a pilgrimage to Jerusalem, from which he would one day return; the version which entered the folklore of Scotland was that like King Arthur he had been miraculously preserved and would return when his country's need was greatest.

The disappearance of mortal remains facilitates both aspects of the myth. As far as the Scots were concerned the body of James IV disappeared completely. One of the corpses from the battlefield was identified as that of the King of Scots, and carried down into England. Henry VIII obtained from the Pope permission to bury it in St Paul's Cathedral; papal permission was required since James had died under excommunication. But for some unspecified reason the corpse was never given either a state funeral or even a Christian burial. What ultimately became of it remains a mystery. However, John Stow, the Elizabethan annalist and antiquary, wrote in his *Survey of London*, in his description of the church of St Michael's, Wood St:

'There is also (but without any outward monument) the head of James IV, King of Scots of that name, slain at Flodden field, and buried here by this occasion: after the battle the body of the said King being found, was enclosed in lead and conveyed from thence to London, and so to the monastery of Skene in Surrey, where it remained for a time. . . . I have been shown the same body so lapped in lead ... thrown into a waste room amongst the old timber, lead and other rubble. Since which time workmen there, for their foolish pleasure, hewed off his head; and Launcelot Young, master glazier to Her Majesty [Elizabeth I], feeling a sweet savour to come from thence, and seeing the same dried from all moisture, and yet the form remaining with the hair of the head and beard red, brought it to London to his house in Wood St, where for a time he kept it for its sweetness, but in the end caused the sexton of that church to bury it among other bones taken out of their charnel.'

An English poet of the later sixteenth century had pity for the fate of James IV. He wrote a poem in which he attributed to the King of Scots these apt words concerning his own fate:

> *The world taketh from me all that he me gave,*
> *Miserere mei, Deus, et salva me.*[1]

[1] 'God have mercy on me and grant me salvation.'

7
James v,
1513–1542

Son port estoit royal, son regard vigoureux
De vertus, et d'honneur, et de guerre amoureux;
La douceur et la force illustroient son visage
Si que Vénus et Mars en avoient fait partage
(Ronsard, of James v)

Pierre de Ronsard first saw James v at the court of France in 1536, and the following year he returned with him to Scotland. His elegant verse, quoted in the original French at the beginning of the chapter, is therefore an impression of the King sketched from life:

> *His bearing was regal, his glance was eloquent*
> *Of honour in war, skill in love's tournament;*
> *Sweetness and strength together in his face*
> *Showed Mars and Venus both had lent him grace.*

If for Ronsard's more complimentary 'sweetness and strength' the translator could be permitted 'hardness and charm', the impression would perhaps be the more exact.

As far as his actual appearance was concerned, James v was universally acknowledged to be a very handsome man. He had inherited the dark auburn hair of his father and the white complexion of his mother. He had finely arched brows and an aquiline profile; his eyes, according to Bishop Lesley's description, were 'grey and sharp'.

Surviving portraits show the adult James v dressed in the fashions of the 1530s; there is no certain likeness of the younger James as a youth or as a boy, and none of the very small child who succeeded in 1513.

James v had been born on 10 April 1512, and therefore at the time of his accession he was only seventeen months old, so far the youngest of the series of child-Kings which the misfortunes of the Stewart dynasty had provided.

The coronation of James V took place in the Chapel Royal of Stirling on 21 September 1513. Despite the splendour with which it was performed it was remembered as the 'Mourning Coronation'. The assassination of James I, the accidental death of James II and the murder of James III had made each succeeding coronation a mournful occasion; but the death of James IV and of so many of the nobility at Flodden made the coronation of James V a more sombre occasion than all the rest.

Besides mourning their King, the Scots were doubtless well aware that they were mourning the passing of peaceful and prosperous times. Each royal minority had witnessed a greater or lesser degree of disorder; the long minority in prospect promised many years of strife. Furthermore, the political situation was fraught with danger. In a will which he had made before he went to war, James IV had appointed Queen Margaret tutrix or guardian of their son, in the event of his death. This appointment made her effectively head of state, though she was the sister, and the devoted sister, of the King whose army had been victorious at Flodden.

The Parliament which met at Stirling in the month of James V's coronation ratified Queen Margaret's appointment as guardian of the King; but a strong party among the nobility and clergy was opposed to her assumption of the headship of state. If Margaret Tudor's authority were to be repudiated, earlier precedent suggested that the regency could properly be offered to the King's nearest adult male kinsman. Robert, Duke of Albany and his son Murdoch had ruled successively during the imprisonment of James I; during the minority of James V, it was likewise a Duke of Albany who was nearest in blood to the King. John, Duke of Albany, the son of James III's traitorous brother by his French Duchess, had been born and brought up in France, and was to all effects a Frenchman; but he was not altogether unknown in Scotland, for James IV had corresponded with him, and had occasionally employed him as an agent in his foreign diplomacy. Those of the Scottish nobility who were opposed to the rule of Margaret Tudor advocated the alternative appointment of the Duke of Albany. A letter of invitation was despatched to him before the end of 1513.

The early months of 1514 saw the increase of Margaret's difficulties. She was in the later stages of pregnancy; in April she gave birth to James IV's posthumous son, Alexander, Duke of Ross, who survived less than two years. While pregnancy and childbirth made it difficult for her to maintain political control, the most powerful members of her council advocated her displacement in favour of Albany. Those who favoured him were the late King's cousin, James Hamilton, first Earl of Arran (the son of James III's sister Mary, by her second husband Lord Hamilton); James Beaton, Archbishop of Glasgow and Lord Home, the High Chamberlain. In order to maintain her position, Margaret was forced to rely increasingly upon the traditionally pro-English House of Douglas.

The young head of the House was Archibald, sixth Earl of Angus, who had recently succeeded his grandfather ('Bell-the-Cat'), whose eldest son had been killed at Flodden. In August 1514 Queen Margaret married the Earl of Angus. Contemporaries supposed that she had married 'for her pleasure', though her situation suggests that her motive may rather have been to acquire a husband who would strengthen her political position and support her pro-English policy. If so, her choice was disastrously mistaken, as the events of the next few years were to show. For the time being she had committed a sufficient mistake in marrying at all. Her opponents were able to announce that by remarrying she had forfeited her guardianship of the King under the terms of James IV's will. Nothing stood in the way of the appointment of Albany in her place.

Scotland was fortunate that while this internal power struggle was in progress Henry VIII did not take the opportunity to attempt the conquest of the country. Probably it seemed to him likely that English domination of Scotland could be achieved through Queen Margaret and the Earl of Angus. Furthermore the quarrel which had originally led to Anglo-Scottish hostilities was brought to an end when Henry fell out with his previous allies and made peace with France. This peace was cemented by the marriage of Henry's younger sister the Princess Mary to the widowed Louis XII. Henry then provided Queen Margaret with an opportunity to secure herself in Scotland by persuading Louis XII to detain the Duke of Albany in France.

On the last day of 1514, however, Louis died, to be succeeded by his cousin, François Ier. The policy of the new King was shaped throughout his reign by his rivalry with the House of Hapsburg, in the person of the Emperor Maximilian's grandson, who in 1519 became Charles V. From time to time François 1er required the alliance of England, but he was well aware of the usefulness to his predecessors of the 'auld alliance' with Scotland. Accordingly he began his reign by ratifying the existing peace with England, and by inviting the participation of Scotland.

When Margaret Tudor's opponents had initially invited Albany to assume the regency, they had expected him to come with French re-inforcements to continue the war with Henry VIII. The new political alignments resulted in the arrival of a pro-French Regent, but one who was, at least temporarily, committed to a peace policy. Albany arrived in Scotland in May 1515, and was ceremonially installed as Regent on 10 July.

No motives of ambition led Albany to accept the regency; indeed, he went somewhat reluctantly to Scotland. As Admiral of France and as the friend of François 1er he could have expected to enjoy a career which would have fulfilled his ambitions in the country of his birth. However, he took it upon himself to serve the 'auld alliance' by attempting to reconcile the duty which he owed to James V and that which he felt towards François 1er.

Albany's integrity was quickly recognized, though at first he had a severe liability in the disgraceful memory of his father. His enemies hastened to suggest that the younger Albany likewise might have designs upon the throne of Scotland. Henry VIII, indeed, wrote to the Scottish Parliament and demanded that Albany be dismissed as a danger to the King. Parliament's reply was an affirmation of confidence in Albany, who had left 'his Maister [François 1er], his Lady, his leving, and indurit grete panis [pains] and charges in the Kingis service . . . and we firmly belief he wald notht attempte in the contrare to have the kinrikis of Frans, [and] Inglaand with Scotlaand . . .'.

Upon his installation as Regent, Albany at first sought the alliance of Queen Margaret, but she, understandably, received him as an enemy. He was well aware that without either the friendship of the Queen-mother or the custody of the King and his infant brother, his authority would remain a dead letter. Therefore, in August 1515, he besieged Queen Margaret in Stirling Castle and demanded the custody of the royal children.

Margaret, who was once again pregnant, and ill-prepared to with-stand a siege, surrendered without resistance. She gave the keys of the castle to the three-year-old King, and leading him by the hand to the outer entry, sent him forward alone to present them to Albany.

It is impossible not to feel sympathy for Margaret, forcibly parted from her children. James and his brother remained at Stirling Castle, in the care of Lord Erskine who was its Keeper. Margaret, who was escorted to Edinburgh Castle, did not see James again for almost two years; her younger son she never saw again, for he died a few months later. Albany, having secured custody of the royal children, was prudent in keeping his distance from them. His residence was the un-finished Palace of Holyroodhouse. Though his enemies spread the calumny that he was responsible for the death of the Duke of Ross, they failed to command general belief. The fact that the King survived and was well cared for soon made it obvious that his brother had died a natural death.

Margaret, encouraged by Lord Dacre, Henry viii's Warden of the Marches, resolved to abduct her children and flee with them to the English court. The abduction plot failed, but Margaret, trusting that her sons would be safe in the hands of Lord Erskine, fled to England herself, accompanied by Angus. In England she gave birth to the only child of her second marriage, Lady Margaret Douglas, destined to become the mother of Lord Darnley, the ill-fated consort of Mary, Queen of Scots.

After the flight of Margaret, Albany was able to consolidate his authority in Scotland. In 1516 he quelled a rebellion led by Lord Home, who had initially advocated his appointment. Home may have hoped to enjoy great power under the rule of a more or less foreign Regent; the discovery that Albany intended to share his authority with no-one may have led Home into the treasonable dealings with Margaret and Henry viii which caused his downfall. Home and his brother were tried and executed in the autumn of 1516.

Albany held office as Regent from 1515 to 1524, during which time he spent three periods of residence in Scotland. The first ended in 1517, when the Regent felt that his authority was sufficiently established to permit his visiting France to attend both to his family affairs and to the foreign affairs of Scotland.

In August 1517 Albany negotiated with François 1er the Treaty of

Rouen, possibly the most influential treaty of the reign. The previous year François had signed with King Charles of Spain (the future Emperor Charles v) a treaty by which he agreed that his elder daughter Louise should marry Charles, and that if Louise should die, her younger sister Charlotte should take her place. Albany persuaded François to agree that Charlotte should be promised to James v, but that if Charles should claim her the King of Scots should marry the next daughter born to the Queen of France. In 1517 the Treaty of Rouen appeared somewhat hypothetical; but by the time of its ratification in 1521 the Queen of France had given birth to a third daughter, Madeleine, who ultimately became the bride of James v.

The long interval between the negotiation and ratification of the treaty was caused by the four years' absence from Scotland of Albany, who was detained in France by a new Anglo-French alliance.

During Albany's absence the good order which he had imposed in Scotland speedily collapsed. The principal agents of disorder were the Earls of Angus and Arran. Angus, as the husband of Queen Margaret, sought supreme power through the pursuit of a pro-English policy. Arran, as the premier nobleman in Albany's absence, found the pretensions of Angus intolerable, and sought to counter them by a pro-French policy. The ensuing power struggle culminated in a street battle in Edinburgh in the spring of 1520, in which the Douglases were victorious.

There was, however, no community of purpose between Queen Margaret and Angus. Had there been, it is probable that the English interest would have triumphed. Margaret returned to Scotland when Albany departed, but in pursuit of supreme power for herself, not in conjunction with her husband. Both of them desired to rule, and each sought to minimize the influence of the other. By 1519 Margaret had resolved to secure a divorce from Angus. Henry viii refused to assist her in so immoral and un-Christian a proceeding; angered by his unbrotherly conduct, Margaret resolved to have recourse to Albany, who was related by marriage to the family of Pope Clement vii.

In 1521 Albany returned to Scotland. The brittle alliance of Henry viii and François i^{er} collapsed shortly after their meeting at the Field of Cloth of Gold. Henry formed a new alliance with Charles v, which committed them to a concerted attack upon France. François accordingly sent Albany back to Scotland to arrange a Scottish invasion of England, the traditional form of support which the Kings of France expected under the terms of the 'auld alliance'.

Upon his arrival, in November 1521, Albany found that his erstwhile enemy Queen Margaret had become his warm supporter. She was gratified when he banished the Earl of Angus to France, though her friendship speedily evaporated when he organized a military expedition against England, and advanced to the Border in July 1522. Margaret never felt so much an Englishwoman as when Scotland and England were at war. She changed her tactics and betrayed Albany's plans to Lord Dacre.

On receiving the information that the Scots were unwilling to follow Albany to war, Dacre offered a temporary truce, which Albany thankfully accepted. After Flodden the Scots felt strongly that they had sustained a heavy defeat on behalf of an ungrateful ally, and while they were ready to defend the kingdom against overt English aggression, they were reluctant to invade England merely because François Ier was at war with Henry VIII.

Albany returned to France in October 1522 to persuade François that if he wished for Scottish help against England he must provide military support. Albany was back in Scotland in September 1523, bringing French reinforcements. Henry VIII, in the meantime, had offered Scotland a five-year truce, and his daughter Mary as a bride for James V. Since the Treaty of Rouen had just been ratified his offer was refused. His reply to the refusal was to burn Kelso and Jedburgh. Albany therefore returned to find anti-English feeling strong enough to make his proposed invasion initially popular. However, once again when the Scots reached the Border they demurred at crossing into England. He induced a reluctant army to besiege Wark Castle, but the sudden onset of winter weather and the approach of an English army forced him to retreat.

In the spring of 1524 Albany left Scotland for the last time, his reputation damaged by two inglorious military expeditions. The Scots at the time of his departure felt that during his regency Scotland had been made the tool of French policy; they did not appreciate the part that he had played in protecting Scotland from English domination.

The departure of Albany gave his political opponents the opportunity to seize power and reverse his policy.

The first to take that opportunity was Queen Margaret. Assisted by

Arran she regained control of the King, and with it her position as head of state. Margaret, however, no longer enjoyed the whole-hearted support of Henry VIII. He still refused to countenance her project to divorce Angus, of whose influence in Scotland he entertained great hopes. Despite her betrayal of Albany in 1522 Margaret appealed to him once more, and in 1525 he obtained her divorce from Clement VII. No doubt his motive was not purely altruistic; probably he hoped that the divorce of Margaret and Angus would weaken the English interest in Scotland. It did not, indeed, derogate from the influence of Angus, but it was remarked that after the divorce Henry 'never carried such respect to his sister as he had done before'. In 1526 she married a third husband, Henry Stewart, younger son of Lord Avondale. Subsequently James V created him Lord Methven.

In the summer of 1524 Margaret and Arran declared the twelve-year-old King to have attained his majority. He was invested with the symbols of sovereignty, and the regency of Albany was formally terminated. But the position of Margaret was extremely insecure. Albany's departure permitted Angus to return from his exile. He did so with the approval of Henry VIII, who had been persuaded that Angus would serve the English interest 'better than five Earls of Arran'. Margaret was forced to accept Angus as a member of her Council, over which he quickly gained an ascendancy. In November 1525 he secured possession of the King by a coup d'état, after which James V remained a virtual prisoner of the Douglas faction until 1528.

After the initial shock of separation from his mother, James V was fortunate that the political turmoil of Scotland left him relatively un-affected. During his early childhood James remained at Stirling Castle, surrounded by the familiar faces of his household. The Master Usher, and later the Master of the Household, was the poet Sir David Lindsay of the Mount, who served the King devotedly and with genuine affection. In one of his best-known poems Lindsay reminded the adult James of how he had attended upon him and entertained him when he was a small child:

> *When thou was young I bore thee in mine arme*
> *Full tenderly, till thou begouth to gang,[1]*
> *And in thy bed oft happit[2] thee full warm,*
> *With lute in hand, syne, sweetly to thee sang. . . .*

[1] began to walk.   [2] wrapped.

And, in another poem he reminded the King

> *How, as a chapman bears his pack*
> *I bore thy Grace upon my back.*
> *And sometimes strydlingis[1] on my neck,*
> *Dancing with many a bend and beck.*
> *The first sillabis that thou didst mute*
> *Was 'Pa Da Lyn' – upon the lute*
> *Then played I twenty springs perqueir[2]. . . .*

Lindsay reminded James also of how later he had done his best to satisfy his insatiable demands for stories, with tales of King Arthur, Hector, Alexander, Pompey and Julius Caesar, Hercules and Samson, all heroes for the King to emulate.

James received his formal lessons from 'ane young clerk', Gavin Dunbar, who subsequently became Archbishop of Glasgow. Evidently he won the liking and respect of his pupil, for in later years James made him his Chancellor. The King learnt Latin, in which he probably received an adequate grounding, and French, which he learnt to read and write sufficiently for diplomatic purposes, though he was never able to speak it fluently. He benefited no further from the scholarship of Gavin Dunbar, for his formal education was ended by his mother's coup d'état when he was twelve.

Margaret was culpably neglectful of her son's education, and Angus, after his counter-coup of 1525, made no arrangement for its continuance. The result was that although James v was by no means illiterate he was much less highly educated than most of the princes of his time; indeed, the scope of his education presents a sorry contrast with that of his father. He was, however, a good musician; all his life he derived pleasure from playing the lute and singing. In horsemanship and martial sports he achieved the ostentatious proficiency which was expected of a King.

Angus decided to make his royal stepson's captivity palatable by indulging him with everything he could desire, except his freedom. James was provided with horses, hawks and hounds, and with some fine weapons, including a sporting crossbow and a hand-culverin. He was allowed to indulge his taste for extravagantly splendid clothes and jewels. He was permitted plenty of ready money, for gaming and for

[1] sitting astride. [2] *par cœur*: by heart.

alms. Open-handed generosity to poor people characterized him all his life. No doubt Angus hoped that James would feel sufficiently like a King to prevent his growing restive. When he grew old enough other pleasures were provided for him. In Buchanan's words, 'those who had the instruction of his youth made him more inclinable to women, because by that means they hoped to have him longer under their tuition'. Sir David Lindsay told the same tale in one of his poems. It appears that Angus was sufficiently unconcerned with the King's welfare to hope that an inadequate education, a course of systematic spoiling, and an early sexual initiation would long keep the King's mind away from his responsibilities, or might even turn him into a *roi fainéant*, unprepared and ultimately unwilling to assume them. Angus probably knew enough history to be aware that James ii, James iii and James iv had all assumed power before they were out of their teens; if James v matured as early as his father and his immediate ancestors the Douglas tenure of power would not be long.

It was fortunate for James v himself and for Scotland that Angus's irresponsible policy was unsuccessful.

During his early childhood James was deprived of close family relationships. He would have had no memory of his father; his unpredictable mother disappeared and reappeared according to the exigencies of the political situation; his younger brother died at less than two years old when he himself was four. As King he would always have been a child without equals, but since he lacked a family he was one surrounded entirely by servants. The most affectionate of his attendants were scarcely his intimates; mental isolation was an early experience. This isolation was enhanced during the regime of Angus, for James was separated from the Household which had served him all his life, and surrounded by men whom he regarded as his enemies.

Sir David Lindsay lost his office as Master of the Household, and his place was taken by Angus's brother, Sir George Douglas. Angus's uncle, Archibald Douglas of Kilspindie, became Treasurer. James Douglas of Drumlanrig became Master of the Wine Cellar; James Douglas of Parkhead became Master of the Larder. The stories of the Livingstones and the Boyds were being re-enacted; but James v probably knew those stories as well as Angus. He determined to escape and assert his authority as successfully as his grandfather and his great-grandfather had done.

Between the ages of thirteen and sixteen, while James remained the captive of his stepfather, despite the latter's efforts to divert and corrupt him, James developed a precocious shrewdness and the characteristics of self-reliance, secrecy and ruthlessness which he retained throughout his life. Perhaps in consequence of the conditions of his childhood and adolescence, James remained always somewhat inaccessible. Few of his relationships with either men or women appear to have been deep or lasting. Though he possessed charm of manner he lacked the genuine warmth which had helped to make his father so greatly loved.

Immediately after Angus's coup d'état James appealed to his mother and Arran to attempt his rescue. They responded to his appeal, but their attempt was a failure. After Margaret's marriage to Henry Stewart in 1526 Arran ceased to support her and allied himself with Angus. James did not despair, however, for during 1526 he initiated two plots to secure his liberty. Both plots were organized by the King's cousin, John Stewart, Earl of Lennox, who had given his support to Angus in 1525.

During 1526 James developed an attachment to Lennox, to whom he appealed to help him regain his liberty. Lennox chivalrously promised that he would rescue James from the Douglases or lose his life in the attempt. He may perhaps have hoped to take Angus's place if not as the King's gaoler at least as the power behind the throne. His first plot, to snatch the King from the Douglases while Angus, accompanied by James, was attending a Justice Ayre on the Border, was a failure.

In August 1526 Lennox left the court, and from Stirling issued a general appeal to the nobility of Scotland to assist in rescuing the King. The response illustrated the unpopularity which Angus had won by his seizure of power. Lennox was joined by Margaret and her husband, by James Beaton, now Archbishop of St Andrews, by the Earls of Argyll, Moray, Cassillis and Glencairn, and a representative selection of the lesser nobility.

Lennox and his party marched on Edinburgh and Angus, supported only by his kinsmen and dependers, prepared to do battle for the possession of the King. On the morning of 4 September Angus led his army out of Edinburgh, and commanded his brother Sir George to follow as quickly as possible, with the King. James did his best to help his friends by delaying Sir George and his contingent as much as he could, '. . . and upon the way would often turn aside to ease nature, as if he had been troubled with a looseness'. Suddenly Sir George lost his temper. 'Sir,' he exclaimed, 'rather than our enemies should take you from us, we will lay hold on your body; and, if it be rent in pieces, we will be sure to take out part of it.' With so brutal an expression of the Douglases' determination to keep their captive, Sir George ensured that the King's resentment would be redoubled and his vengeance certain. It was a black day for James. In the battle, which took place near Linlithgow, the King's would-be rescuers were defeated and scattered, and Lennox was murdered after he had surrendered. In triumph the Douglases brought the King to Stirling, still a prisoner.

Angus retained power for a further twenty-one months. His victory made him confident that no more attempts to rescue the King by force of arms would be made for some time to come; but there were changes in the political climate which should have given Angus less cause for confidence. After Linlithgow, Arran again withdrew his support, which meant that the Douglas regime was not supported by a single member of the greater nobility. Numerous though the Douglases were, Angus had not enough kinsmen to staff the whole administration. He was forced to rely upon the services of careerists from baronial families. Ultimately, James benefited, for upon the fall of Angus he inherited some able public servants who had no wish to fall with Angus when the opportunity arose to transfer their loyalty to the King.

After the Battle of Linlithgow James learnt to bear his captivity patiently, until he could procure his liberation. In the ensuing twenty-one months he took time to observe the political situation and to formulate his own views upon it. From his mother James had learnt to dislike and distrust Angus; but Margaret had always been pro-English, and had sought to foster pro-English sympathies in her son. Captivity clarified any confused attitudes which James might have derived from his mother. He accepted and followed her detestation of Angus, but since Angus was the ally of Henry VIII and willing to become the chief agent to English influence in Scotland, the English alliance together with his anglophile stepfather became repugnant to James V.

The King escaped during the last days of May 1528. According to the vivid narrative of Pitscottie, James escaped from Falkland at a time when Angus, Kilspindie and Sir George Douglas were absent, attending to their own affairs, and James Douglas of Parkhead was left in charge of the King.

James announced that he planned a hunting expedition and retired to bed early, bidding Parkhead a courteous goodnight and reminding him to rise in good time. When all the Household was asleep, James got up again, disguised himself in clothes which he had borrowed from one of his Yeomen of the Stable, escaped unrecognized and rode hard for Stirling.

Next morning, when the King's bedchamber was found empty, someone suggested that he had 'passit to Banbreich to ane gentill woman'; but more disquieting to the Douglases was the rumour that he had 'passit the brige of Stirling'.

The Douglases quickly foregathered at Falkland and rode in pursuit, but as they drew near to Stirling they were met by a herald with a proclamation which forebade them to approach within six miles of the King.

Doubts have been cast upon Pitscottie's story because certain entries in the Exchequer Rolls suggest that the King's escape was made not from Falkland but from Edinburgh. But, whatever the starting point of his journey, his destination was Stirling. There, less than two months after his sixteenth birthday, James v began his personal rule.

Some further months elapsed before the young King was able to rid himself of the hated presence of the Douglases in Scotland. Angus defended himself in Tantallon Castle, and it was November before he surrendered and withdrew with his principal kinsmen to England.

Henry viii received Angus favourably. But, since he had begun his long struggle to obtain a divorce from Catherine of Aragon, and anticipated trouble with Catherine's nephew Charles v, he had no wish to embroil himself in hostilities with Scotland. Accordingly, he made only a formal protest against Angus's banishment. In December, when a five years' peace was signed between Scotland and England, it was agreed that Angus should be permitted to reside at the English court. Douglas family history was repeating itself.

During the summer and autumn of 1528 James had been principally occupied in breaking the power of the Douglases. His victory enabled him to turn his attention to the task of ruling his kingdom. The immediate problem which faced him was the imposition of orderly living throughout the country, especially in those perennial problem areas, the Highlands, the Isles and the Border. George Buchanan criticized the early efforts of James v to deal with these problems as 'eager and over-violent'.

Just before the surrender of the Douglases James made his first attempt to quell disturbances in the Highlands. On 10 November 1528 he issued 'Letters of Fire and Sword' to his half-brother the Earl of Moray, by which he, with the assistance of four other lords, was commanded to exterminate the notoriously disorderly Clan Chatten, sparing only priests, women and children, who were to be deported and set ashore on the coasts of Shetland and Norway. Happily for the intended victims, there is some doubt that this drastic remedy was put into effect.

In 1529 and 1530 James gave his attention to the condition of the Border, which had grown increasingly disturbed in the years after Flodden. On the expedition of 1529 James captured and executed two notorious freebooters, Scott of Tushielaw and Cockburn of Henderland. The expedition of 1530 resulted in the more famous incident of the capture and execution of John Armstrong of Gilnockie.

'Johnie Armstrong', the hero of a well-known ballad, was said to have boasted that he acknowledged the authority of neither the King of England nor the King of Scots. He might have been confident that he would never encounter the King of England, except in the persons of his Wardens of the Marches; the King of Scots was too near a neighbour for such a boast to be anything but foolhardy.

According to Pitscottie, the King's expedition to the Armstrongs' district of Liddesdale had the appearance of a large-scale hunting party, and Gilnockie was invited in friendly fashion to come and meet him. When he and his followers unsuspectingly approached they were seized and summarily executed. The ballad 'Johnie Armestrong' gives a dramatic account of how Gilnockie pleaded desperately for his life, making the King increasingly extravagant promises of tribute in money and in kind. To each promise and entreaty James answers

> *Away, away, thou traitor strang,*
> *Out of my sight soon mayest thou be.*
> *I granted never a traitor's life,*
> *And now I'll not begin with thee.*

Finally Gilnockie realizes that prayers are fruitless. He submits himself to death with dignity, saying as he is led to execution

> *To seek hot water beneath cold ice*
> *Surely it is a great follie.*
> *I have asked grace at a graceless face,*
> *And there is none for my men and me.*

Cold and 'graceless' (i.e. ruthless) was the face which James v habitually showed to malefactors. The most notorious of the Border reivers paid for their misdeeds with their lives, and some of the more powerful Border lords and lairds were imprisoned during the early years of the reign. The good order that ensued impressed the contemporaries of James v; especially it impressed them that the King was able to keep vast flocks of sheep in Ettrick Forest as unmolested as if they had been 'within the bounds of Fife'.

The King's dealings with the Highlands and the Isles were equally dedicated to the imposition of orderly living; but after 1529 his methods were less 'over-violent' than those which had inspired his savage orders concerning the Clan Chatten.

In the Highlands James v followed the policy of his father by making use of the influence of the Gordons of Huntly. The fourth Earl of Huntly was slightly younger than the King, and had been the ward of Angus; consequently James and Huntly had become closely acquainted under circumstances which tended to create mutual sympathy. Huntly became the King's friend, and therefore James readily trusted him to keep order in the north in the best interests of the Crown.

James looked less favourably upon the Campbells, who during the previous reign had been entrusted with keeping order in the Isles. When the third Earl of Argyll died in 1529 James did not renew his commission of lieutenancy in favour of his son. Instead he gave the commission to Alexander MacDonald of Islay, who had informed him that the Campbell policy had been to foment disorder in the Isles and then gain credit and profit by stamping it out. The Isles remained quiet until 1539, when Donald Gorm of Sleat rose in rebellion and laid claim to the Lordship of the Isles. The rebellion was abortive, but no doubt its occurrence influenced the King's decision to make a circumnavigation of the north in 1540. In the course of his voyage the King visited Orkney and the Western Isles, and took prisoners and hostages from several clans whose loyalty he doubted. He also brought home with him a number of chiefs' sons for education at court, no doubt with the intention of producing a more tractable generation to succeed to estates in the turbulent parts of his kingdom. Upon his return he finally annexed the Lordship of the Isles to the Crown.

James's efforts to impose law and order throughout his kingdom won him considerable popularity with his poorer subjects who had suffered greatly from lawlessness during his minority. According to Buchanan, James would 'sit on horseback night and day, in the coldest winter, so that he might catch the thieves in their harbours at unawares: and his activity struck such terror into them, that they abstained from their evil purposes, as if he had been always present among them'.

His popularity was further enhanced by his habit of wandering among his people in the guise of a farmer, 'the Gudeman o' Ballengeich', supposedly the tenant of one of the royal farms. With his regal and striking appearance James was not a man who could have disguised himself easily; and the fact that 'the Gudeman o' Ballengeich' became almost synonymous for 'the King' suggests that he was recognized more often than he thought. However, he enjoyed the possibilities for informal adventure which disguise permitted, and many tales of his encounters with tinkers, beggars and outlaws, and his seductions of country girls, passed into the folklore of Scotland.

Most of the King's adventures probably took place in the years between his escape from the Douglases and his marriage to Madeleine of France in 1537. That this event was so long deferred was due to the intricate marriage diplomacy into which he was forced by the tortuous course of international politics. Like his father, however, James V did not live celibate while he negotiated for the hand of a suitable princess; apart from the informal adventures already referred to, James had numerous affairs with young women of noble birth. By Elizabeth Shaw of Sauchie he had a son who was given the royal name of James Stewart, and by Margaret, daughter of Lord Erskine, a second James Stewart, who as Earl of Moray played a prominent part in Scottish politics during the next two reigns. Margaret Erskine was recognized as the King's favourite mistress, but she shared his favour with Euphemia Elphinstone, Elizabeth Carmichael, Elizabeth Stewart and Elizabeth Beaton, all of whom bore him children.

In 1529 James wrote to the Duke of Albany, stating that it was expedient he should marry, for the good of his kingdom, to secure the succession, and 'pour evyter la procréation des batardz'. The passage of time lent a certain unconscious humour to the third consideration. In writing to Albany James was inviting him to use his influence to persuade François 1er to honour the Treaty of Rouen. James had grown up with the idea that he was destined to marry the Princess Madeleine; but not only had time made the idea familiar, politics had made it necessary.

Though James had signed a convenient peace with England in 1528, the terms of the peace permitted Henry VIII to give protection to Angus, an exile whose family tradition was one of treasonable intercourse with England. Furthermore, with Angus at the English court were his brother and uncle. The perceptive observation of an eighteenth-century historian was that Henry VIII 'in supporting the infamous Douglases against their sovereign ... in a manner forced James to fix a connexion with France'.

After the French defeat by the Imperial forces at the Battle of Pavia in 1525, François became concerned for a time to retain friendly relations with England, in preference to reaffirming the traditional alliance with Scotland, the lesser power. James V responded astutely to François's hesitations. Although he was eager to induce the French King to honour the Treaty of Rouen – not only for political but for financial reasons, since he stood in great need of the Princess Madeleine's dowry – James played upon François's basic unwillingness to see him marry elsewhere by inviting counter-proposals. He negotiated with the Emperor, for his sister Mary of Hungary; with the deposed King of Denmark for one of his daughters, who were also the Emperor's nieces; with Henry VIII for his daughter Mary Tudor; and with the Duke of Albany and Pope Clement VII, for Catherine de' Medici, who was Albany's niece and the ward of the Pope.

It is futile but nonetheless intriguing to speculate upon what might have been the course of Scottish history had Catherine de' Medici married James V. However, Henry VIII had no wish to see his old enemy Albany reappear in Scotland as the Queen's uncle. He suggested to François that she would make a suitable bride for his younger son, Henri, Duc d'Orléans. The marriage took place, and the unforeseen succession of Henri made Catherine Queen of France.

Though Clement VII preferred the French to the Scottish marriage for his ward, his dealings with Henry VIII had taught him the deleterious effects that matrimonial disappointment could have upon the relations between the Papacy and the temporal powers. The interest which James had shown in Catherine de' Medici's dowry suggested that a financial consolation for the refusal of her hand would greatly assist in retaining James V as a faithful son of the Church.

James was an orthodox Catholic by personal conviction and by policy, and never did he show any inclination to imitate the religious policy of Henry VIII. But he was well aware that the defection of England enabled him to drive a hard bargain with the Pope, virtually to name the price of his obedience to Rome. Obviously an ecclesiastical subsidy from Scottish sources would provide a form of *douceur* convenient for the Pope to impose and easy for the King of Scots to collect.

In 1531 the Pope wrote to the prelates of Scotland asking their opinion on the imposition of a permanent tax of £10,000 a year to be levied on their prelacies for 'the protection and defence of the realm', a form of words open to wide interpretation. In the event the Pope imposed a tax for this purpose, which was known as the 'Three Teinds', or three tenths, of a tenth of the income of all benefices worth more than £20 per annum, for three years. For the 'Great Tax' of £10,000 a year a better-defined purpose had to be found.

The purpose suggested to the Pope was the foundation and endowment of a 'College of Justice', a body of salaried professional judges in Scotland. As a means of guaranteeing that the results of the foundation would be beneficial to the Church it was agreed that in the membership of the College of Justice ecclesiastics would predominate. Of the fifteen 'senators' to be appointed, seven were to be spiritual and seven temporal persons, and the president was always to be an ecclesiastic.

The foundation of the College of Justice was not the great innovation with which James V has sometimes been credited. Of the fifteen senators who were appointed in 1532, fourteen had served on the Session the previous year, and eleven had served on it since 1527. Basically what happened was that the 'Lords of Session', the existing unsalaried judges, became 'Senators of the College of Justice' and received salaries. This provision might have been expected to encourage efficiency and impartiality; but unhappily the proportion of the

'Great Tax' allotted to providing the salaries was extremely small. The foundation of the College of Justice had been the pretext for, rather than the purpose of, the imposition of the 'Great Tax', most of the proceeds of which went to the Crown. Furthermore, the Scottish prelates, who understood James's dealings with the Pope, resented the 'Great Tax' and paid the annual instalments grudgingly. James therefore made a new arrangement with them, permitting them to compound for the sum of £72,000 to be paid in four instalments. The judges' salaries were to be paid out of a tax of £1,400 per annum, to be paid from the incomes of benefices assigned for the purpose, with the addition of £200 per annum from benefices in the patronage of the Crown. This somewhat meagre provision was ratified by a bull of Pope Paul III in 1535.

Though he was not above driving a hard bargain with Papacy and clergy, James was concerned to demonstrate his own orthodoxy and to defend his kingdom against heresy. In 1532 an Act of Parliament recorded James's resolution to 'defend the authority, liberty and freedom of the seat of Rome and halikirk [i.e. The Holy Church]'. Though the purpose of the act was to illustrate that the Pope's generosity over the 'Three Teinds' and the 'Great Tax' would be properly repaid, it also provides evidence that the coming of the Reformation to Scotland was no longer a matter to be decided by the King alone. For some years the dissemination of Lutheran ideas had been regarded as a threat to the orthodoxy of Scotland.

The explanation of Scotland's receptiveness to heresy lies in the preceding century, when the Catholic religion was the Christian religion, and its observances the unquestioned background of life. The later fifteenth century was not an age of great faith, but one of pious observances. The hollowness of much observance and the overlaying of faith by superstition, which were the worst aspects of the religious life of the age, may have done much to make the clear statements and theological simplifications of the Reformers attractive to people whose spiritual diet had gradually become over-elaborate and under-nourishing.

In 1525 an Act of Parliament had been passed forbidding the importation of Lutheran books; but such acts are difficult to enforce, and Lutheran literature continued to be smuggled into the country by way of the East Coast ports, especially St Andrews.

As a major port, an intellectual centre, and the primatial see, St Andrews played a leading part in the Reformation conflict. It was the scene of the first Protestant martyrdom, that of Patrick Hamilton, in 1528. Hamilton was the author of a widely read religious treatise, setting forth Lutheran ideas, and he was also a relative of Archbishop Beaton, who, with embarrassed reluctance, condemned him to death. The interest aroused by his writings and the sympathy inspired by his martyrdom caused a servant of the Archbishop to say to his master that if he proposed to burn more heretics, then 'let them be burnt in deep cellars, for the reek of Master Patrick Hamilton has infected as many as it blew upon'.

Beaton did not heed the warning. In 1533 or 1534 a man named Henry Forrest was burnt at St Andrews, and in 1534 he was followed by two more named Straiton and Gourlay. James v presided at the latter trial, and was disposed to acquit Straiton, whose only fault was refusal to pay his tithes. However, the ecclesiastics on the tribunal informed the King that in cases involving heresy he did not possess the prerogative of mercy.

The reek, or smoke, of these burnings infected those it blew upon not only with Lutheranism but with anti-clericalism, which, though it had existed during the Middle Ages, increased in virulence and intensity as the sixteenth century progressed. The later years of James v witnessed a rapid increase in anti-clericalism to which reference will be made in the context of those years. In the meantime, while the threat of the coming Reformation developed in the background, the King continued to negotiate the French marriage and alliance which were the principal aims of his diplomacy.

In 1534 the peace which James had signed with England at the beginning of his personal rule was due to expire. Both James v and Henry viii were eager to renew the peace, James because he was desirous of maintaining peaceful relations with all his neighbours, Henry because he was fully occupied with the metamorphosis of the old Catholic into the new Henrician England.

In May 1534 a peace was signed which was to last for the joint lifetime of both Kings, and for one year beyond the death of whichever should die first. Henry viii also offered James the hand of his daughter Mary, but James had the object lesson of his father's misfortune to discourage him from an English marriage. He declined the hand of

Mary Tudor, who in any event could no longer be regarded as a worthy match; for, after the birth of Elizabeth, Henry's daughter by Anne Boleyn, Mary had been displaced from the succession and declared a bastard. However, James made a gracious concession to Henry's sensibilities by acknowledging the validity of his divorce from Catherine of Aragon and his marriage to Anne Boleyn. Henry, gratified at receiving this recognition from a Catholic sovereign, bestowed upon James the Order of the Garter. At the same time he sent envoys to Scotland instructed to persuade James to imitate the Henrician policy of dissolving religious foundations and annexing Church property, and by way of encouragement to 'inculce and harpe upon the spring of honour and profit'. James, who had other notions of honour and other sources of profit, remained deaf to these persuasions.

At the end of 1534 François Ier, probably influenced by James's partial *rapprochement* with Henry VIII, overcame his hesitancy to honour the Treaty of Rouen. He remained unwilling to part with his daughter Madeleine, not unreasonably since she was only fourteen years old and was in delicate health, but he offered James Marie de Bourbon, the daughter of the Duc de Vendôme, with a dowry of 100,000 crowns.

James accepted reluctantly. Though his youthful expectation and his adult ambition had been to marry the Daughter of France, he had recently experienced a temptation to abandon the ambition for which he had negotiated so patiently, and marry his mistress, Margaret Erskine. He had gone so far as to arrange her divorce from her husband, Douglas of Lochleven, and to request from Pope Paul III a dispensation for his own marriage to her. The Pope, however, refused to recognize the validity of the Scottish divorce or to grant the dispensation. James, accepting the papal decision in a more obedient spirit than Henry VIII had done in similar circumstances, made preparations for his marriage to Marie de Bourbon.

In September 1536 James paid an informal but nonetheless magnificent visit to France, to claim his bride. Accompanied by an entourage which filled seven ships, he sailed to Dieppe and went thence to St Quentin, where the Duc de Vendôme held his court. According to Pitscottie, the King, in order to see Marie de Bourbon while remaining unrecognized, disguised himself as the servant of one of his own servants. However, in the course of the marriage negotiations Marie had been presented with a portrait of the King of Scots; despite his disguise she recognized him as readily as one of his own subjects might have recognized the Gudeman o' Ballengeich. At once she went up to him and 'tuik him be the hand and said, "Schir, ye stand ower far assyde",' and greeted him as 'your Grace'. Then, 'the King heirand this was a lyttill eschameit that he had dissagyssit him self to be wuknawin and syne was so hastallie knawin be the meanes of that gentillvoman'. He was obliged to acknowledge his identity and allow himself to be presented to the Duc de Vendôme.

At St Quentin James was lavishly entertained for eight days. But he was disappointed with the appearance of Marie de Bourbon whom he found 'bossue et contrefaicte' [i.e. hunchbacked and mis-shapen]. His thoughts turned to the Daughter of France. Apparently he resolved to visit the French court and demand the Princess Madeleine under circumstances which would make it almost impossible for François to refuse.

He offered courteous and non-committal excuses to the Duc de Vendôme, and made his way to Lyons, where the French court was in mourning for the death of François's eldest son. When James reached Lyons François was in his bed, sick with grief; but, when he heard of James's arrival, he 'bownit [bounded] from his bede . . . and ressawit the King of Scotland in his armes'. Though it had pleased God, he said, to take away one of his sons, it had also pleased him to send 'that nobill prince', the King of Scots, to take his place. James responded to this welcome by requesting François to treat him not with the formality due to a visiting sovereign, but with the informal affection proper to a son.

To the marriage of James and Madeleine there was no further obstacle. Traditionally the marriage is said to have been a love-match, probably because of James's repudiation of Marie de Bourbon and his impetuous journey to Lyons, and because of Pitscottie's statement that the Princess Madeleine, 'fre tyme scho saw the King of Scotland . . . scho became so inamorit witht him and luffit him so that scho wald haue no man on lyffe bot him allanerlie [only] . . .'. However, Pitscottie did not suggest that James fell in love with the French Princess. Having described how the enamoured Madeleine determined to marry him, he declared that James 'consentit thairto hastelie ffor . . .

he knew thair was great profeit, freindschip and alya [alliance] to be gottin at the King of France's hand'.

The French memoirist Brantôme gives an equally unromantic account of the marriage. Madeleine, according to Brantôme, did not desire to marry the man with whom she had fallen in love at first sight, but to become a Queen, 'so proud and lofty was her heart'. Madeleine, whose elder sisters had predeceased her, was so delicate that her whole life had been lived in expectation of an early death. But, to warnings that marriage and child-bearing might prove fatal to her, Madeleine's answer was, 'At least I shall be Queen for so long as I live; that is what I have always wished for.' In both the Scottish and the French versions there is little suggestion of romantic love. Possibly both the King and the Princess loved in each other the being who represented the fulfilment of ambition.

The marriage took place in the Cathedral of Notre Dame in Paris on 1 January 1537, and thereafter James and his Queen remained in France until the beginning of May. Besides paying Madeleine's dowry of 100,000 livres, François Ier bore the whole cost of James's visit, and at his departure presented him with several suits of gilded armour, twelve warhorses with rich accoutrements and two ships to assist in transporting the enlarged entourage of the King and Queen to Scotland.

On 19 May they landed at Leith, where Madeleine knelt upon the shore, 'thankit God that he had saiflie brocht hir witht hir husband till [to] thair awin contrie', and then took up two handfulls of Scottish earth and kissed it. Madeleine's gesture of respect for Scotland endeared her to the Scots; but the young Queen did not find her new country congenial, for the climate, even in May, was 'very different from her sweet France'. However, the young Ronsard, who was a member of her entourage, told Brantôme that 'without one word of repentance, she said nothing except these words: "Alas! I would be Queen" – covering her sadness and the fire of her ambition with the ashes of patience as best she could.' But patience was not a quality which Madeleine was long required to display, for the early death which had been prophesied for her awaited her in Scotland. Less than two months after her arrival, on 7 July, she died at Holyrood, and was buried in the Abbey which was to have been the scene of her coronation.

The grief which James v experienced at her death was no less sincere for being accompanied by anxiety that the Franco-Scottish alliance should not suffer in consequence. The ambassador who carried the news of Madeleine's death to her father was also instructed to negotiate a second French marriage for the King of Scots. François 1er accepted James's request with complete understanding. Madeleine's death was no cause of surprise to him, and though he grieved for it he did not experience resentment against his son-in-law. James's visit to France proved at this point to have been of great political value, for it had gained him the affection and respect of François, who after James's return to Scotland showed a far greater solicitude for the 'auld alliance' than he had shown before. Without hesitation he offered James a second French bride, in the person of Marie de Guise, the widow of the Duc de Longueville.

The marriage negotiations were dramatically interrupted by a counter-bid from Henry VIII, who had just lost his third wife, Jane Seymour, who died after giving birth to his son Prince Edward. François, however, was not tempted to withdraw his offer to James, who, he declared, 'J'estime comme mon propre filz'. He gave substance to his words by providing Marie de Guise with a dowry of 150,000 livres and granting her the honorary rank of a Daughter of France. It was agreed that the marriage should take place in the summer of 1538, when James would have observed a decent period of mourning for his Queen, and Marie de Guise for her husband. Henry VIII, disappointed of Marie de Guise, married, and swiftly divorced, Anne of Cleves.

In the eleven months which elapsed between the death of Queen Madeleine and the arrival of Marie de Guise James dealt with a series of problems apparently connected only with the Douglas family, but symptomatic also of the uneasy relations which had arisen during the years of James's personal rule between the King and the nobility.

In too many instances James V's dealings with his nobility were high-handed and ill-advised. Perhaps exalted by his early and apparently easy successes, he did not stop to consider the extent to which he was dependent upon retaining the goodwill of his most powerful subjects. To permit the development of a disaffected opposition could prove fatal, as it had done in the instance of James III. James IV had learnt the lesson of his father's fate, and his policy towards the nobility had shown his awareness of the importance of blending the imposition of authority with the winning of support.

James V, however, did not apply the lessons of the past to his dealings with his most influential subjects. He relied upon the use of his powers of intimidation, backed by the sanctions of imprisonment, forfeiture and ultimately execution. It was small wonder that though a majority of the nobility had rallied to the support of the King in 1528 and assisted in the overthrow of Angus, by 1537 a contemporary observer could write 'so sore a dread King and so ill-beloved of his subjects [the writer was referring specifically to the nobility] was never in this land'. The misdeeds of Angus were forgotten, and the exiled Douglases pitied as victims of royal oppression.

James returned from France to discover that during his absence his mother had been attempting to negotiate a divorce from Lord Methven, with a view to being reunited with Angus. Since the 'auld alliance' had always been against her Tudor instincts, Queen Margaret may have aspired by remarrying Angus to strengthen the English interest in Scotland. James regarded her negotiations as scarcely less than treasonable. He quashed the divorce proceedings and ordered her to return to Lord Methven; she did so with great resentment, and remained married to him until her death in 1541.

Besides discovering his mother's intrigues, James probably also learnt that while he was in France plots had been taking place to secure the recall of Angus from exile. James naturally feared a revival of sympathy for the Douglases; therefore, when two relatives of Angus were executed in July 1537, it appeared that he was indulging in a purge of those Douglas connections which remained in Scotland.

John, Master of Forbes, Angus's brother-in-law, was condemned to death for the 'abominable imagination' of shooting the King when he went to Aberdeen to preside at a Justice Ayre, and Lady Glamis, Angus's sister, was likewise condemned for 'treasonably conspiring and imagining the King's slaughter or destruction by poison'. Public opinion held neither of them guilty. But the death of Lady Glamis in particular aroused much ill-feeling against the King, principally because she was a woman of great beauty who endured the terrible sentence of burning with 'manlike fortitude'. Such ill-advised severity increasingly alienated the King and the nobility, and in this instance it is possible to refer to the nobility *en bloc*. As early as 1536 an English ambassador had observed that of the greater nobility not one was a member of the King's Council, which consisted of 'none else but the papistical clergy'. By 1537 the King's position was growing dangerously isolated.

James V's marriage to Marie de Guise in 1538 inaugurated the final period of the reign.

The marriage was performed by proxy in May, and the following month Queen Marie arrived in Scotland. The Nuptial Mass was celebrated in the Cathedral of St Andrews by David Beaton, Archbishop Beaton's nephew and coadjutor, who officiated on behalf of his uncle who was now a frail old man. The occasion served not only to solemnize the marriage of the King and Queen, but to bring together the political trinity which was to dominate the remainder of the reign.

Marie de Guise was a beautiful woman, tall, graceful and fine-featured, with blue eyes and red-gold hair. Besides beauty she possessed great intelligence, and the right connections to foster her husband's policy. If the Guise family was not yet the powerful Catholic interest that it became later in the century, it was nonetheless a great Catholic family of increasing influence, marriage with which served both to strengthen the King's policy and to reaffirm the 'auld alliance'. Queen Marie gave her patronage and friendship to David Beaton, who from 1538 to the end of the reign became increasingly indispensable to James V.

Beaton was a cosmopolitan prelate who held the French bishopric of Mirepoix before he succeeded his uncle as Archbishop of St Andrews. At the end of 1538 he became a Cardinal. Early in his career he had been employed on diplomatic missions in France by the Duke of Albany, and throughout his life he remained a dedicated supporter of the 'auld alliance'.

The influence of the Queen and Cardinal Beaton provided an additional source of strength to James's already strong personal commitment to the 'auld alliance' and the Catholic Church. But although James supported the Church and in turn relied upon it to support him politically and financially, he was not unaware of its shortcomings, or of the anti-clericalism which they encouraged.

Most of the Bishops previously mentioned in this book were churchmen first and politicians second. The same could not be said of the Bishops of the early sixteenth century. The Chancellor, Archbishop Dunbar, was admittedly a churchman in the best medieval tradition;

but the Beatons, uncle and nephew, were renaissance politicians in Holy Orders.

Cardinal Beaton typified what was least praiseworthy in the pre-Reformation clergy by leading a life that was openly non-celibate. On the credit side, he was a scholar, who had studied at the universities of Glasgow, St Andrews and Orléans; but learning was no longer typical of most of his contemporaries among the Scottish Bishops. Probably the most shocking example of episcopal ignorance was provided by Bishop Crichton of Dunkeld, who cheerfully admitted to an apostate priest on trial before him in 1539 that he had never read either the Old or the New Testament. 'And yet,' he said, 'thou seest I have come on indifferently well.'

The lower clergy hastened to follow the poor example set by the Bishops. In the religious orders discipline was lax and immorality common. The parish clergy on the whole were ignorant and poverty-stricken. Frequently they were hated for the greed with which they extracted their 'mortuary dues' from parishioners who were poorer than themselves. These mortuary dues, death-duties paid in kind to the Church, were the 'upmost cloth', the coverlet of the dead person's bed, and the 'corpse-present beast', usually a cow, which was payable upon burial. A series of deaths could reduce a family to destitution; yet it was seldom indeed that the mortuary dues were unclaimed. While parish priests dealt ungenerously with their flocks, they sought the same pleasures and fell victim to the same temptations. The lecherous priest and the drunken priest were as commonplace figures of sour mockery as the rapacious priest. Even instances of clerical criminality were not unknown.

The churchmen of Scotland may not, indeed, have been intrinsically worse than their counterparts in the rest of Europe; but the realization was slow in reaching them that, in order to combat Protestantism, they must put their house in order, and institute a counter-reformation.

James v fully recognized the need for reform within the Church, probably because he saw the vulnerability of his own position in relying upon the support of an institution which had forfeited public respect and was coming increasingly under attack. The King's position, however, was very difficult, for he was still receiving instalments of the £72,000 composition for the 'Great Tax' for the collection of which he relied upon the goodwill of his prelates. Furthermore, he was himself a party to a particularly profitable form of ecclesiastical abuse, since he had persuaded Pope Paul iii to appoint his bastard sons as Commendators, or titular Abbots, of six of the richest abbeys and priories in Scotland, the revenues of which were thus diverted to the Crown. Financially, James v could not afford either to offend the prelates or to reform the abuses. Though he was aware of the need for reform, he could not play the part of a reforming King with any seriousness of purpose. He attempted, indeed, to induce the clergy to abolish the mortuary dues, but since he himself set no example in voluntarily foregoing any source of profit, his attempt was a failure. He fell back upon the encouragement of anti-clerical satire as a means of stimulating the churchmen to reform themselves.

Two satirists who enjoyed the King's patronage were the young scholar George Buchanan and the King's old friend Sir David Lindsay of the Mount. With the King's encouragement Buchanan wrote two anti-clerical poems, the *Palinodia*, and the *Franciscanus*, an attack on the degeneracy of the Franciscan order. Buchanan, however, was disposed to hunt with the hounds and run with the hare since he held the post of tutor to the eldest of the illegitimate Commendators, James Stewart, Abbot of Kelso and Melrose. By 1539 his anti-clericalism had made Scotland too dangerous to contain him, and he fled the country. Sir David Lindsay did not, like Buchanan, abjure the religion in which he had been born. His attitude to the Church has been described as that of 'one of the disgusted faithful', yet his satires made an influential contribution to the Scottish Reformation. All the sins of commission of which the clergy was guilty, and the complete lack of spiritual values which characterized the clerical estate, were castigated in his play *The Satire of the Three Estates*, which was performed on Twelfth Night 1540 in the Great Hall of Linlithgow Palace, before James v and Marie de Guise, and the assembled court, which included several Bishops.

James v was deeply affected by the play. At the close of the performance, a contemporary observer wrote:

'The King of Scots did call upon the Bishop of Glasgow, being Chancellor, and divers other bishops, exhorting them to reform their fashions and manners of living, saying that unless they so did he would send six of the proudest of them to his uncle of England, and as those were ordered so he would order the rest that would not amend.'

Archbishop Dunbar answered 'that one word of his Grace's mouth should suffice them to be at commandment, and the King hastily and angrily answered that he would gladly bestow any words of his mouth that could amend them . . .'.

This incident was reported for the benefit of Henry VIII, who probably misinterpreted James's purpose in patronizing *The Satire of the Three Estates,* and assumed him to be entering a personally anti-clerical phase. In February 1540 Henry sent an ambassador, Sir Ralph Sadler, to Scotland, with instructions to attempt to undermine the influence of Cardinal Beaton, to urge upon James the advantages of suppressing religious houses and to persuade him of the value of a close alliance with England by hinting at his proximity to the succession.

Since the birth of Prince Edward the last argument had lost some of its force; neither did James show himself amenable to the two preceding ones. He stoutly affirmed his confidence in Cardinal Beaton, and on the subject of Scottish religious houses he pointedly demanded of Sadler, 'What need I to take them to increase my livelihood, when I may have anything that I can require of them?' He went on to assure the ambassador that his policy was the reform and not the suppression of religious foundations.

Perhaps James believed that despite his own ambiguous position he would be able to initiate sufficient reform in Scotland to stem the tide of the Reformation; perhaps he merely hoped for the best, for at the beginning of 1540 his mood was sanguine. Despite the undercurrents of trouble suggested by his uneasy relations with the nobility, to outward appearances his position was secure and his power increasing.

In the spring of 1540 Marie de Guise gave birth to their first child, a prince who was named James, and who seemed 'fair and lifelike to succeed us', as his father triumphantly informed Henry VIII. The following year the succession seemed doubly assured when Queen Marie bore a second son, who was named Arthur.

In the early months of 1541 James V seemed to have reached the apogee of his achievement and his prosperity. Of all his achievements perhaps the most satisfactory to himself was the success with which he had built up the finances of the Crown. During his minority the extravagance of Queen Margaret and of Angus had left James the heir to an almost empty exchequer. But, with the aid of the generous dowries which he had acquired with his two Queens, of the 'Great Tax' and the 'Three Teinds' and of some dubious forms of extortion from various members of the nobility who had fallen into disfavour, James had, in Bishop Lesley's words, 'wonderfully enriched' himself, and his realm.

After his return from France in 1537 James began to spend lavishly. Evidently he had derived great inspiration from his visit to France, for according to Lesley 'there were many new "ingynes" and devices, as well of building of palaces, habiliments, as of banquetting and of mens behaviour, first begun and used in Scotland at this time, after the fashion which they had seen in France. . . .'

At a time when princes were greatly concerned with the magnificence of their public image, James v had fallen under the influence of the most magnificent of renaissance princes, François 1er. Thereafter James sought to make the image of the Crown of Scots measure up as well as possible to the more glorious image of the Crown of France.

To this end he spent increasingly upon personal splendour, and he ordered the refashioning of the regalia. The crown itself was converted from a gothic diadem into an arched imperial crown. The motive for this innovation may have been that because Henry VIII claimed 'imperial' power over his dominions, James wished to make visually clear the independence of Scotland from Henry's 'empire'. François 1er had similarly refashioned the crown of France to illustrate his independence from the Holy Roman Empire.

James further imitated the splendour of his father-in-law's court by the enlargement and elaboration of his own Household, until £10,000 a year of the clerical taxation had to be diverted to meet the increased cost. The King's most extravagant expenditure, however, was upon an ambitious programme of architectural embellishment of the royal residences, undertaken with the intention of making them worthy of comparison with the royal châteaux of France.

James v inherited a group of essentially medieval residences, on which a certain amount of improvement and expansion had been begun during his father's reign. This relatively recent reconstruction served very well as a basis upon which his own principally decorative ideas could be carried out. To the new Palace of Holyroodhouse he made additions which were destroyed during the minority of Mary, Queen of Scots. The best work surviving from the reign of James v is at Stirling and Falkland. The palace-building at Stirling has been described as 'a curious mixture of late medieval structure and renaissance ornament'; it exemplifies admirably James v's decorative metamorphosis of an earlier and simpler structure. At Falkland the twin-towered gatehouse with its conical roofs, and the graceful South Range of buildings completed by James v, gives the Palace the appearance of a French château, which has caused it to be described as 'the finest monument to the "auld alliance" '. That is perhaps the very description of his architectural achievements which would best have pleased James v.

While James was occupied in the creation of splendour to surround himself and to enhance the image of the Crown of Scots, he must have appeared powerful, prosperous and fortunate; but the last year of his reign was to provide a dramatic illustration of the proverbial mutability of human affairs.

Since 1537 the King had been in declining health. In that year he had a hunting accident, and though he refused to take his hurts seriously, it is probable that he was more severely injured than anyone realized at the time. Increasing sums of money were spent on obtaining medicines for him from abroad, and his correspondence contains a number of references to unspecified illness.

To the increasing burden of ill-health was added the burden of nervous stress as political difficulties multiplied during 1541. Disaster supervened in a year which had begun auspiciously, when both the King's sons died suddenly in April. The King's grief was so great that Queen Marie concealed her own and endeavoured to offer him comfort. 'They were young enough,' she is reported to have said, 'and God would send them more succession.'

In August Sir Ralph Sadler came again to Scotland, bringing the apparently friendly proposal that James v and Henry viii should meet in person at York.

At the time of Sadler's previous embassy Henry had been in fear of a *rapprochement* between François 1er and Charles v, which led them to plan a joint crusade against heresy, including heretical England. Paul iii, attempting like Julius ii before him to act as the puppet-master of Europe, excommunicated Henry viii and encouraged the formation of a coalition of the Emperor, the French King and the King of Scots against England. When Sadler arrived in Scotland for the second time Cardinal Beaton was on embassy in France, and the obvious supposition was that he had gone to negotiate James's part in the papal project.

After his excommunication Henry, fearful of becoming the victim of a tripartite alliance, began putting his coastal defences in order to repel invasion from Europe, and organizing a military build-up along the Border to resist invasion from Scotland. These preparations led James in his turn to fear English aggression, and possibly the purpose of Beaton's embassy to France was defensive rather than offensive.

By 1541 the habitual rivalry of François Ier and Charles V had begun to reassert itself; but when the threat of a tripartite alliance evaporated, Henry VIII sided with the Emperor against François, while James remained true to the 'auld alliance'. War between Scotland and England was on the verge of being brought about by mutual suspicion and international alignments.

While the purpose and outcome of Beaton's embassy were in doubt, Henry was playing for time. Accordingly, while amassing his military power in the north he invited James to meet him at York. James, likewise playing for time, agreed to do so. He allowed Henry to make the most northerly journey that he made in the whole course of his reign, and left him to wait at York for twelve days, before making a Border incident for which he had demanded and not obtained redress the excuse for his own non-appearance. Henry, enraged by the public humiliation to which he had been exposed, returned south, to be greeted with the revelation of the infidelities of his fifth Queen, Catherine Howard, who was duly executed. Henry's mood was intolerant as the year 1541 approached its end; he had no doubt that James intended trouble, whether as a member of a European coalition or as the ally of France.

Henry's resolution for the new year was to invade Scotland rather than wait upon James's intentions. Cardinal Beaton returned from France without either having linked Scotland and the European powers in a crusade against England, or having obtained a promise of French support against English invasion. François failed the King whom he had said he regarded as his 'propre filz'. He was too heavily engaged in his preparations to make war upon the Emperor. Henry VIII was preparing to make war on France as the ally of the Emperor;

James like his father before him was committed to act as the ally of France. A situation not unlike that of 1513 was developing, but the old configuration was altered by a new element – the influence of the Reformation.

It was as the ally of both France and the Papacy that James faced the impending invasion, and neither the 'auld alliance' nor the Catholic Church commanded universal loyalty. In 1523 and 1524 Albany had discovered that Flodden was remembered and that the Scots were unwilling to risk another such slaughter for what seemed only the benefit of France. James v was shortly to make the same discovery. Furthermore, in the course of the reign a considerable number of the Scottish nobility had embraced Protestantism, and were not willing to take arms against the English enemies of the Pope. At the end of the reign James was said to be in possession of a 'blacklist' of 350 noblemen against whom he could institute proceedings for heresy, if he chose.

Besides the influence of political and religious considerations, the King now experienced the consequences of the personal unpopularity which he had won by his high-handed treatment of the nobility throughout the reign. Many of the men whom he summoned to the defence of the realm had suffered from disfavour and imprisonment, from fines and forfeitures. The army of 30,000 men which the King mustered on the Burgh Muir of Edinburgh in the autumn in no way resembled the enthusiastic host which had followed James iv to Flodden. The mood of the commanders was dangerously like the mood of those who had accompanied James iii to Lauder.

Unmolested, the Duke of Norfolk led an English army into Scotland and made a tour of the Borders, looting, spoiling and burning. His invasion was backed by the old claim of English overlordship, which Henry viii made on 5 November. James, knowing that he could expect no help from François, who was now at war with the Emperor, appealed to the Pope, declaring that Henry was only making war upon him because he would not desert the Holy See or the King of France. Norfolk, however, encountered difficulties of his own. His army was poorly provisioned, and his soldiers grew mutinous when beer ran short. He retreated to his own side of the Border.

Meanwhile James with a more seriously disaffected army was marching south. He encamped on Fala Muir, a plateau near the western end of the Lammermuir Hills, where tidings of Norfolk's retreat brought matters to a crisis. James, realizing that Norfolk's discomfiture offered the Scots an unexpected advantage, wished to pursue him and bring him to battle. But his orders to advance into England brought him face to face with the failure of his relations with the nobility. The commanders refused to obey him, and there was talk of a repetition of the Lauder Bridge massacre. However, though tempers ran high against those who wished to obey the King, the rest 'could not agree among themselves about those who should stretch the ropes, everyone striving to save his kinsman or friend'. In the end there were no hangings, but the army disbanded, and the King, utterly humiliated, had no choice but to ride back to Edinburgh.

James was still resolved upon military action against England, in which he was still convinced that the Scots possessed the advantage. At his instigation, his half-brother Moray and Cardinal Beaton raised a force which marched to Haddington, as though intending to invade England on the east. The King, with Lord Maxwell, the Warden of the Marches, gathered a second army, which finally numbered about 10,000 men, and marched to the west. At Lochmaben the King was suddenly taken ill. He remained at Lochmaben Castle to await the result of the invasion, which he insisted should take place even though he could not lead it.

The invading army marched south during the night of 24 November, and in the morning encountered an English force under Sir Thomas Wharton, the Governor of Carlisle, near the Solway Moss, a marshy area beside the River Esk. The result was the total rout of the Scots by an English force which numbered no more than 1,200 men. Though the occasion of the defeat was a last-minute quarrel over who should command in the King's absence, the basic reason was that the King's war did not inspire the enthusiasm of his subjects, nor his commands their obedience. There were few Scottish casualties, but the number of prisoners equalled that of the English soldiers. Perhaps the most damning comment on the failure of James V's relations with his nobility, which led to the shameful episode, is Professor Donaldson's observation that many Scottish lords were 'not unwilling to become prisoners rather than die in the service of a King in whom so many of his subjects had completely lost confidence'.

When the news of Solway Moss was brought to James V, who was evidently extremely ill, its effect was devastating, and indeed proved fatal. According to John Knox, who wrote a detailed account of the conclusion of the reign, James was 'striken with a sudden fear and astonishment, so that he could scarcely speak, or hold purpose with any man'.

The defeat appeared to be a disaster beyond exaggeration, for after the mutiny of his main army at Fala Muir, his second force had been a private army, raised by 'privy letters', and not a national muster. After Solway Moss he had no further military resources upon which to draw, and he did not doubt that Henry VIII would gather his strength, invade Scotland and assert his claim to overlordship with overwhelming force.

James gave way to despair, and abandoned all concern with a future over which he felt that he could exert no control. He left Lochmaben, and, increasingly ill and uncaring, he rode purposelessly from place to place. His wanderings took him first to Edinburgh, where he met Cardinal Beaton, returned from his abortive expedition to Haddington; thence he rode to Tantallon, and then to Linlithgow, where Queen Marie was in the last month of her third pregnancy. He did not remain long with her, but crossed the Forth and wandered on through Fife towards Falkland, where, early in December, he took to his bed.

On 8 December Marie de Guise bore the daughter who was to become Mary, Queen of Scots. The story of how James received the news of her birth is well-known. When the messenger from Linlithgow told him that the Queen had borne him a fair daughter, he replied, remembering that the Crown had come to the house of Stewart through Margery Bruce, 'Adieu, farewell, it came with a lass, it will pass with a lass.' Drummond, in his version of the story, gives the King a speech which elucidates the mental processes behind the well-known but incorrect prophecy: 'The Crown came by a woman, and it will with one go; many miseries approach this poor kingdom; King Henry will either take it by his arms or marriage.'

James V survived the infliction of this ultimate despair by one week, during which time he spoke little but lay awaiting death with his face turned to the wall. On 14 December he 'turned him back' to see Sir David Lindsay, Cardinal Beaton and a group of courtiers and officials standing round his bed. He 'gave a little smile and laughter', kissed his hand to them, 'and thereafter held up his hands to God and yielded the spirit'.

Though he died 'ill-beloved of his nobility' he was still popular with the common people who remembered the Gudeman o' Ballengeich.

John Knox, who seldom attempted impartiality as a historian, summed up the King's character with sufficient fairness for his words to do duty as an epitaph:

'He was called by some a good poor man's King; of others he was termed a murderer of the nobility, and one that had decreed their whole destruction. Some praised him for the repressing of theft and oppression; others dispraised him for the defouling of men's wives, and virgins. . . . And yet none spoke altogether beside the truth; for . . . as the virtues could not be denied, so could not the vices by any craft be cloaked.'

8

Mary, Queen of Scots,
1542–1567

The noble famous Queen
Who lost her head of late
Doth show that Kings as well as clowns
Are bound to Fortune's fate,
And that no earthly Prince
Can so secure his crown
But Fortune with her whirling wheel
Hath power to pull them down
(Sixteenth-century song, on the fate of Mary,
Queen of Scots)

THE MINORITY

Now is Protestantis risen us amang
Saying thay will make reformatioun . . .
(*Papistis and Protestantis*, Sir Richard Maitland of Lethington)

Mary, Queen of Scots was six days old when her father 'yielded the spirit' at Falkland. Her kingdom faced a minority of unprecedented length.

The death of James v was followed by a brief power struggle between Cardinal Beaton and James Hamilton, second Earl of Arran. The Cardinal's prestige was at a low ebb, for he was closely identified with the unpopular policy of the King whose reign had ended in disaster. Arran, besides, had the better claim. As the grandson of James III's sister Mary, he was the new Queen's nearest adult male kinsman, and could claim that precedent supported the appointment of the heir presumptive to the regency.

Arran's claim was successful, and he was appointed Governor of the Realm and 'tutor' or guardian of the Queen, while Cardinal Beaton suffered a short spell of imprisonment. As the Queen was a small baby, inevitably she remained in the care of her mother. Marie de Guise was not, at the beginning of the minority, a candidate for the regency; possibly she, like the Cardinal, was too closely identified with an unpopular and defeated policy.

The Earl of Arran was a Protestant of a sort. It was said that his name had headed James v's 'blacklist' of heretics. But in both religion and politics he showed himself inconstant, and readily influenced by stronger personalities. The only principle which he held with any tenacity was that of the advancement of the House of Hamilton.

The eclipse of Cardinal Beaton and Marie de Guise gave Henry VIII the opportunity to intervene in Scottish politics more effectively than he had been able to do since the minority of James v. The fears which had haunted the dying James v had not been altogether chimerical; Henry VIII did not indeed think of achieving the English domination of Scotland by direct conquest, but he hoped ultimately to achieve it through the marriage of the Queen of Scots to his son Prince Edward.

To assist him in this ambition he proposed to make use of the ageing Earl of Angus, who had lived in England since 1528, and of the Scottish nobles who had been captured at Solway Moss. These prisoners, who included the Earls of Cassillis and Glencairn, and the Lords Maxwell, Fleming, Somerville and Gray, returned to Scotland as pensioners of England, pledged to support the English interest and to further the projected marriage. Thenceforward they were referred to in Scotland as the 'English Lords'. The name was more justified than was generally known, for some of them had pledged themselves to assist in making Henry King of Scots if Queen Mary should die young.

Under the influence of this group Arran negotiated with Henry VIII the Treaties of Greenwich, which provided for peace between Scotland and England, and the betrothal of the Queen of Scots to Prince Edward. Henry wished to have the little Queen sent to England as soon as she was old enough to be parted from her mother, but such over-eagerness to secure her person aroused suspicion in Scotland, and the best that Henry could obtain was the agreement that she should be sent to the English court at the age of ten.

Henry's long-term policy was that the political union of the two kingdoms, under the descendants of his son and the Queen of Scots, should be accompanied by uniformity of religion in accordance with the English pattern. To this end he recommended to Arran that the Scottish Parliament should 'let slip the Bible', or authorize the importation of vernacular translations of the Scriptures into Scotland. Arran's Parliament did so, and the influence of the Bible in Scotland proved to be greater, and longer-lasting, than that of the Treaties of Greenwich, which were repudiated before the end of 1543.

The explanation of this sudden change of front was a reversal of the influences which directed Arran's policy. Cardinal Beaton regained his liberty in the autumn, and quickly achieved an ascendancy over Arran. He was well aware that Arran's principle interest was in the reversionary rights of the Hamiltons to the Scottish succession, and he was able to point out to Arran that his legitimacy, and therefore his claim, was dependant upon whether or not his parents had been legally married. This matter, upon which some doubt existed, was a matter for the Church courts to decide. Arran's Protestantism withered, together with his enthusiasm for the English alliance.

Further point was given to Beaton's arguments by the arrival in Scotland of the man who would take Arran's place as heir presumptive if the Church should declare him illegitimate. This dynastic rival, whose relationship to the Royal House was through a female line, was Matthew Stuart, fourth Earl of Lennox, the son of that Earl who had been murdered after the Battle of Linlithgow in 1526. The young Earl of Lennox and one of his brothers had been brought up in France by their kinsman Robert Stuart d'Aubigny, and in 1537 had taken French nationality. In 1543 Lennox returned to Scotland and presented himself as a suitor for the hand of Marie de Guise.

To the conjoint influences of Lennox's arrival and Beaton's veiled threats were added the persuasions of Arran's half-brother John Hamilton, Abbot of Paisley, who was convinced that the best interests of Scotland and of the Hamiltons would be served by an anti-English policy. Presently it was observed of the pliant Arran that 'what the English lords decide him to do one day, the Abbot changes the next'.

Henry VIII had left a loophole for his opponents by inexplicably failing to ratify the Treaties of Greenwich within the agreed period of two months. Accordingly Arran was within his rights when he repudiated the Treaties. Nonetheless, Henry's reaction to disappointment was to order the invasion of Scotland. Henry showed his recognition of Cardinal Beaton as the principal architect of the reversal of Scottish policy by instructing the Earl of Hertford who was to command the invading army to 'turn upside down the Cardinal's town of St Andrews . . . sparing no creature alive within the same'.

Hertford led two invasions, in 1544 and 1545, to which the Scots with sour humour gave the name of the 'Rough Wooing'. Neither invasion reached St Andrews, but Hertford did untold destruction in southern Scotland, to buildings, to the population, to farms and livestock. Edinburgh, and the Palace and Abbey of Holyrood, were burnt, and the Border abbeys reduced to ruins. The capital repaired itself, and Holyroodhouse was eventually rebuilt, but the ruins of the abbeys still provide evidence of the violence of the 'Rough Wooing'.

Inevitably Hertford's savagery caused a revulsion of feeling against England. Though Arran retained the governorship he was obliged to yield increasing influence to Cardinal Beaton and Marie de Guise. But the 'Rough Wooing' redounded to his advantage in that the 'English Lords' ceased to advocate the English marriage for Mary, Queen of Scots, and supported the more patriotic project for her marriage to Arran's son, the Master of Hamilton.

The pro-English party in Scotland was reduced to one, the Earl of Lennox. Disappointed of recognition as heir presumptive, and of the hand of Marie de Guise, in 1544 Lennox married Lady Margaret Douglas, the daughter of the Earl of Angus and Margaret Tudor. His policy of self-advancement through matrimony was thus remarkably successful, for though he had failed to secure the Queen-dowager of Scotland he linked his family to the Royal House of England with momentous effects upon the future of both countries.

Though the 'Rough Wooing' had achieved nothing but the increase of anti-English feeling in Scotland, Henry VIII did not admit the failure of his policy. He was satisfied that the spread of Protestantism could be relied upon slowly to undermine the Catholic government. In the meantime he continued to regard Cardinal Beaton as the member of that government who was most obstructive to his designs. After the failure of the Treaties of Greenwich and the 'Rough Wooing' to further the English interest, Henry VIII gave his countenance to more than one plot to assassinate the Cardinal.

Whether the conspiracy which succeeded enjoyed the backing of Henry VIII is uncertain. However, in May 1546 a group of conspirators which included Norman Leslie, the son of the Earl of Rothes, and William Kirkaldy of Grange, the son of James V's Treasurer, gained access to Beaton's Castle of St Andrews, murdered the Cardinal, seized the castle, and appealed for English help. The expectation of receiving English assistance suggests the certainty at least of English approval for the deed.

The occupation of St Andrews Castle by the Cardinal's murderers precipitated an international incident. Arran laid siege to the castle, but since his son was a hostage in the hands of the garrison the siege was but hesitantly conducted. Eventually the castle fell to a French expeditionary force, Arran's son was rescued and the castle garrison, including its chaplain, John Knox, was captured by the French and condemned to service in the galleys, a relatively moderate punishment when a death sentence might have been expected.

The failure of the English government to intervene on behalf of the murderers of Beaton is probably explained by the mortal illness of Henry VIII and his death in January 1547.

The Earl of Hertford became Duke of Somerset and Regent for the new King Edward VI. He continued the late King's policy by retaliating to French intervention in Scotland with yet another invasion. In the face of Somerset's invasion the Scots displayed political unity but military ineptness. In September 1547 Somerset won an overwhelming victory at Pinkie, near Musselburgh. After the battle the English policy was to leave garrisons in Scotland, not for purposes of conquest, but to assist the infiltration of Protestantism.

Defeat at Pinkie brought Arran's prestige even lower than it had fallen after the 'Rough Wooing', and the decline of his influence was illustrated by the withdrawal of Scottish support from the projected marriage of Queen Mary to the Master of Hamilton. Marie de Guise, whose influence had commensurately increased, seized the opportunity to appeal for French help to evict the English, and to secure the French alliance by offering Mary as a bride for the Dauphin François, the eldest son of Henri II and Catherine de' Medici. The treaty was swiftly concluded, and the Queen, who after the Battle of Pinkie had been sent for refuge to the island priory of Inchmahome in the Lake of Menteith, was taken to Dumbarton, and thence in July 1548 she sailed for France. At the French court she received the upbringing and education which conditioned her responses to the religious and political problems which she encountered in Scotland thirteen years later.

The unfortunate Master of Hamilton, the hostage of first one side and then the other, was also sent to France, to ensure the acquiescence of his father in the schemes of Marie de Guise. Arran retained his governorship of Scotland, and to reward his compliance and encourage his further support he received the French title of Duke of Châtelherault. His half-brother the erstwhile Abbot of Paisley, lately the Bishop of Dunkeld, was advanced to the Archbishopric of St Andrews.

From 1548 onwards the influence of Marie de Guise steadily increased. In 1550 she paid a visit to France, taking with her a group of Scots who might have been likely to react against the strengthening of the French alliance. Among them were the Earls of Huntly, Glencairn, Cassillis and Marischal, the Lords Maxwell and Fleming, and the Lord James Stewart, Commendator of St Andrews, the son of James v by Margaret Erskine. It was reported that the King of France, with flatteringly lavish entertainment and generous *douceurs*, 'bought them completely'. At least he did so temporarily, as Henry viii had done with some of them eight years previously.

Marie de Guise was carefully preparing the way for her own assumption of the regency. Her plans for the displacement of Châtelherault were elaborately laid. Châtelherault's 'tutory' or guardianship of the Queen was to run conjointly with his governship of Scotland, to which he had been appointed 'during the Queen's non-age'. According to Professor Donaldson, 'tutory lasted, by a well-understood rule, until the "pupil", if a girl, reached the age of twelve, which Mary would not do until December 1554'. However, 'in December 1553, when Mary was entering her twelfth year, an opinion was obtained in Paris that she was now of age to choose her own curator in place of a tutor, and so to dispose of the regency'. Upon the pronouncement of this specious theory, Châtelherault was persuaded to resign his governorship, and in April 1554 Marie de Guise was appointed Regent in his place.

Under the regency of Marie de Guise Scotland was once again fully committed to the 'auld alliance', and as had happened in the past, was manipulated in the interests of France.

In 1553 the Protestant Edward VI had died, to be succeeded on the English throne by his Catholic half-sister Mary Tudor, who married Philip II of Spain. France and Spain were at war, and by 1557 it appeared that in the interests of France Scotland might once again be forced unwillingly into war with England. The principal inducement that France could offer was the assistance of French troops to recover Berwick, an attack upon which could be timed to coincide with a French attack upon Calais, the last remnant of England's medieval empire in France. The chance of recapturing Berwick might have stimulated a King of Scots into action, not least for reasons of prestige; but it did not arouse the enthusiasm of the Scottish nobility, many of whom had grown disenchanted with the increase of French influence in Scotland, and especially with the presence of the French garrisons in Scottish fortresses, which had been sent to assist the Queen-Regent to maintain her authority. In January 1558 Calais fell to the French without the Scots having moved against Berwick.

It was an unhappy but incontrovertible fact that during the minority of Mary, Queen of Scots, Scotland, torn by the strife of rival political factions and rival religions, was too weak to stand alone. The attempts of Henry VIII and Somerset to impose English domination had been frustrated at the cost of permitting a form of French domination which was beginning to appear scarcely more palatable.

Marie de Guise was not principally concerned to maintain the independence of Scotland, which, since she was an intensely practical politician, she may have believed impossible. Her prime concern was to conserve her daughter's inheritance, which, since her daughter was destined to be Queen of France, could best be achieved from her viewpoint by linking the two countries under the rule of Mary and her French husband.

On 24 April 1558 Mary, Queen of Scots, was married to the Dauphin François, in the Cathedral of Notre-Dame in Paris. They assumed the titles of 'King and Queen of Scots, Dauphin and Dauphiness of France'. The Scottish commissioners who negotiated the marriage secured from Queen Mary documents which acknowledged the reversionary rights of the Hamiltons and safeguarded the laws and liberties of Scotland. But in secret documents signed three weeks before the marriage Mary bequeathed her kingdom to the Royal House of France in the event of her death without issue. In France it was generally believed that by the marriage the sovereignty of Scotland had been transferred to the House of Valois. In Scotland, though Mary's secret pledge remained secret, the degree of French domination permitted by the marriage was sufficiently unpopular. It was without the enthusiasm of his Scottish subjects that in November François was granted the 'Crown Matrimonial', which gave him the right to reign in Scotland should his wife predecease him. Though the Hamiltons insisted that this privilege was granted without prejudice to their rights, there was no reason for them or anyone else to expect that the marriage would be without issue.

It appeared that Scotland, like Britanny, had been absorbed into France by matrimony, though geographical considerations made the permanence of the arrangement inherently less likely. The remoteness of Scotland from a French centre of government, and the desire to reassert national independence would surely have led the Scots eventually to rebel against French domination; but rebellion occurred with unexpected swiftness, stimulated by the religio-political forces which Marie de Guise had been powerless to control.

To the influence of Lutheranism which had begun to permeate Scotland during the reign of James v and the early years of Mary's minority, succeeded the stronger influence of Calvinism which gained a tenacious hold upon the country during the 1560s.

Both the Lutheran and the Calvinist religions eliminated the superstructure of elaborate observance which had characterized Catholicism during the fifteenth and early sixteenth centuries. Those who embraced either form of Protestantism found that in the place of relying upon such subsidiary aids to spiritual life as invocation of saints, pilgrimages and indulgences, they were required to make a single, immense act of faith. Luther postulated the doctrine of justification by faith alone. Calvin, emphasizing the omnipotence of God and the powerlessness of man to approach Him, produced the doctrine of predestination: that some men are preordained to salvation, or union with God, others to separation from Him, and eternal reprobation. 'Predestination,' Mrs Rosalind Mitchison observes, 'can only be lived with as doctrine if it is coupled with the notion that one oneself belongs to the unreprobate. This idea is formulated in the doctrine of assurance, that those who are saved have the certainty of it in their faith. . . .' The great strength which Calvinists derived from these doctrines was the equal certainty that those who opposed them were *ipso facto* the reprobate. This idea, which is almost unimaginable from the standpoint of twentieth-century ecumenism, may have seemed to have a certain obviousness at the time when it was formulated. The faults of the Church from which Calvin had broken away were indeed worthy of reprobation in the ordinary sense of the word, and the challenge which Calvinism presented in Scotland during the 1550s elicited a late and indeed a desperate response.

The international and concerted effort of the Church to combat the Reformation began in 1546 with the inauguration of the Council of Trent. Scotland did not send representatives, but the Church in Scotland, led by Archbishop Hamilton, held its own councils, in 1549, 1552 and 1559, by which it attempted to oppose the challenge of Calvinist doctrine, and to amend the abuses which brought the Church into contempt.

The Council of 1552 produced a Catechism, to assist parish priests to instruct their flocks in basic Christian doctrine. It was a tactful document which dealt with the Ten Commandments, the Creed and the Sacraments, but avoided mention of the Papacy. If the priests for whom it was intended had had the skill to put it to good use, its effect could have been salutary. Unhappily the accompanying instruction that it was to be read to the people on Sundays and Holy Days 'clearly, articulately, and with attention to the stops', suggests that the Council was well aware of the educational shortcomings of the parish clergy.

As for the grosser failings, pluralism, non-residence and clerical immorality were more easily legislated against than cured. And, as the Bishops had set a poor example to the lower clergy in worldly living, so they were reluctant even at the eleventh hour to give up their comfortable lives for the sake of setting a good example. The efforts at reform that were made in the 1550s were too little and twenty years too late; for even had greater efforts been made in the 1530s at the instance of James V, time would have been short.

While the Church somewhat feebly attempted to put its house in order, Calvinism gained an increasing hold upon Scotland, not merely in terms of religious conversion, but of organization. The predominant name connected with the establishment of Calvinism is that of John Knox.

After his release from the French galleys in 1549, Knox pursued his vocation in England, where he was for a time a chaplain to Edward VI. After the accession of Mary Tudor he retired to Geneva. 'His retreat,' Mrs Mitchison remarks, 'would have been entirely respectable if he had not later accused Queen Elizabeth of cowardice for keeping her head down and conforming in Mary's reign.' However, he returned to Scotland in 1555, and during a short period in that and the following year he was instrumental in forming a Calvinist group among the Scottish nobility. Under the leadership of the Lord James Stewart this group formed the nucleus of the association of Protestant nobles who later called themselves the 'Lords of the Congregation', and became the secular leaders of the Reformation rebellion.

In the meantime Marie de Guise, pursuing a pro-French policy which commanded decreasing sympathy, did not risk the unpopularity which would have been the concomitant of vigorous persecution of the Protestants. She deferred turning upon them until her daughter's inheritance had been safely united with the strong Catholic monarchy of France. But by the time the young Queen of Scots married the Dauphin François the metamorphosis of Scotland from a Catholic into a Protestant country was already far advanced.

To predict the course of events is seldom possible for the participants, but for those who lived through the events of the next two years the political convulsions must have appeared bewilderingly swift, and the conclusion contrary to any expectation.

In November 1558 Mary Tudor died, to be succeeded by her half-sister Elizabeth, who, as the daughter of Anne Boleyn, was illegitimate in the eyes of Catholic Europe. Whatever may have been her personal preference in religion, Elizabeth was debarred from adopting Catholicism by her faulty title to the throne. She adopted her father's religious position which gave her supremacy over the national Church and eschewed the more revolutionary doctrines of continental Protestantism. Elizabeth's anti-Catholic position brought about the situation to which Henry VIII had looked forward in 1543: the death of the old Anglo-Scottish enmity under the influence of common religious interest. The Calvinists of Scotland began to look hopefully towards Elizabeth as an ally against Marie de Guise and the overshadowing power of France.

Elizabeth, however, had troubles of her own to face, and France constituted the greatest threat to her new and insecure authority. At the beginning of 1559 France and Spain made peace, and in April signed the Treaty of Cateau-Cambrésis. In France, as in Scotland, the 1550s had witnessed the rapid spread of Calvinism, and shortly after the peace with Spain was signed Henri II turned his attention to the problem of heresy in his own kingdom. He declared war upon the Protestants in France, and threatened Protestant England by causing his son François and his daughter-in-law Mary, Queen of Scots to quarter the arms of England with their own. As the grand-daughter of Margaret Tudor, the Queen of Scots was in Catholic eyes the legitimist claimant to the English throne. An arrogant Latin verse which adorned the side of a triumphal chariot in which Mary appeared at a tournament in 1559 proclaimed (in translation):

> *The armies of Marie Quene Dolphines of France,*
> *The nobillest lady in earth for till advance;*
> *Of Scotland Quene, of Ingland also,*
> *Of Ireland also God hath providit so.*

The French offensive against Protestantism was linked with a similar movement in Scotland. Marie de Guise likewise turned upon the Calvinists who had hitherto almost enjoyed an unofficial immunity.

The Catholic offensive precipitated the Reformation rebellion in Scotland. In May 1559 Knox returned again from Geneva, and his inflammatory preaching led to outbreaks of iconoclasm in Perth, St Andrews, Stirling, Linlithgow and Edinburgh. The Lords of the Congregation gathered their followers in arms, and appealed for English assistance to resist Marie de Guise and the French troops which constituted the mainstay of her authority.

On 6 July Henri II, participating in the tournament referred to, was accidentally killed. François and Mary became King and Queen of France and Scotland. The 'auld alliance', in the last months of its existence, became a complete incorporation of the two countries. The situation of the Scottish rebels appeared desperate, for they did not at this stage receive the help of English arms. Elizabeth hesitated to encourage rebellion, for she was as yet uncertain of her hold upon her own kingdom. The only hope for the Lords of the Congregation seemed to be a more extreme form of rebellion than had been contemplated at first: the substitution of a Protestant head of state for the absentee Catholic sovereign, who as Queen of France seemed likely to remain absent. The Lord James Stewart was considered and rejected on the grounds of his illegitimacy. The Duke of Châtelherault, whom Marie de Guise had been able to control as long as his son remained a hostage in France, became the nominal leader of the rebels when his son, with English assistance, escaped and returned to Scotland in September. The following month the rebels formally declared the regency of Marie de Guise at an end, and transferred her authority to a council headed by Châtelherault.

Marie de Guise, however, though expelled from the capital, fortified herself in Leith and appealed for reinforcements from France. The rebels might yet have been defeated, but English intervention came before French help. Elizabeth intervened at this point for reasons of self-interest. The Treaty of Berwick which she signed with the rebels in February 1560 was a treaty of mutual defence. She would aid them, but they were likewise to aid her if the French should invade England. An English army, the first which ever received a welcome in Scotland, arrived in March, and English ships stood off the coast to intercept the French reinforcements. The defence of Leith was resolute, but the victory of the rebels was assured at the last by the death of the indomitable Marie de Guise on 11 June.

The unforeseen triumph of the Reformation rebellion was followed by the Treaty of Edinburgh, signed the following month. Under the terms of the Treaty French and English troops withdrew from Scotland; England and France stated their pacific inclinations towards each other; France recognized Elizabeth's title to the throne of England; and François and Mary were no longer to display the English arms. By her timely intervention Elizabeth had gained for herself a measure of security by neutralizing the threat of France; the Lords of the Congregation had won an opportunity to remake Scotland in accordance with their own ideas. The result was a conservative political settlement and a religious revolution.

The Parliament which met in August was summoned in the names of François and Mary. It was a crowded session, attended by many lesser barons and lairds, who invoked the non-implemented legislation of James I in defence of their right to be present. It was religious not political change which aroused their enthusiasm. The Reformation Parliament abolished the authority and jurisdiction of the Pope in

Scotland, prohibited the celebration of Mass and adopted a Calvinist *Confession of Faith* as the definition of the new state religion.

At this point the revolution stopped. Knox and his brethren, the ministers who were to serve the new Protestant Kirk, had hoped to see the adoption not only of their *Confession of Faith*, but also of their *Book of Discipline*, the product of an optimistic committee which had worked out a plan for a nationwide ecclesiastical and educational system which was to be endowed by the total revenue of the old Church. However, the wealth of the Church had largely fallen into the hands of the nobility; noble families had obtained benefices for cadets and illegitimate sons in the same manner as James v had done; latterly certain lords had 'greedily gripped' the Church lands to which they had such ready access, while commendators had tacitly secularized themselves.

The adoption of Protestantism served many secular interests, and not all who supported the Reformation wished to become members of the godly society which was the original ideal of the Reformers. The old poet Sir Richard Maitland of Lethington, who provides a necessary reminder that not all pre-Reformation Catholics had forgotten what their religion was about, wryly described the Reformation's less edifying converts:

> *Thay think it weill an thay the Pape do call*
> *The Antichrist and Mess idolatrie*
> *And syne eit flesche upoun the Frydayis all,*
> *That thay serve God richt then accordinglie,*
> *Thoch in all thing thay leve maist wikkitlie:*
> *Bot God commandit us His law to keip –*
> *First honour Him, and syne haif charitie*
> *With our nichtbour, and for our sinnis weip.*

The victors of the Reformation rebellion rendered to God the things which they conceived to be God's: the *Confession of Faith*, the repudiation of the Pope and the prohibition of Mass. Caesar's portion was to be fought over for some time to come.

The moderation of the political measures which followed the Treaty of Edinburgh may mirror the cautious ambitions of the House of Hamilton. The Queen of Scots was Queen of France, and Châtelherault may have hoped that if no provocative gesture of defiance were made, the reality of power and perhaps ultimately the title might be transferred to himself or his heir. Châtelherault's son, on whom had been bestowed his father's original title of Earl of Arran, was offered as a suitable bridegroom for Queen Elizabeth, a proposal which may have been intended to facilitate the union of Scotland and England under a Protestant monarchy.

These cautious manoeuvrings were brought to a sudden end by the last and most unforeseen of the royal deaths which had brought about so many political changes within so short a time. On 5 December 1560 the young King of France died, leaving the Queen of Scots a childless widow. The future had little to offer her as Queen-dowager of France; as Queen of Scots it offered her the challenge of a Protestant kingdom for a Catholic sovereign.

PERSONAL RULE

Welcum, illustrat Ladye, and our Quene!
(*Ane New Yeir Gift to the Quene Mary . . . 1562*, Alexander Scott)

Burn the whore!
(Edinburgh mob, 1567)

It is a commonplace of history that Mary, Queen of Scots was beautiful. '. . . As her youth grew on,' wrote Brantôme, 'we saw her great beauty and her great virtues grow likewise; so that, coming to her fifteenth year, her beauty shone like the light at mid-day.'

On the evidence of her portraits, Mary bore a strong resemblance to her father and her immediate ancestors. She had a long, oval face, finely drawn brows and an aquiline nose. Her complexion was very pale and her eyes hazel. In youth she had fair-red hair which darkened gradually to auburn and then to dark chestnut. During her imprisonment in England her hair turned prematurely grey, and was cropped short and concealed beneath an auburn wig.

She was tall, athletic and elegant, a courageous horsewoman and a graceful dancer. Her beauty, accomplishments and *élan de vie* combined to inspire the admiration of all beholders.

Mary's education at the court of France was that of a European renaissance princess. In addition to her native Scots, she learnt Latin,

French and Italian. Ronsard taught her the art of verse-making. Despite the death of her father and her separation from her mother, she was not altogether deprived of a family: domestic relationships were provided by her maternal grandmother, Antoinette de Guise, and by her mother's brothers, the Duc de Guise and the Cardinal de Lorraine. The Queen's uncles were doubtless influential in forming her political attitudes, but the overshadowing influences of her childhood were Henri II of France, his Queen, Catherine de' Medici, and his mistress, Diane de Poitiers, who, during Mary's childhood and adolescence, was the dominant figure at the French court.

In religion Mary's upbringing was automatically Catholic. Though the Council of Trent was summoned two years before Mary was sent to France, its final session did not close until after she had returned to Scotland; the militant Catholicism which resulted from it characterized the following generation. In this context Archbishop Mathew's comments on Mary's religion are very pertinent: 'She was formed before the Counter Reformation . . . She came from the old lax Catholic world.' The resultant religious attitude was not fanatical, and it enabled her to respond to the challenge of her kingdom in an adaptable and intelligent fashion.

While the death of Mary's French husband left her little choice but to return to Scotland, the manner of her return could accord with one of three courses. The Earl of Huntly, the friend of James V and the leading Catholic nobleman, wished her to head a conservative reaction; he offered to raise an army of twenty thousand men to restore Catholicism by force. The Hamiltons, endeavouring to salvage as much as possible from the wreck of their ambitions, wanted her to be constrained to embrace Protestantism and to marry the young Earl of Arran. A more moderate Protestant party, led by the Lord James Stewart, advised her to 'press no matters of religion', in other words to adopt a *politique* position designed to conciliate both Catholics and Protestants, thus avoiding the danger of becoming identified exclusively with either party. Huntly's offer and Lord James's advice show by how narrow a margin the Lords of the Congregation had gained their victory; however, it was a victory, which even the accession of a Catholic sovereign would not overturn.

Mary chose to follow the advice of the Lord James. To have accepted the proposals either of Huntly or of the Hamiltons would have been to allow herself to become the tool of a religio-political faction; the proposal of her half-brother and his supporters would allow her a more independent political rôle. Furthermore, to adopt a *politique* position in Scotland might encourage support in England for her claim to the English throne, which she tacitly maintained, by refusing to ratify the Treaty of Edinburgh. Although she ceased to use the style of Queen of England or to display the English arms, so long as she refused formal acknowledgement of Elizabeth's sovereign rights, her own claim was maintained by implication. Mary, as an indisputably legitimate claimant, who might appeal to the loyalty of Catholics in England without arousing the enmity of Protestants, was a potential enemy whose arrival in Scotland Elizabeth could not be expected to welcome.

Much fruitless argument has taken place concerning the rights and wrongs of the diplomatic duel between Mary, Queen of Scots and Elizabeth of England. Surely at the outset there were no rights and wrongs, for both Queens had positions to defend and ambitions to pursue. Resolutely and adroitly, each of them endeavoured to serve her own interests.

The opening manoeuvres took place before the Queen of Scots left France. Since Mary had refused to ratify the Treaty of Edinburgh, Elizabeth retaliated by refusing Mary a safe-conduct to pass through England. Furthermore, English ships waited to intercept the convoy which brought Mary and her entourage to Scotland. Elizabeth, who had refused the hand of the Earl of Arran for herself, at this stage advocated a marriage between him and the Queen of Scots. She had an understanding with the Hamiltons, and her ships may have been intended to force Mary to take the western route to Scotland, and land at Dumbarton where the Hamiltons awaited her.

Sea mists came to the assistance of the Queen of Scots. Her ships evaded coercion or capture and brought her safely to Leith on 19 August 1561. It has never been uncommon for Leith to be enveloped in a *haar*, but John Knox chose to see a normal mist as an evil portent: 'the very face of heaven, the time of her arrival,' he wrote, 'did manifestly speak what comfort was brought into this country with her, to wit, sorrow, dolour, darkness, and all impiety. . . . The sun was not seen to shine two days before, nor two days after. . . .'

The anger of extreme Protestants at the coming of a Catholic sovereign erupted in violence on the first Sunday after Mary's arrival, when the celebration of Mass in the Chapel Royal of Holyroodhouse provoked a riot. The Lord James Stewart defended the door of the Chapel, and two more of Mary's equally Protestant half-brothers protected the life of the priest from those who shouted, 'The idolator priest should die the death.'

Archbishop Mathew has observed, of Mary's resolution to practise her religion, that 'according to her status, and the age in which she lived, her chapel was a royal appurtenance which it was against her dignity to surrender'. Her insistence upon her personal right to have her Mass was almost the limit of Mary's defence of Catholicism. Upon her arrival in Scotland she issued a proclamation which forbade 'alteration or innovation of the state of religion . . . which her majesty found public and universally standing at her majesty's arrival in this her realm'. Thereafter she several times reissued a proclamation under which priests were prosecuted for saying Mass beyond the confines of the court.

Knox and a few other extremists remained vociferously inimical to the Queen; but under the guidance of the Lord James Stewart, and of her Secretary of State, William Maitland of Lethington, Mary contrived to make herself acceptable to the Kirk as a whole. Unlike the Reformation Parliament of 1560, she was prepared to admit that the Kirk should have some share of the revenues of the old Church. An agreement was reached that two thirds of the income of all benefices should remain in the hands of those who held them, for their lifetimes, and that the other third should be shared between the Crown and the Kirk. 'The principal weakness of the scheme,' Professor Donaldson observes, 'was that the share of the reformed Church was not defined and that year by year the Crown's share tended to increase, but the plan was not unstatesmanlike in its attempt to reconcile conflicting interests.'

Less successful was the attempt, made principally by Lethington, to reconcile the potentially conflicting interests of the Queen of Scots and the Queen of England.

Lethington's first mission to England took place shortly after Mary's arrival in Scotland. Without the aid of the French armies which Henri II might have contemplated employing for the purpose, Mary could not lay immediate claim to the throne which Elizabeth occupied. However, as the legitimate claimant to the throne of an unmarried Queen, she requested recognition as Elizabeth's successor.

Elizabeth informed Lethington that she was unwilling to make any pronouncement concerning the succession, and she renewed her demand that Mary should ratify the Treaty of Edinburgh. Mary's answer was that she might ratify the Treaty if Elizabeth would commit herself on the subject of the succession. This compromise was the solution which Lethington desired to bring about. Mary had great hopes that it might be effected by a personal meeting between herself and Elizabeth. She proposed that their meeting should take place in September 1562; Elizabeth agreed, and then subsequently withdrew from the arrangement. The meeting never took place.

Some historians have been sanguine enough to suggest that if the two Queens had met they might have reached an understanding. However, there was so much suspicion, so much potential hostility between them, that it seems more likely that their meeting would have been a feminine equivalent of the Field of Cloth of Gold. Their failure to meet has perhaps deprived history of an entertaining, though surely unproductive, episode.

Though Mary failed to reach a settlement with Elizabeth, she continued to make headway in establishing her authority in Scotland. The autumn of 1562 witnessed a minor outbreak of trouble, apparently caused by her advancement of the Lord James Stewart to the earldom of Moray. The Earl of Huntly had been administering the lands of Moray, and he may have hoped to lay claim to some of them. In addition to the resentment aroused by disappointment, he may also have been disillusioned by the lukewarmness of Mary's Catholicism. Though unsupported by any other noblemen except his own sons and his cousin the Earl of Sutherland, he rose in rebellion and was defeated by the new Earl of Moray at the Battle of Corrichie, on 28 October 1562. Huntly himself collapsed and died, apparently of a stroke, immediately after the battle, and one of his sons, who was said to have aspired to marry the Queen, and to have contemplated attempting to abduct her, was executed. A single execution was the limit of her severity, and no further disaffection was shown with her *politique* rule.

Although Mary refused to marry the Earl of Arran, which was fortunate since he had long shown signs of mental instability and soon became insane, and although Huntly's son paid for his presumptuous aspirations with his life, Mary was resolved to marry as soon as a suitable bridegroom could be found. It was, of course, expedient that she should marry to secure the succession in Scotland; besides, if Mary produced an heir while Elizabeth remained unmarried, Mary's claim to recognition as her successor would appear increasingly attractive in England.

To find a suitable husband was not, however, an easy matter. In particular, to find a suitable husband for a sovereign Queen presented a problem in a period when the dominance of the male was the accepted order of nature. John Knox was presenting an entirely orthodox view when he wrote his famous tract *The First Blast of the Trumpet against the Monstrous Regiment* [i.e. Rule] *of Women*; and it is significant that most of the Queens regnant of the sixteenth century exercised their 'regiment' alone. Marie de Guise and Catherine de' Medici ruled as regents in their widowhood; Elizabeth, despite many matrimonial negotiations, in the end remained the 'Virgin Queen'. The sovereign Queen who had married did not provide an encouraging precedent. Mary Tudor's marriage to Philip II of Spain caused much political unrest in England, and the fact that he was largely an absentee husband probably saved his wife as much trouble as it caused her personal sorrow.

Mary, Queen of Scots was well aware of the danger of domination by a foreign power inherent in making such a marriage. She refused several foreign suitors, including the Kings of Sweden and Denmark, and the Archdukes Ferdinand and Charles, the sons of the Emperor Charles v. However, she conducted serious negotiations with a view to marrying Don Carlos, the son of Philip II. This marriage, uniting her to a great Catholic monarchy, would automatically have ended Mary's policy of conciliation in Scotland; but, at the cost of Spanish domination, it might have provided her with the resources to assert her claim to the English throne by force.

Moray and Lethington, aware of these considerations, supported the negotiations not in the hope of bringing them to a successful conclusion, but of using them to coerce Elizabeth into naming Mary as her successor. Elizabeth, indeed, went so far as to say that if Mary married Don Carlos she would regard her as an enemy; whereas, is she married with Elizabeth's approval the reward would be her recognition as

Elizabeth's successor. This interesting deadlock was broken when Don Carlos became insane in the spring of 1564.

To marry with Elizabeth's approval was at least worth consideration. But, when she was asked to name a candidate who would meet with it, Elizabeth made the extraordinary nomination of her own favourite, Lord Robert Dudley. Whether or not Elizabeth intended the offer seriously, the man himself was scarcely acceptable, and was not made much more so by Elizabeth's creating him Earl of Leicester. However, he provided a central figure for several months' fruitless negotiation, until early in 1565 Elizabeth suddenly announced her intention to make no declaration concerning the succession until either she had married or made public her resolve never to marry.

Mary, freed from inhibiting political considerations, made no further delay in choosing a husband. She chose her cousin Henry Stuart, Lord Darnley, the elder son of Matthew Stuart, Earl of Lennox, and his Countess, Lady Margaret Douglas. If the names of Mary's rejected suitors are considered, it becomes obvious that while Darnley was perhaps the last suitable candidate for her hand, he was also perhaps the most suitable on genealogical grounds. If the marriage did not enjoy Elizabeth's approval, it offered the compensation of linking the two strongest claimants to the English succession, the grandchildren of Margaret Tudor.

Lord Darnley had been brought up in England, where Lennox had lived since 1544, when he had been forfeited and banished from Scotland for his treasonable dealings with Henry VIII. In 1564, Lennox was permitted to return and was reinstated in his Scottish possessions; his son followed him north at the beginning of 1565.

Mary, Queen of Scots was delighted with her cousin; she pronounced him 'the lustiest and best proportionit lang man that sche had seen'. She may have been disposed to fall in love, for she had been a chaste widow for a little more than four years, and Darnley was physically attractive. He was tall, slender and graceful with 'sharp yellow' hair; he had 'a virginal look which he would lose'. That he should marry the Queen of Scots had long been his mother's ambition, and to this end she had caused him to acquire certain courtly accomplishments. He could sing, play the lute, dance and make verses. Attributed to him is a poem called *Advice to a Prince*, which contains these lines:

Be to rebellis strong as lyoun eik,
Be ferce to follow thame quhair evir thay found,
Be to thy liegemen bayth soft and meik,
Be thair succour and help thame haill and sound,
Be knaw thy cure and caus quhy thow was cround,
Be besye evir that justice be nocht smord,[1]
Be blyith in hart, thir wordis oft expound,
Be bowsum[2] *aye to knaw thy God and Lord.*

This was, unfortunately, a conventional literary exercise, the sentiments of which he did not take to heart. When his best behaviour had
worn off he proved to be arrogant and flaccid, addicted without dis-
crimination to sexual pleasures, and to the bottle.

The Queen of Scots, however, married him before she had discovered his faults. The marriage took place in accordance with
Catholic rites, though before the arrival of the necessary papal dispensation, on 29 July 1565. Darnley received the titles of King of
Scots and Duke of Albany; Mary's good sense prevailed to the extent
that she did not also grant him the Crown Matrimonial.

The Lennox Stuarts were Catholic in the same wavering manner as
the Hamiltons were Protestant. Darnley was prepared to be married by
Catholic rites, but also prepared to conciliate Protestant opinion. To
that extent the marriage was not injurious to Mary's policy of conciliation. In other respects, however, it was disastrous. The Hamiltons
saw the Queen's marriage to a Lennox Stuart as the final ruin of their
regal aspirations; Moray resented a marriage which simultaneously
put an end to his policy of reaching an understanding with Elizabeth
and threatened his ascendancy in the counsels of the Queen of Scots.

Moray and Châtelherault made common cause, and supported by
the Earls of Argyll and Glencairn, rose in rebellion, and were soundly
defeated by the Queen of Scots, who rode herself at the head of her
army and chased them across the Border into England. Moray took
refuge at the English court, where Elizabeth publicly berated him for
his rebellion, but probably made an ally of him in private.

From this point the ambitions of the Earl of Moray and the Queen
of Scots diverged. The character of Moray is difficult to assess. At the
beginning of her personal rule he appears to have intended to serve

[1] smothered.   [2] humble.

his half-sister loyally; however, his relationship to her left room for much suspicion and resentment. He was the eldest surviving son of James v, who had come near to marrying his mother; he probably knew that but for the intransigence of Pope Paul III he might have been the King. He was a consummate politician, and he knew his own ability. Though he was prepared to follow a conciliatory policy, he was a Calvinist by personal conviction. From the time of the Queen's marriage onwards he was increasingly disposed to follow his own religious ideals, and the radical Protestant policy which they dictated. If he required justification, it was provided by the increasing political ineptitude which the Queen of Scots displayed after her marriage to Darnley.

The halcyon days of Mary's second marriage, if they existed at all, were very brief. Before the end of 1565 she had become aware of all her husband's shortcomings, and had turned for political advice, and to some extent for more congenial company, to a foreign favourite, David Riccio.

In 1561 Riccio had arrived in Scotland in the household of the ambassador of Savoy. He had at first attracted the Queen's attention as an accomplished musician and singer; she retained him in her service and subsequently appointed him secretary in charge of her French correspondence. Though his official position was modest, he was considered to possess great influence.

The rise of Riccio was a cause of disaffection among the Scottish nobility, who resented the intrusion of an upstart foreigner, whom they suspected probably groundlessly of being a papal agent, into the centre of the political scene. A group of lords who had sympathized with Moray, although they had not participated in his rebellion, plotted the death of the detested foreigner and the recall of Moray and his associates. They won the support of Darnley, who already resented the influence of Riccio, by inflaming him to murderous jealousy with the suggestion that Riccio was the lover of the Queen. The conspirators required the participation of Darnley, for his authority was needed to cancel the Parliament which was to try Moray and his associates on 12 March 1566. The double intention of the conspirators was to slaughter Riccio and coerce the Queen into pardoning Moray and the rest.

In return for his participation, the conspirators promised to support Darnley's claim to the Crown Matrimonial, which he had many times requested, and the Queen had steadfastly refused. The dispute over the Crown Matrimonial had already played its part in damaging the relationship of Darnley and the Queen before it was altogether poisoned by his suspicions concerning Riccio.

In March 1566 the Queen was six months pregnant and Darnley, believing that the child was Riccio's not his, may have hoped that the shock of a murder committed in her presence would cause the Queen to miscarry. He may even have hoped that it would cause her death, naïvely trusting that if she died his fellow conspirators would help him to assert what he conceived to be his right to rule.

Darnley's fellow conspirators were the Earl of Morton, and the Lords Lindsay and Ruthven, who were supported by a gang of willing helpers, including Ruthven's son. In a sense the conspiracy was a family affair, for Darnley was the grandson of Margaret Tudor's Earl of Angus and Morton was his nephew, while the wives of Lindsay and Ruthven were both Douglases. However, though the conspirators may have promised to support Darnley's ambitions as his kinsmen, they made use of him in the most cynical fashion; for Darnley did not inspire their loyalty, and their principal purpose was to coerce the Queen on behalf of Moray and the rest. A latent aspect of the conspiracy was that it represented a resurgence of extremist Protestantism, for the rise of Riccio and the banishment of Moray had led to renewed suspicions of the Queen's Catholicism and of her intentions towards the future of Protestantism in Scotland.

The murder of Riccio took place on the evening of 9 March. The Queen was at supper in a little room which opened off her bedchamber in Holyroodhouse, with the Countess of Argyll who was her half-sister, a daughter of James V. Riccio was with them, not indeed sitting at table, but eating 'meat from ye Queen's table from ye cupboorde [i.e. sideboard] as ye servants of ye privie chamber uses to do'. To the Queen's surprise, Darnley came to join them, and seated himself at her side.

The informal scene was interrupted by the appearance of Lord Ruthven, who had recently been believed to be dying, 'so sick as he was not able to come out of his chamber, and yet he undertakes this bloody action'. His macabre figure, clad in armour and a dressing-gown, was followed by the rest of the conspirators, who pushed their way into the little room, overturning the table as they came. Darnley flung his arms round the Queen and held her in her place, while one Andrew Ker of Fawdonside 'held a pistol to her breast which refused to give fire'. The rest of the conspirators seized Riccio, who clung to the Queen's skirts until his fingers were bent back to force him to let go. Shrieking in polyglot terror, 'Justizia! Justizia, Madame! Save ma vie! Save ma vie!', he was dragged from the room and stabbed with many weapons, including Darnley's dagger, which the murderers left stuck into the corpse, to ensure that Darnley was inextricably identified with themselves. This gesture, however, proved to be of little advantage, for it failed to secure Darnley's adherence to them. He did indeed cancel the Parliament which was to have tried Moray, while the Queen remained a prisoner in Holyroodhouse, guarded by the followers of Morton. Moray and his associates entered Edinburgh the following day, to receive the pardon which Mary was powerless to withhold.

Although the conspirators were apparently triumphant and the Queen helpless, the situation was swiftly reversed by her own resolute action. The Queen did not miscarry, neither did she yield any further to Darnley's wishes; indeed, she infected him with such terror of his kinsmen and late allies that he was willing to join her in fleeing from them.

Mary and Darnley escaped to take refuge in the Earl of Bothwell's Castle of Dunbar, where they were joined by the Earl of Athol, the new Earl of Huntly, and by Lords Fleming and Seton. With their support, and that of the pardoned Moray, Argyll and Glencairn, Mary was able to return in triumph to Edinburgh. Morton, Lindsay, Ruthven and sixty of their followers fled to England. But, though temporarily discomfited, they were free and alive, and they were not disposed either to forget or forgive the treachery of Darnley.

Neither did Mary forgive him. Their relationship had deteriorated considerably during recent months, but not even the poorest pretence at a relationship could have survived the murder of Riccio. For Darnley, besides participating in a crime of violence which had endangered her life and insulted her sovereignty, had committed the irreparable offence of accusing his wife of infidelity. No-one of sense has ever taken Darnley's accusation seriously, but to the child of Mary and Darnley the slur upon his paternity was ever painful. Those who desired to compliment King James vi were wont to compare him to the wise King Solomon; his enemies could sour the compliment with references to 'Solomon the son of David'. James was born in the early summer of 1566.

'The Kingdom and Court was at quiet [wrote Mary's adherent Lord Herries, in his memoirs]. . . . the Queen, growing great with child . . . retired her from Holyroodhouse unto the Castle of Edinburgh, where, upon the nineteenth day of June she brought forth a son, betwixt nine and ten o'clock in the morning. About two o'clock in the afternoon the King came to visit the Queen, and was desirous to see the child. "My Lord," says the Queen, "God has given you and me a son, begotten by none but you!" At which words the King blushed, and kissed the child. Then she took the child in her arms, and, discovering his face [i.e. unwrapping him enough for his face to be seen] said, "My Lord here I protest to God and as I shall answer to Him at the great day of Judgement, that this is your son and no other man's son. And I am desirous that all here both ladies and others bear witness; for he is so much your own son, that I fear it will be the worse for him hereafter!" Then she spoke to Sir William Stanley [an English servant of Darnley]. "This," says she, "is the son whom I hope shall first unite the two kingdoms of Scotland and England!" Then Sir William answered, "Why, Madam? Shall he succeed before your Majesty and his father?" "Because," says she, "his father has broken to [i.e. with] me." The King was by and heard all.'

The Queen, as Lord Herries's anecdote reveals, had come to regard her husband with revulsion and contempt. Darnley responded by absenting himself from her and from the court as much as possible. The principal place in the Queen's counsels was taken by the Earl of Bothwell, who had so loyally supported her after the murder of Riccio.

Bothwell was described as 'a man high in his own conceit, proud, vicious, and vainglorious above measure, one who would attempt anything out of ambition'. In his qualities and in his faults Bothwell was the very antithesis of Darnley, which for Mary may not have been the least of his attractions. But she committed a great error when she allowed herself to fall in love with him. Though her infatuation was probably brief, it was disastrous.

The birth of an heir made Darnley dispensable, and by the autumn of 1566 Mary was considering the possibility of finding an 'outgait' from her burdensome marriage. At Craigmillar in November a conference upon the subject took place between the Queen herself, the Earls of Moray, Bothwell, Huntly and Argyll, and William Maitland of Lethington. The Queen rejected the possibility of obtaining a divorce, although consanguinity and marriage before the papal dispensation might have provided adequate grounds, for fear of affecting the legitimacy of her son. Her counsellors therefore assured her that they would devise some other 'outgait' for her, which would not be detrimental to her honour. There, for the present, the matter rested.

The following month witnessed the baptism of Prince James. It took place on 17 December, in the Chapel Royal of Stirling, in accordance with Catholic rites. The occasion was one of great splendour. The Prince's godparents were the King of France, the Duke of Savoy and the Queen of England, whose representatives came bearing costly gifts: France sent jewels, Savoy sent a jewelled fan trimmed with peacock feathers, and Elizabeth provided a golden font. The baptism appeared to mark the Queen's triumph over disaffection in her kingdom; but despite appearances the troubles in the background could not be altogether concealed. Darnley was in residence at Stirling, but his unwelcome presence was kept out of sight; the French ambassador was not permitted even to see him privately.

After the baptism Mary left her son at Stirling Castle, in the custody of John Erskine, Earl of Mar. Stirling had provided a safe refuge for James v during the turbulent years of his minority, and for Mary herself during the earliest years of her childhood. The Queen could be confident that her son would be safe, though she did not reflect that in a crisis he might also be out of her control. She turned her mind to other matters, of which the 'outgait' promised by her counsellors took precedence over all the rest.

On 24 December the Queen pardoned the murderers of Riccio. She was aware that they would not lightly forgive Darnley's defection after the murder; and if they were to avenge themselves by killing him it would not be detrimental to her honour. The pardon shows that she was consenting in principle to obtaining her 'outgait' through Darnley's death; what part she played in the events that followed remains a matter of controversy.

In January 1567 the murderers of Riccio returned to Scotland. Bothwell did not intend to leave their vengeance to chance. He went to meet Morton, and invited him to join a conspiracy to murder the Queen's husband. Morton refused, though not on humanitarian grounds. The reason for his refusal was that since he had just been pardoned for his part in one murder, he did not wish to invite fresh trouble by helping to commit another. Determined to act prudently, he concealed his knowledge that Darnley was likely to meet a violent death.

The following month Darnley, who had been ill at Glasgow since Christmas with a complaint which is thought to have been syphilis, was brought by the Queen to convalesce at Kirk o'Field, a house on the outskirts of Edinburgh. He met his end on the night of 9 February, when the house was blown up, though he himself was found dead in the garden, killed by strangulation and uninjured by the explosion. Many ingenious and specious theories, including the existence of more than one conspiracy, have been invented to explain the mysterious circumstances; but hitherto the murder of Darnley has retained its mystery, which includes the apportioning of responsibility.

Morton's was not the only cautious absence from the scene of the murder. Moray also, considering that he had been Darnley's enemy, was ostentatiously not there; the previous day he had gone to visit his wife at St Andrews, and thence he went to France. Though there were numerous suspects, and if anything their number increased with the years, the populace of Edinburgh had no doubt at the time that the murder was the work of Bothwell.

Mary's actions during the ensuing months had the appearance of an insensate policy of self-destruction.

The public outcry against Bothwell made it necessary that he should be put on trial. But the prosecution was not initiated by the Crown; it was left to Darnley's father the Earl of Lennox. Bothwell was tried on 12 April and acquitted for want of evidence against him, which was lacking because Lennox dared not enter Edinburgh which was filled with Bothwell's followers, in arms.

This travesty of justice created the impression that Bothwell was protected because the Queen shared his guilt. Even Elizabeth felt that it behoved her to send the Queen of Scots a warning:

'O Madam [she wrote], I would not do the duty of a faithful cousin and affectionate friend, if I thought more of pleasing your ears than saving your honour. I will not conceal from you what most people are saying . . . that you have no desire to touch those who have done you such pleasure. . . . I exhort you, I council you, I beg you to take this event so to heart that you will not fear to proceed even against your nearest.'

Mary received this, and other more forthright warnings, without heed. Instead, she committed what appeared to be the ultimate act of folly and abandonment of principle: on 15 May she married the Earl of Bothwell, in the Chapel Royal of Holyroodhouse, in accordance with Protestant rites. Previously, Bothwell had hastily divorced his wife Lady Jean Gordon, whom he had married only the year before.

Those who have seen Mary's marriage to Bothwell as motivated by passion have found it hard to explain why, shortly after the marriage, the Queen was crying out for a knife to kill herself, and threatening otherwise to drown herself.

The explanation of Mary's actions during the spring of 1567 is that she was pregnant by Bothwell, which was proved by a subsequent miscarriage. It was essential that Bothwell should be acquitted of the murder of Darnley and that the Queen should marry him, because it was public knowledge that she had not cohabited with Darnley for many months, so that a child born in the late summer or early autumn of 1567 could not be his. When Mary brought Darnley from Glasgow to Kirk o'Field she had promised to resume marital relations with him as soon as his convalescence was over. This makes it likely that Mary already suspected her pregnancy, and that she brought him to Kirk o'Field with the intention of preserving his life long enough to implement her promise, a repulsive prospect which only desperate need could have led her to contemplate. His death, which upon this hypothesis occurred before the Queen intended, left her no choice but to marry Bothwell.

Mary knew well enough that the acquittal had failed to clear Bothwell's reputation, and she made a desperate effort to protect her own by presenting herself as Bothwell's victim when she permitted him to carry her off by force to the Castle of Dunbar before the marriage. The Queen's tale of abduction, rape and enforced marriage convinced nobody; and her anguish and thoughts of suicide after the marriage clearly illustrate that far from persisting in a passionate determination to marry her lover, she had married him only out of expediency, and had recognized that the marriage would bring about her political ruin.

Though Bothwell held office as Warden of the Marches and was a Border magnate in whose possession were the castles of Bothwick, Crichton, Hailes, Hermitage and Dunbar, his career had resembled that of a freebooter rather than that of a great nobleman. He was not supported by a network of alliances, in the manner of Moray, Châtelherault or Morton. Bothwell had many enemies who, after the marriage, became if only temporarily the enemies of the Queen. Mary herself, who had made a remarkable political recovery after the murder of Riccio, and had contrived to hold the balance of power until the murder of Darnley, forfeited the support of her nobility and most of her subjects by her conduct during the early months of 1567. The marriage left the Queen and her husband isolated and vulnerable.

The situation of the Queen of Scots closely paralleled that of James III in the last months of his reign: in each instance the sovereign had provoked the existence of a strong opposition, which held Stirling Castle, and in it the heir to the throne.

Only a month after their marriage Bothwell and the Queen faced their enemies in arms at Carberry Hill, near Musselburgh. There was, however, no battle. The Queen's army, which was dwindling through desertion, faced a much stronger force commanded by the Earl of Morton. Bothwell wished to decide the issue by single combat, and sent Morton a challenge; but Morton preferred to let the lack of enthusiasm for the Queen's cause win the day for him. At the Queen's insistence, Bothwell was permitted to make his escape. After a variety of adventures he reached Denmark, where a discreditable past caught up with him and he was imprisoned. He died in captivity, and probably insane, in 1578. Mary, who never saw him again after he left the field of Carberry Hill, surrendered to her enemies and was led into Edinburgh as a prisoner. The populace of her capital showed its opinion of her conduct during the last months by crowding about her and shouting, 'Burn the whore! Burn the murderess of her husband!' She was protected from the anger of the mob by William Kirkaldy of Grange, who years before had participated in the murder of Cardinal Beaton; the misfortunes of Mary won him to her cause, in which he ultimately lost his life.

After her surrender Mary was imprisoned in the island fortress of Lochleven, where her gaoler was Moray's half-brother. The formidable chatelaine of Lochleven was his mother, and Moray's mother, who had been Margaret Erskine, long ago the favourite mistress of James v. She, who firmly believed that she should have been Queen, and her son King of Scots, spared no opportunity to insult the unfortunate Mary. In these unhappy circumstances, some time between 18 and 24 July, Mary miscarried of twins. The pregnancy was evidently well advanced for the miscarriage was described as 'deux enfants'.

The annals of the Stewart dynasty did not provide an example of the supersession of a living sovereign by the heir. The lords who had defeated and imprisoned their discredited Queen desired to replace her with an infant King whose sovereignty would not carry the stigma of usurpation. They required, accordingly, to secure her voluntary abdication. Mary defended her sovereign rights with as much resolution as was possible in the circumstances; but ill and alone as she was, it was impossible for her to withstand the threats and physical force which were offered her. On 24 July she was compelled to issue under her Privy Seal a document of abdication and acknowledgement of the 'government of her young son', and an authorization of the regency of the Earl of Moray. The coronation of the thirteen-month-old James vi took place five days later.

The new King, who had been baptized as a Catholic, was crowned as a Protestant. His coronation completed the process which had been begun by the Reformation rebellion. To this extent the reign of Mary, Queen of Scots, the events of which are the best-known events in the whole of Scottish history, can be seen as a parenthetical interlude between the victory of Protestantism in Scotland and its complete establishment. Whether Mary could have maintained successfully the policy of conciliation which she followed during the early years of her reign under the guidance of Moray and Lethington remains questionable; but it seems probable that even had she continued to rule as intelligently as she had begun, the problem of a continued Catholic dynasty in a Protestant country would have proved insuperable.

The reign of Mary, Queen of Scots was over, but it had a dramatic epilogue. Mary, who possessed as much courage and indomitability as any of her family, abandoned her belief in her sovereignty, and her hope of reasserting her authority, only with her life. On 2 May 1568

Mary escaped from Lochleven Castle, revoked her abdication and contested Moray's victory.

Inevitably the circumstances of her overthrow caused a revulsion of sympathy in her favour. Furthermore, the regime of Moray did not command the support of the Hamiltons, who formed the nucleus of a resurgent Queen's party. That the successful early years of her rule were not forgotten is attested by the fact that nine earls, eighteen lords, nine bishops and twelve commendators rallied to her cause. Their combined followings raised a force of between five and six thousand men. However, the Queen's hope of regaining her throne was destroyed when her army was defeated by Moray, on 13 May, at Langside, near Glasgow.

Mary fled, by way of Sanquhar and Terregles, and took refuge at the Abbey of Dundrennan, near the shore of the Solway Firth, where she spent her last night in Scotland. From nearby Abbeyburnfoot she took boat to England, on 16 May.

Mary's choice of a refuge was her own. Had her pride permitted her to return as a fugitive to France, or had she looked for sanctuary and support in Spain, the end of her story might have been very different. As it was, she committed not the least fateful of her errors by seeking refuge in the kingdom of a rival whose title she had once assumed, and whose successor she claimed to be. In extenuation of the error it must be said that during her imprisonment at Lochleven Elizabeth had displayed sympathy with her cause, and Mary may have convinced herself that Elizabeth might be persuaded to negotiate her reinstatement, in preference to giving her indefinite asylum in England.

If this was Mary's hope, the outcome was bitter indeed. The Queen of Scots was received as a guest and detained as a prisoner. The conditions of her imprisonment, at first courteous and comfortable, increased in rigour with the passage of the years. Elizabeth, far from being prepared to reinstate her rival, though she occasionally allowed the idea to be canvassed for purposes of diplomacy, preferred to retain her as a hostage who ensured the alliance, or at least the non-enmity of the government of Scotland. The imprisoned Queen served this purpose throughout the minority of James vi. Her attenuated influence upon Scottish politics will be referred to in the context of his reign.

As a prisoner Mary, Queen of Scots continued to hope and plot for her liberation and reinstatement, and even for the Catholic coup d'état or foreign invasion which would give her the ultimate triumph of the English throne. The plots which centred around her and which she encouraged were not too chimerical to be a source of fear to Elizabeth and her ministers. Ultimately they brought the Queen of Scots to the block at Fotheringay.

During her imprisonment the religion which Mary had done so little to maintain in Scotland became increasingly important to her. After her Protestant marriage to Bothwell the Pope had declared that 'unless in time to come he shall see some better sign of her life and religion than he has witnessed in the past' he would hold no further communication with her. Imprisonment transformed her into a devoted daughter of the Church. It was not policy alone that made Mary offer herself as the hope of disaffected Catholics in England and of Elizabeth's enemies abroad. In adversity she sought and found the solace of religion. A sonnet which she wrote during her imprisonment conveys the desolation of spirit which she sometimes experienced, and the hopes of Heaven which came to seem more real than the hopes of worldly triumph. The original French is here translated: [1]

What am I, alas, what purpose has my life?
I nothing am, a corpse without a heart,
A useless shade, a victim of sad strife,
One who lives yet, and wishes to depart.
My enemies, no envy hold for me;
My spirit has no taste for greatness now.
Sorrow consumes me in extreme degree;
Your hatred shall be satisfied, I vow.
And you, my friends, you who have held me dear,
Reflect that I, lacking both health and fortune,
Cannot aspire to any great deed here.
Welcome, therefore, my ultimate misfortune.
And pray that when affliction ends my story,
Then I may have some share in Heaven's glory.

Before Mary went to her execution on 8 February 1587, she declared, 'I am settled in the ancient Catholic Roman religion, and

[1] Author's translation.

mind to spend my blood in defence of it.'

Strong feelings can still be aroused in academic debate and in discussion as to whether Mary, Queen of Scots was an immoralist and murderess or a martyr for her religion. The answer perhaps is that neither is a true description. She was a Queen who accepted the challenge of a difficult inheritance, played a dangerous political game, made several disastrous mistakes and lost.

9
James VI,
1567–1603

Since thought is free, think what thou will
O troubled heart, to ease thy pain!
Thought unrevealed can do no ill,
    But words past out turn not again.
      Be careful, aye, for to invent
      The way to get thine own intent ...

Since fool haste is not greatest speed,
    I would thou shouldest learn to know
How to make virtue of a need
    Since that necessity hath no law.
      With patience then see thou attend
      And hope to vanquish at the end.
(The King's verses, when he was fyfteene year old,
James VI)

King James VI was crowned on 29 July 1567, in the church of the Holy Rude, the parish church of Stirling.

A Protestant coronation was an event without precedent, and the ceremonial of the occasion represented an attempt to reconcile disparate elements of Catholicism and Protestantism.

Tradition demanded crowning and anointing by the Archbishop of St Andrews or the Archbishop of Glasgow, and it seemed expedient to adhere to tradition as closely as possible, since the King's predecessor was still alive and the legality of his sovereignty rested only upon her enforced abdication.

Neither of the Archbishops was available to perform the ceremony, for Archbishop Hamilton of St Andrews was a resolute opponent of the new regime, and Archbishop Beaton of Glasgow (a nephew of Cardinal Beaton), had been in exile since 1560. However, there was a suitable Bishop, whose career bestrode the Reformation, and who fulfilled both the demands of tradition and the requirements of innovation. Adam Bothwell, Bishop of Orkney, had been provided to his see by the Pope and duly consecrated in 1559; upon the success of the Reformation rebellion he had prudently reformed himself and become a Protestant Bishop. He anointed the King 'on ye croune of the head, shoulder blaides, and palmes of ye hands, saiing certain prayers befor in the English tongue'. When the crowning itself had been performed, James's guardian the Earl of Mar held the crown above his head, since the thirteen-month-old baby could not possibly support its weight.

The Protestant elements of the coronation are evident in the choice of the parish church in preference to the Chapel Royal, in the use of vernacular prayers, in the coronation oath taken by the Earl of Morton on behalf of the King, promising to 'maintain ye religion then professed in Scotland' and in the presence of John Knox who preached a sermon on the coronation of Joash. The reformers were understandably fond of comparing James VI to the Old Testament child-King Joash, and Mary, Queen of Scots to the evil Queen Athaliah whom he rightfully supplanted.

To complete the solemnities and to stress the legality of the occasion, the Queen's abdication was read out, and her authorization of the regency of the Earl of Moray. The King was then carried back to the castle, and his coronation was celebrated with 'fyre works, and shotting of canon, and feasting'.

The precariousness of the new regime, despite all precautions, was illustrated the following spring, when Mary, Queen of Scots escaped from Lochleven Castle, revoked her abdication and showed that she was still capable of attracting strong support. From the viewpoint of history the Battle of Langside appears decisive; to the Earl of Moray the consequence of Mary's flight to England seemed much less certain.

Elizabeth's diplomacy, following Mary's arrival in her kingdom, was characteristically subtle. While Mary remained in courteous detention, Elizabeth held a conference to decide her future. Moray was summoned to attend what purported to be a trial of himself and his partisans on the charge of rebellion against his sovereign, before her commissioners, though in reality it was a trial of the Queen of Scots herself, for the murder of Darnley. On the question of her guilt or innocence depended the righteousness or otherwise of Moray's rebellion. The result, after tortuous negotiations, was the kind of non-result which Elizabeth so frequently contrived to turn to her advantage: she declared that nothing had derogated from the honour of either party, but she sent Moray back to Scotland to resume his regency with the benefit of limited English support, while Mary remained in England, with her guilt neither established nor cleared, but with her reputation smeared by the Casket Letters and poems, of which Moray had produced copies. Whether Mary had written these incriminating letters and passionate poems to Bothwell, or whether they were the forgeries of her enemies, will probably remain for ever as controversial as her part in Darnley's murder; their importance lies in the use to which Moray put them, which was to alienate some of Mary's influential supporters, and to strengthen the bonds of her captivity.

The following year the dangerous but ill-co-ordinated Northern Rebellion on Mary's behalf served to illustrate to Elizabeth the desirability of maintaining friendly relations with the anglophile Regent of Scotland. Moray in his turn was desirous of strengthening the bond with England and of confirming the results of the Reformation in Scotland. His policy looked ultimately towards the uniting of the two countries under the succession of the King of Scots, a prospect which became increasingly probable as the years passed and Elizabeth remained unmarried.

The events of Moray's regency in general epitomize the trend of events throughout the King's minority. There was a gradual increase in the strength of the King's party, and a corresponding decline in the strength of the Queen's. At the time of his coronation the King was unacknowledged by a sizeable proportion of his own subjects and by the majority of the nobles, whose sympathy had veered back again to the Queen. At the time of the Battle of Langside the King appeared to be no more than the figurehead of a faction. But by the end of Moray's regency he was nearer to being the true King. Respect for his sovereignty grew in proportion to the respect which the regency commanded. Moray proved himself a capable ruler. His desire to impose law and order and to provide the troubled kingdom with the benefits of peace and good government led the people to consider him the best ruler that they had had 'sen [since] James in Falkland deit'. After his death they remembered him as the 'Good Regent'.

Moray's principal weakness lay in his failure either to defeat the Hamiltons decisively or to win their support. Though defeated in the field at Langside, their castles, the centres of their strength, remained in their hands, and Moray lacked both the resources to move against them and the power to invoke against them the sanctions of the law. If the Hamiltons were little disposed to exert themselves further on be-half of the Queen, they were no more disposed to give their support to the regency of Moray. The Hamiltons, as always, were for the Hamiltons.

The Duke of Châtelherault had been pardoned for his part in the rebellion at the time of Mary's marriage to Darnley, the single occasion on which he had acted as Moray's ally, on condition of his living abroad for five years. He failed, upon his return, to regain the influence which he had lost, and the appointment of Moray to the regency left him aggrieved that he was excluded from the office which he had occupied during the early minority of Mary, and which he felt was his by right. Châtelherault himself showed a certain lethargy during his later years, but his half-brother the Archbishop and his two younger sons, the Lords John and Claud Hamilton, more than supplied his lack of vigour. It was their enmity which terminated simultaneously the regency of Moray and his life.

On 23 January 1570 Moray was shot from the 'forestair' of a house as he rode through the town of Linlithgow, by one James Hamilton of Bothwellhaugh. According to Lord Herries Moray had been warned of an attempt upon his life, but had confidently expected to frustrate it by riding swiftly through the town. However, either the crowd which thronged to see him impeded his progress, or the assassin was an exceptional marksman, even with the primitive 'fyrlock' which was the best weapon at his disposal. The house in which Bothwellhaugh positioned himself belonged to Archbishop Hamilton, and after the fatal shot he made his escape on a fast horse lent him by Lord John Hamilton. Châtelherault made arrangements for his escape to France.

Moray's death was a severe blow to the King's party, but once again English intervention ensured its continued ascendancy. A Border raid led by some of the Queen's partisans, for which the Hamiltons were held ultimately responsible, provided the pretext for a small-scale

English invasion to take reprisals. The King's party joined forces with the English, and destroyed the palace, Castle and town of Hamilton.

The new Regent, who was elected with Elizabeth's approval, was the King's paternal grandfather, the Earl of Lennox. Personally Lennox commanded little respect, but his relationship to the King gave him a very good claim to the regency. The King remained in the care of his guardian the Earl of Mar, while the effective leadership of the King's party devolved increasingly upon the Earl of Morton.

At the time of Moray's death the Queen's party still held a number of fortresses of strategic importance, including the Castles of Doune, Dumbarton and Edinburgh. Moray had attempted and failed to take Dumbarton immediately before his murder. Lennox gained increasing prestige for the King's party by taking both Doune and Dumbarton early in 1571. In the latter castle Archbishop Hamilton was taken prisoner. After the murder of Cardinal Beaton no priest could expect to enjoy ecclesiastical immunity; the Archbishop was drawn to the gallows like a common criminal, and hanged in Stirling on 7 April.

Lennox and Morton made the possession of the capital their next objective. The castle was resolutely held for the Queen by Kirkaldy of Grange and Maitland of Lethington, who were joined for a time by Châtelherault and Lord Claud Hamilton. Morton took charge of what promised to be a long campaign, and based his forces at Leith. Most of those citizens of Edinburgh who supported the King left their houses upon the orders of Grange, and throughout the summer of 1571 Edinburgh was a half-empty battleground.

Though this 'war between Leith and Edinburgh' dragged on indecisively the advantage was clearly with the King's party. In August a Parliament was held at Stirling which was the strongest gathering that had yet mustered for the King. The successes of Lennox had won him the support of a number of noblemen who had hitherto adhered to the Queen. Among them were three Earls, Eglinton, Cassillis and Argyll.

The Queen's party decided to take advantage of the absence of Morton, who had left his base at Leith, and gone up to Stirling, and of the fact that the King's lords were in a vulnerable group at Stirling, lodged about the town and confident that their opponents would not leave the safety of Edinburgh. Grange planned a night attack on Stirling, his intention being that as many of the King's lords as possible should be taken prisoner and brought to Edinburgh Castle, where they could be compelled to come to such terms as the Queen's party should dictate. He was certain that negotiations backed by force would give the Queen's party its last chance of recovery.

Whatever hopes his plan may have held were frustrated when Grange's companions refused to let him lead the attack, 'alledging that their only comfort, under God, consisted in his preservation'. The raid on Stirling was led by Huntly and Lord Claud Hamilton, who speedily forgot Grange's orders to bring back the prisoners in safety. The attack was neither swift enough nor quiet enough. Though some of the King's lords were initially captured, their removal was delayed by street-fighting and looting; the Earl of Mar led a sally from the castle, the raiders were repulsed and most of the prisoners rescued. The Regent, however, was shot in the back and died of his wound. The little King, now five years old, saw his grandfather carried mortally wounded into Stirling Castle in the early morning.

Grange, it was reported, 'greatly lamented the Regent's slaughter', and bitterly abused Huntly and Lord Claud Hamilton as 'disorderly beasts'. He saw more clearly than they did that the murder had lost the Queen's party the last chance of advantageous negotiation, and that without a miracle defeat was only a matter of time.

The Parliament at Stirling, which had been on the point of dispersing when the attack occurred, met again to elect a new regent. There were three candidates, the Earls of Mar, Morton and Argyll. The choice fell upon Mar.

The election of the Earl of Mar as the third in the swift succession of regents illustrates the respect which his contemporaries felt for his qualities of character. He was known to be a man of high integrity, dedicated to the King's cause and desirous of attaining peace. The King's lords were well aware that peace could not be looked for before the defeat of the Queen's party, but they knew that in the necessary military enterprises Mar would have the experience of Morton at his disposal.

Mar, however, was never given the opportunity to display his qualities as a ruler in time of peace. The bitter civil war continued in Edinburgh during the winter, and the spring of 1572. During the summer an 'abstinence' or truce was arranged, and Châtelherault, Lord Claud Hamilton, Huntly and Lord Seton took the opportunity to leave the castle. Grange was left, with Lethington who was slowly dying of a paralytic disease, to hold the castle and await the inevitable defeat.

The last act of their tragedy was prolonged by the death of the Earl of Mar, which necessitated the election of yet another regent, with all the accompanying political rearrangements. Mar was said to have died because 'he loved peace and could not have it', which may mean that he broke under the magnitude of his task. A more sinister rumour was reported by Sir James Melville:

'The Regent went to Edinburgh [he wrote] to convene the lords of council, to show them the calamities that civil wars produced, and to let them see how necessary an agreement would be to the whole country. In the meantime until the appointed council day, he went to Dalkeith, where he was nobly treated by the Lord of Morton; shortly after which he took a vehement sickness, which caused him to ride suddenly to Stirling, where he died regretted by many. Some of his friends and the vulgar suspected he had gotten wrong at his banquet.'

The fourth and last of the regents elected to rule on behalf of James VI was the Earl of Morton, whose regency was destined to be more enduring than those of his predecessors.

James Douglas, fourth Earl of Morton, who was born about 1516, was the son of Sir George Douglas, the younger brother of Margaret Tudor's Earl of Angus. When James V attained his majority and banished Angus and his kinsmen, the young James Douglas fled to the north of Scotland, and is said to have worked 'as the grieve and overseer to him with whom he lived'. He married Lady Elizabeth Douglas, daughter of the third Earl of Morton, and succeeded to his father-in-law's title in right of his wife.

Morton's rise to power had been closely bound up with the progress of the Reformation. He had been an able henchman of Moray and the *éminence grise* of Lennox and Mar. After the death of Mar, as 'the man in that time of greatest courage and counsel' he was the obvious choice as the next regent. His regency, in Archbishop Mathew's words, was 'the last great showing of the Douglas blood'. It was also, in terms of service to the state, the most creditable. Morton possessed much personal ambition and few amiable qualities, but he showed a profound understanding of the nature of his office when he wrote, 'The bearing to the charge of the government of the realm, indeed mon lead us, or any other that shall occupy that place, not simply to respect ourself, but his Majesty's roume which we supply. . . .'

Morton was formally installed as Regent on 24 November 1572, which was the day of John Knox's death.

The death of Knox, the most influential of the first generation of Scottish reformers, may conveniently be regarded as marking the end of the first phase in the development of the Kirk. Since the establishment of Protestantism in 1560 the Kirk had developed its own system of government under the General Assembly. As the Kirk was intended to comprehend the whole nation, the representative assembly of the Kirk could be regarded as a representative assembly of the nation in its ecclesiastical aspect; possibly for this reason it was structured like a Parliament, to include nobles, lairds and burgesses as well as ministers. This meant that the Kirk possessed the means to present efficient and nationally-organized opposition to the sovereign and Parliament if circumstances demanded it.

The circumstances in which the Kirk became almost an official opposition party to the government arose from the development of the Presbyterian movement. The basic tenet of Presbyterianism was the parity of ministers, which required that the Kirk should be governed not by higher ecclesiastical dignitaries, since such could not be admitted to exist, but by local, regional and national ecclesiastical courts and assemblies, the Kirk Sessions, Presbyteries, Synods and ultimately the General Assembly. The first necessity in establishing this form of organization was the elimination of episcopacy.

In this development Knox was a transitional figure. He condemned the Catholic hierarchy, and in the *Book of Discipline*, adopted by the Kirk but rejected by the Reformation Parliament, he and his brethren urged the abolition of the title 'Bishop'. In the system of ecclesiastical polity established by the Kirk after the Reformation Bishops were replaced by 'Superintendents' who were appointed to dioceses and performed a Bishop's administrative functions. The Superintendent did not entirely supersede the Bishop, however, and even Knox on occasion showed tacit acceptance of the existence of Bishops, for example when he attended the coronation of James VI. In 1572 the Kirk, not yet powerful enough to resist the authority of the government, was obliged to accept the Concordat of Leith, by which Bishops were officially imposed upon it.

By this time the powers which a pre-Reformation Bishop had enjoyed had been greatly curtailed. Indeed, it appeared that the office of Bishop existed no longer for the benefit of clergy or laity, but for that of some noble patron. For instance, Morton, after the execution of Archbishop Hamilton, received the temporalities of the see of St Andrews, which he enjoyed for some time without appointing anyone to the benefice. When eventually he made an appointment he selected a minister venal enough to accept a small stipend in return for the title and dignity of Bishop while allowing Morton as patron to continue to receive the greater part of the revenues. The ministers of the Kirk scornfully called such a travesty of an ecclesiastical dignitary a 'tulchan bishop', because as David Calderwood, the historian of the Kirk, explained, 'a tulchan is a calve's skinne stuffed with straw to caus the kow give milk'.

Knox and Morton had a bitter quarrel over Morton's tulchan appointment to St Andrews shortly before Morton was elected to the regency, and Knox, who was requested to induct the Bishop, refused to do so, and 'in open audience of many . . . denounced anathema to the giver, anathema to the receiver', the venality of the transaction being the aspect of it to which he took particular exception. It was little wonder that after Knox's death Morton described him as one who 'nather fearit nor flatterit any flesh'.

Morton's tulchan Bishop, however, was duly inducted, and the Concordat of Leith regularized the existence of Bishops for the time being. A new and more vigorous phase of the Kirk's war against episcopacy began in 1574 when the reformer Andrew Melville returned to Scotland from Geneva, assumed Knox's position as acknowledged leader of the Kirk and set about imposing upon it a purer form of Calvinist discipline and a Presbyterian organization. Morton took no direct action against Melville, for, as Professor Donaldson observes, 'the place of bishops in ecclesiastical administration . . . was founded in statute law; the assembly could produce a programme, but only Parliament could put it into effect'. In 1578 the General Assembly condemned the office of Bishop, a challenge which the government was bound to take up sooner or later. Ultimately the challenge was taken up by James VI. During the 1570s Morton was more concerned with the problems of secular government than with the aspirations of the Kirk.

The first problem which faced Morton upon his assumption of the regency was that of Grange and Lethington, still in occupation of Edinburgh Castle. With characteristic practicality Morton saw that, aside from the unlikely eventuality of their receiving help from abroad, the only help which would come to the aid of Grange and Lethington would be from the Hamiltons. However, the situation of the Hamiltons was materially weaker than it had been at the time of the assassination of Moray; to come to terms with the Regent clearly offered them more advantages than to persist in fighting for a cause which was obviously lost in Scotland. Morton offered terms, and in 1573 he signed with the Hamiltons the Pacification of Perth, assent to which was the last public act of the Duke of Châtelherault, who retired from political life and died in 1575.

Having isolated the defenders of Edinburgh Castle, Morton negotiated for English help in reducing the fortress. At the beginning of May 1573 Elizabeth sent a force under Sir William Drury, with '20 grate pieces' of ordnance to batter down the defences. Grange was forced to surrender on 29 May. Some weeks later he was hanged at the Mercat Cross of Edinburgh. Lethington, who would undoubtedly have shared his fate, had died a little earlier, possibly by suicide. The fall of Edinburgh Castle ensured that James VI was at last established as the indisputable sovereign of Scotland, and removed any lingering impression that his government was merely that of a successful faction.

Morton turned his attention to the restoration of stability to a kingdom which had known little but political and religious turmoil since the death of James V in 1542. Considering the magnitude of the problem, his achievement was substantial.

In his foreign policy Morton followed his predecessors in sedulously cultivating the English alliance; but in his dealings with Elizabeth he was strong enough to retain a measure of independence for himself, and freedom from English domination for Scotland. In internal policy he concentrated upon restoring the rule of law and, in the words of Sir James Melville, he kept the kingdom 'under great obedience, better than for many years before or since'. His economic policy was less successful. 'No sixteenth-century ruler after James V,' Mrs

Mitchison comments, 'had strength to do more than live from hand to mouth, and none of them had enough grasp of currency and elementary economics to do even this in an intelligent way.' Morton had recourse to the old and ineffective expedient of depreciating the coinage, with the result that the pound Scots sank from being worth one quarter of the pound sterling in 1560 to being worth one twelfth of it by 1600. James VI was no better than Morton at solving economic problems, and neither were his ministers.

Morton's greatest failure, however, was in his personal relationship with the King. He ruled with a strong sense of the duty of the Regent towards the sovereign; but, concerned with the affairs of the kingdom, he did not concern himself with the child who was the King. '. . . as soon as ever his Majesty shall think himself ready and able for his own government,' Morton wrote during the minority, 'none shall more willingly agree and advance the same nor [than] I, since I think, never to set my face against him, whose honour, safety and preservation have been so dear to me.'

James VI remained unaware, or else incredulous, of these sentiments and Morton paid dearly for permitting him to receive a false impression.

The childhood world of James VI was circumscribed by the walls of Stirling Castle. From the beginning of his conscious life he lived in the care of the Earl of Mar and his Countess.

The Earl himself, especially when he became the Regent, may have seemed a somewhat remote figure to the little King. The Countess of Mar, his foster-mother, though probably kindly intentioned, was austere in character. 'My lady Mar,' wrote Sir James Melville, 'was wise and sharp, and held [kept] the King in great awe.' But she had a basic respect for the fact of his sovereignty; she referred to him as 'the Lord's Anointed', and objected when he was beaten for his childish misdemeanours.

Though he had honourable and responsible foster-parents, James VI, like most of his ancestors, lacked the love and support of family relationships.

The earliest portrait of the King shows a small, sturdy boy clad in unrelieved black, a hawk on his hand, and a black cap adorned with a band of pearls set aslant on his fair red hair. His face is pale and serious, his grey eyes have a strangely bleak expression for so young a child. There was little in his childhood, however, to make James VI lighthearted.

He was subjected to an intensive education as soon as he was old enough to absorb knowledge; his tutors were appointed soon after his third birthday in 1569, and his education began early the following year. He had two tutors, George Buchanan, of whom some previous mention has been made, and Peter Young.

Buchanan, who had lived for some years in exile in France and Portugal, had returned to Scotland after the Reformation, and for the last year had been principal of St Leonard's College in the University of St Andrews. He was considered one of the most eminent of Scottish scholars; he was a poet, historian, satirist, political theorist and author of tragic dramas, in Latin. He was also a virulent enemy of Mary, Queen of Scots. As a Lennoxman he was an unquestioning supporter of the Lennox Stuarts, and an apologist for the unfortunate Darnley. Though Mary had shown him favour, and had kept up her Latin by reading Livy with him in her brief times of leisure, after Darnley's death he had utterly turned against her. To his lasting discredit he had lent his scholarship to the writing of a book entitled *Detectio Mariae Reginae Scotorum*, a compilation of all the foul gossip which could be put to use by her enemies. Part of his task was to ensure that James VI should be brought up to regard his mother as an enemy.

As far as his actual education was concerned, Buchanan's task was to instil into James a thorough knowledge of the classical languages, history, political theory, and above all, the Protestant religion. Buchanan showed a conscientious determination to make his pupil a fine classical scholar, a responsible ruler, and the exemplar of Protestant princes.

James proved to be an apt and indeed a precocious pupil, whose scholarship did Buchanan credit. His influence on James's political ideas, however, was entirely negative. Whereas Buchanan believed in constitutional monarchy, James came to believe in absolute sovereignty. Buchanan attempted to instil into James his own belief that tyrannous rule justified tyrannicide; James, with a background of generations of kingship, could scarcely have been expected to find such a view acceptable. His response was to develop the theory of Divine Right, whereby a King 'acknowledgeth himself ordained for his people, having received from God the burden of government, whereof he must be countable'; in other words a conscientious ruler would be guided by his responsibility to God, and controlled by his awareness of impending judgement.

James was intensely aware of God. He accepted the Calvinist theology in which he was educated, and became as well-versed in it and as zealous to defend it as Buchanan could have wished. But superimposed upon his orthodox Calvinism was his entirely personal conviction that between Godhead and Kingship there existed a particular and intimate connection.

Buchanan endeavoured to inculcate his ideas into an extremely obstinate boy who developed strong ideas of his own. With the advantage of sixty years' seniority he could terrorize James so much that half a lifetime later he confessed to trembling at the memory of Buchanan; but Buchanan entirely failed to mould him in accordance with his theories. With the passing of years, the mutual dislike of master and pupil became cordial and unconcealed.

With the second tutor James had a pleasanter relationship. Peter Young, who had been educated at Geneva as a pupil of Calvin's successor Theodore Beza, was only twenty-seven at the time of his appointment. He treated the King with kindly consideration and was rewarded with his affection and trust. It was fortunate that James's dislike of Buchanan did not lead him to a dislike of learning; perhaps Young's encouragement was in the end more influential.

The remarkable progress of James's education received outside testimony in 1574, when the English ambassador Sir Henry Killigrew was permitted to visit him at Stirling:

'His Grace is well grown both in body and spirit since I was last here [1572]. He speaketh the French tongue marvellous well; and that which seems strange to me, he was able to extempore (which he did before me) to read a chapter of the Bible out of Latin into French, and out of French after into English, so well, as few men could have added anything to his translation. His schoolmasters, Mr George Buchanan and Mr Peter Young, rare men, caused me to appoint what chapter I would; and so did I, whereby I perceived that it was not studied for. They also made his Highness dance before me, which he likewise did with a very good grace; a Prince sure of great hope, if God give him life.'

He gave the King some books, which, he must have concluded, had been a well-chosen present.

Books were welcome, for Peter Young made it his particular concern to build up a library for the King. The resulting collection numbered six hundred volumes. It included theological works, especially those of Calvin, innumerable Bibles and Psalters, which were presented by ministers and other Protestant zealots; the works of many Greek and Roman writers; modern history, political theory and many handbooks for the guidance of rulers, a literary *genre* which flourished in the sixteenth century. From his mother's library, left behind in Scotland, came some medieval romances and some French poetry. By the time James reached adulthood he was an extremely well-read man, and his pleasure in books lasted throughout his life.

To revert to his childhood, the political turmoil and civil war which were endemic during the first three regencies impinged upon the King's world but little, except on the occasion when he saw his grandfather Lennox, a victim of that background of violence, carried dying into the castle. It became, however, common knowledge that James VI was afraid of violence, and the psychological effect of that single occasion when he witnessed its consequences may well be to blame. For his notorious fear of naked steel it may not be incorrect to blame his pre-natal experience on the night of Riccio's murder. The Erskine family successfully protected James from physical danger; it was less easy to protect him from his own nervous terrors.

After the death of the Earl of Mar his brother Sir Alexander Erskine of Gogar took his place as the King's guardian. The pattern of James's life remained unchanged, but in the course of the next few years a gradual alteration took place in the political atmosphere of Stirling Castle. Enmity towards the Earl of Morton slowly permeated the King's household. While the Regent Mar lived, Morton had been secure in the alliance of the Erskine family. After Mar's death Morton remained on friendly terms with the young Earl his son, who was about eight years older than the King of Scots; but the rest of the King's household and familiars 'had no kindness for him', as a neutral observer put it. Sir Alexander Erskine, though not actively factious, disliked him; John Cunningham of Drumwhasel, the Master of the Household, 'became his great enemy', apparently because he felt that the Regent was ungenerous; George Buchanan had a personal grudge against him, which was unfortunate for Morton, as Buchanan had a well-developed talent for enmity; even Peter Young had little liking for him. Under the influence of all the talk against Morton, casual or deliberate, that he must have heard, it was scarcely surprising that the young King also turned against him; the more so as the Regent appeared to him an awesome and authoritarian figure with whom he had little contact.

The first plot against Morton, which was the occasion of the King's political initiation, occurred in 1578, shortly before James's twelfth birthday. The plot was the consequence of a feud between the Earls of Athol and Argyll. Morton attempted to discipline them as rigorously as he was accustomed to discipline all breakers of the peace, whatever their degree. The two Earls were summoned before the Council to answer for their actions; firstly, for levying private war, and secondly for refusing to lay down their arms in response to the Regent's commands. In this predicament Athol and Argyll laid aside their feud and made common cause against the Regent. In accordance with their simple and effective plan, Argyll went to Stirling Castle, to which he was readily admitted by Sir Alexander Erskine, and requested the King to summon a meeting of the nobility, to which he would submit his cause and Athol's for judgement. James, flattered by the offer of responsibility as arbitrator in the dispute, and by the apparent submissiveness towards him of two of his most powerful subjects, at once agreed. Morton, to whom these proceedings could not be acceptable, wrote the King a letter of protest, in which he requested James either to accept his resignation or to permit him the untrammelled use of his disciplinary powers. Athol and Argyll at once urged the King to accept Morton's resignation, which he did.

On 12 March 1578 the King's 'acceptance of the government' was proclaimed in Edinburgh. Like his grandfather James v, he became the nominal ruler two years before his official majority; but, of course, the fact that he was still a child was an open invitation to men of ambition who aspired to rule. The next nine years witnessed a series of coups d'état, from which the King emerged 'un vieux jeune homme', as a French visitor described him, and an extremely subtle and disillusioned ruler.

Athol and Argyll did not remain long in control of the situation. Morton, despite his previous protestations, clearly considered that the

King was not yet 'ready and able for his own government'. He swiftly organized a counter-coup, and with the aid of the young Earl of Mar regained control of Stirling Castle and of the King's person. Athol and Argyll mustered an army, with the ostensible purpose of delivering the King from Morton's tyranny; and Morton, who had been an indomitable fighter all his life, prepared to do battle with them. A new English ambassador, Robert Bowes, offered to mediate, and with the assistance of two ministers managed to compose a dangerous situation.

In essence, Morton regained power, though he was not restored to the regency. A kind of coalition was formed, with Morton as First Lord of the Council, and Athol officially next in dignity. The King was still nominally ruling, and it appeared that he had taken a liking to Athol, to whom he turned for advice and encouragement.

In the spring of 1579 Athol died suddenly and, as in the instance of the Regent Mar, it was rumoured that he had been poisoned by Morton. For the next few months Morton dominated the political scene as completely as he had done during his regency, and the King endured relegation to the conditions of childhood with resentment, and awaited impatiently an occasion to rid himself of a man he had come to fear and detest.

During the summer of 1579 Morton occupied himself in destroying what remained of the influence of the Hamiltons. He invoked the Pacification of Perth, which had contained a general pardon for all who had fought against the King's party during the civil war, and claimed that the pardon did not include any who had been connected with the murder of the Regent Moray. Accordingly an act of forfeiture was passed against the Lords John and Claud Hamilton, both of whom fled the country. Subsequently all but one bearer of the name of Hamilton were banished from Edinburgh and from the court. These measures, together with the destruction of a number of castles belonging to the Hamilton kindred, may have given Morton the impression that he had secured his position. The fall of the Hamiltons, however, had other implications.

The place of the Hamiltons in the succession had arguably been taken by that of the Lennox Stuarts, whose position increased its strength through the forfeiture of Châtelherault's sons. After the death of Darnley's younger brother Lord Charles Stuart, in 1576, the heir of the House of Lennox was the next brother of the Regent

Lennox, Lord Robert Stuart, titular Bishop of Caithness, who was childless. The next in succession was the son of the Regent's younger brother Lord d'Aubigny, who had inherited the Aubigny possessions and settled in France. The fall of the Hamiltons and the prospects of the Lennox inheritance disposed d'Aubigny's son Esmé Stuart to visit Scotland, to secure his position in the line of succession, and his rights to the Lennox title. His arrival, in the autumn of 1579, had a transforming effect upon the life of James VI.

Esmé Stuart d'Aubigny was handsome and amiable, possessed of rare and powerful charm, and, since he was concerned with the future, intent upon securing the favour of the King. James, after years of having been bullied by Buchanan and fought over by his Regents and their rivals, was intoxicated by the experience of being treated like a King, with honour and reverence. His response was to love his kinsman with an intensity which astonished everyone, not least the object of his affections. At the height of the attachment, a year or two later, James was reported to be 'in such love with him as in the open sight of the people, oftentimes he will clasp him about the neck with his arms and kiss him'.

Before the end of 1579 James bestowed on Esmé Stuart the Abbey of Arbroath, one of the forfeited properties of the Hamiltons, and early the following year he persuaded Lord Robert Stuart, who had recently been granted the title of Earl of Lennox, to resign it again in Esmé's favour.

For the new Earl of Lennox the natural concomitant of supremacy in the King's favour was aspiration to supreme power. Morton was the only obstacle, and his removal was a service which the King would value. Morton had made many enemies, and there were many more who would not have taken action against him, but who were ready to stand by and watch him fall. His ruin was brought about with surprising ease, for which the best explanation is simply that time had run out for him. His erstwhile allies felt that the future belonged to the King, and, if only temporarily, to Lennox.

The instrument of Morton's ruin, selected for the task by Lennox, was a well-born soldier of fortune, Captain James Stewart, the younger son of Lord Ochiltree. On 31 December 1580 he accused Morton before the Privy Council of having been 'art and part' in the murder of Darnley. Upon accusation, Morton was imprisoned.

The Queen of England was prepared, within very narrow limits, to attempt to save her ally. She sent an ambassador to demand his release, or failing that to insist upon the assurance of a fair trial. Morton was tried, but the result was undoubtedly a foregone conclusion. Though Morton denied 'art and part', or participation, in Darnley's death, he was obliged to admit foreknowledge and concealment, which was considered a degree of guilt sufficient to be worthy of death. On 2 June 1581 Morton was publicly executed in Edinburgh, by a guillotine known as 'the Maiden' which he himself had introduced into Scotland as the common instrument of execution.

Esmé Stuart, as the prime mover in Morton's ruin, was rewarded with the Dukedom of Lennox, and Captain James Stewart, for his part in it, was created Earl of Arran. Stewart's grandmother had been Châtelherault's half-sister, which provided some sort of excuse for bestowing the title upon him; the insane Earl of Arran, however, was still alive, and he survived until 1609.

Lennox was now supreme, and he has been described by Archbishop Mathew as a 'pseudo-Regent'. Certainly his influence with the King was paramount, and as James began to participate in politics he cooperated with Lennox in a way that he would never have done with Morton. But Lennox, as a man scarcely acquainted with Scotland, and insufficiently provided with the necessary alliances, was unequipped to become a strong ruler. Furthermore he was a Catholic, and therefore an object of extreme suspicion to the Kirk. Even before Morton's death he had realized the danger of the situation, and in order to allay suspicion had permitted the King to convert him to Protestantism. Unfortunately the Kirk remained unconvinced of the genuineness of the conversion. Lennox, like Riccio, was suspected of being a Papal agent. He was also rumoured to be an emissary of the Catholic powers, commissioned to attempt the reinstatement of Mary, Queen of Scots.

These suspicions were insular and alarmist, for the Queen of Scots, in her post-Darnley disillusionment with the Lennox Stuarts, regarded the Duke of Lennox with the deepest disfavour. Her Guise relations in concert with the King of Spain at this period evolved a scheme for Mary's return to Scotland, and restoration as joint sovereign with her son. This scheme, known as 'the Association', completely lacked reality, and would have been very much against the interests of James and Lennox. Nevertheless, the mere fact that Lennox was visited by

Guisard and Spanish agents who hoped to win his co-operation was sufficient to cause a kind of anti-Catholic hysteria in the Kirk and among its more extreme supporters.

By the 1580s a *politique* approach to religion was not good enough for the Kirk. Lennox did his best to quieten his adversaries by signing in 1581 the *Negative Confession*, a document which condemned in detail many aspects of Catholic belief and practice. This effort was completely unavailing, and the following year his ascendancy was ended by an extreme Protestant coup d'état, led by William Ruthven, first Earl of Gowrie, who invited the King on a hunting expedition and detained him at Ruthven Castle, near Perth. Lennox was ordered to leave the country, and he died in France in 1583. At his death he declared himself a Protestant, and bequeathed the King his embalmed heart.

Lennox was the first of a long series of favourites, each of whom in turn dominated the King's emotional life and played a leading part in the political life of Scotland, and later of England. But, although this first attachment had an overtly homosexual element, it was also important to the King as a familial relationship. Lennox had several children by his French wife, and James made himself responsible for their welfare. The eldest son, Ludovic, was brought to Scotland in 1583, to inherit his father's honours and to be educated as the King's *protégé*.

In the meantime the King, as the victim of Gowrie's coup, which was known as the 'Raid of Ruthven', remained a grief-stricken and angry prisoner. However, he had an exact appreciation of the degree of blame which attached to the various participants in the coup. The Kirk, which had begun its long history of political interference by its enmity to Lennox, won the King's bitter resentment when the General Assembly passed an act registering its approval of the Raid of Ruthven. The Kirk was not over-nice in its choice of allies. Gowrie was the son of the old Lord Ruthven who had risen from his deathbed to take part in the murder of Riccio, and had also been a participant in it himself. His extreme Protestantism was political; it does not appear to have contained doctrinal or moral elements. James resolved to discipline the Kirk and to be revenged upon the Earl of Gowrie as soon as possible. Most of Gowrie's supporters in the Raid were not regarded as beyond forgiveness. They were the young Earl of Mar, Morton's nephew young Angus, the Earl of Glencairn and the Master of Glamis. The Earl of Bothwell, the nephew of Mary's third husband, was an ally of theirs who was destined to cause the King much future trouble.

The ascendancy of Gowrie was very brief. In July 1583 the King repeated the exploit of James V. He slipped away from his captors, who at the time were holding him at Falkland, and rode off with only two companions, one of whom was Sir James Melville who likened him to 'a bird flown out of a cage'. His destination was St Andrews, where he was joined by the Earls of Montrose, Rothes, Argyll, Huntly and Crawford, and by the recently created Earl of Arran, who was to become the last pseudo-Regent.

Sir James Melville described Arran as 'a scorner of all religion, presumptuous, ambitious, covetous, careless of the commonwealth, a despiser of the nobility, and of all honest men'. The King seems to have been attracted by his masterful self-assurance, but he was not a favourite for whom he felt a strong bond of affection or loyalty. However, his ascendancy allowed James the satisfaction of executing the Earl of Gowrie in 1584, and in the same year of passing the 'Black Acts' against the Kirk. In these acts, so named by the Kirk, James proclaimed himself head of both Church and State. He declared that under him the Kirk should be governed by Bishops, and that no assembly should be held without his permission. He forbade sermons against himself or in contempt of the proceedings of his council; there had been a great many of these during the ascendancy of Lennox. After the passing of the 'Black Acts', Andrew Melville and a number of the more intransigent ministers who supported him retired to England. This triumph over the Kirk was very transitory; it was merely the end of one round in a fight which was to last many years. At least the King had stated his intentions.

Arran had a taste for authority which led him to encourage the King to leave affairs of state in his hands and enjoy more leisure. During 1584, apart from spending a great deal of time in the hunting field, James produced his first book. He had begun to write poetry when he was fifteen, probably with the encouragement of Lennox, and had gathered around himself a group of court poets of whom the acknowledged leader was Alexander Montgomerie. During the next few years the court was the scene of much literary activity, in which James participated with enthusiasm. His first collection of poems was called *Essays of a Prentise in the Divine Art of Poesie*. It contained a brief sonnet sequence, translations by James from Lucan and the contemporary French poet Du Bartas, a long poem of lament for the exile and death of Lennox, and a treatise on Scottish verse. It was published in 1584, and James offered it to the public with some humility, requesting the 'good reader'

> *. . . when as thou does read*
> *These my first fruits, despise them not at all*
> *Who wots but these may able be indeed*
> *Of finer poems the beginning small.*

They were not the beginning of any great development as a poet. James had a very variable talent, but his verse is of interest for the sidelights it provides upon his thoughts and feelings.

His time of leisure was short-lived; for Arran, like his several predecessors, was not destined to a long ascendancy. The Earl of Gowrie's allies had fled to England after the King's escape to St Andrews. There they plotted the last in the series of coups d'état which had kept Scotland almost perpetually in turmoil since 1578. In the autumn of 1585, with a measure of English support, they returned to Scotland. On 2 November they appeared before Stirling in force, and Arran was driven from the court. The King appears to have taken his downfall with equanimity. The following year he was deprived of his earldom, and he lived in obscurity until 1595, when he was murdered by James Douglas of Parkhead, a nephew of Morton.

Possibly the King found Arran dispensable since he now had a more pliant favourite in Patrick, Master of Gray. Though Gray was personally favoured, and employed in diplomacy, neither he nor any other man was ever again permitted a total ascendancy while the King reigned in Scotland.

When James had escaped from the Earl of Gowrie in 1583 he had expressed his desire to 'draw his nobility to unity and concord and to be known to be a universal King'. The coup against Arran provided his first real opportunity to put this desire into effect. Concord, indeed, was far to seek, but James was at least successful in creating a workable coalition made up of what remained of the various factions which had held power in turn. The new administration included Angus, Mar and

the Master of Glamis, who became Treasurer, and their late opponents, Huntly, Crawford and Montrose. It also included John Maitland of Thirlestane, the younger brother of Mary's Secretary of State,
Maitland of Lethington. Thirlestane became Keeper of the Great Seal
in 1586, and Chancellor in 1587. He was a minister of the Crown
whose influence depended upon service to the King and not upon the
support of family alliances. His service was of the greatest benefit in
assisting the King to lift the Crown clear of faction and establish the
'universality' which he desired.

The great achievement of 1586 was the establishment of a formal
league with England. Preliminary negotiations had already taken place
during the ascendancy of Arran, when James had given Elizabeth a
solemn assurance that he would have nothing to do with 'the Association', and Elizabeth had proposed to reward him and secure his
future alliance with a yearly subsidy of £4,000. James would have
liked to improve the terms by inducing Elizabeth to recognize him as
her successor; Elizabeth, however, declined to grant James the recognition which she had refused to his mother. The best she would
promise was to do nothing that should derogate from his rights, unless
she were provoked by 'manifest ingratitude'. On these terms the league
was established.

The extent to which James had accepted Buchanan's view of his
mother is uncertain. He may not have wished to believe that she was,
as Buchanan had tried to teach him, an adulteress and a murderess, but
he would not have found it easy to forgive her favour to Riccio. A
King's privileges were not extended to a Queen. Furthermore, the
revocation of her abdication cast a shadow upon his sovereignty. As
long as the Queen of Scots was alive, the position of the King of Scots
was ambiguous. He inherited her claim to the English succession, but
while she lived, what was the relative validity of the two claims?
Elizabeth notoriously disliked to contemplate her own mortality; the
most disagreeable aspect of an unpleasing subject was the possibility
that she might predecease the Queen of Scots. That possibility, and the
political dangers which accompanied it, must have contained for the
King of Scots all the elements of a nightmare.

Only a few months after the conclusion of the league between
Scotland and England came the revelation of the complicity of the
Queen of Scots in the Babington conspiracy against Elizabeth's life.

Mary has been frequently blamed for her complicity, in tones which imply that she owed Elizabeth gratitude for her hospitality. Certainly, from Mary's viewpoint, where she had sought help and found imprisonment she did not owe gratitude. But unfortunately for her, she had lost touch with the realities of the outside world; the fragile and amateurish plot did not offer her the means to reverse her fortunes. Instead, it brought her to face trial for her life. On 12 November she was found guilty of conspiracy against the life of Elizabeth, and from then onwards Elizabeth was subject to increasing pressure from her ministers and her Parliament to condemn the Queen of Scots to death.

James was in an unenviable position. He had neither personal acquaintance with, nor affection for, his mother; her death would ease his political position in many ways. Yet decency and common humanity demanded that he should defend her life. He sent two ambassadors to Elizabeth, the Master of Gray and Sir Robert Melville, who were commissioned to protest against a death sentence. Gray at least was without illusions concerning the political background. On a previous mission to London, a few months before, he had said to Elizabeth, with reference to the Queen of Scots, 'Mortui non mordent [the dead do not bite]'. No doubt Elizabeth remembered. Besides, she was capable of appraising James's position with perfect exactitude.

With great reluctance, genuine reluctance since anything which threatened the sacrosanct nature of sovereignty was anathema to her, she signed the death warrant of Mary, Queen of Scots on 1 February 1587. Thereafter she refused to take any cognizance of the proceedings, leaving it to her Council to send the warrant and take responsibility for the execution. The Queen of Scots was executed at Fotheringay on 8 February, and Elizabeth wrote to James declaring that the execution had taken place without her knowledge and against her intentions.

To James the episode was profoundly distasteful and deeply disturbing. His conscience was not easy, and it probably afflicted him the more because his mother's death was so greatly to his advantage. His reply to Elizabeth's letter maintained his dignity as well as possible, and at the same time, without damaging diplomatic relations, did nothing to ease Elizabeth's conscience. 'Whereas ye purge yourself of yon unhappy fact [the execution],' he wrote, 'I dare not wrong you so far as not to judge honourably of your unspotted part therein, so I wish that your honourable behaviour in all times hereafter may fully persuade the whole world of the same.'

Hot-heads in Scotland talked wildly of revenge. But the Queen of England and the King of Scots understood each other, and the matter was closed. James continued to press for recognition as Elizabeth's successor, and Elizabeth continued to refuse.

The execution of Mary, Queen of Scots simplified for James the great problem of 1588: what position he should adopt in the face of Philip II's attack upon England. There was still a Catholic interest in Scotland, and certain Catholic or pro-Catholic noblemen, including Huntly, Lord Maxwell and Lord Claud Hamilton (who with his brother had been permitted to return to Scotland in 1585), were in favour of the Spanish invasion, which they envisaged as being accompanied by the King's conversion to Catholicism. James was aware of their intrigues, to which he gave discreet countenance, because, as Professor Donaldson puts it, he 'felt that his pro-Spanish nobles might offer a faint chance of survival should Spain defeat England'. His preference, however, was that the Armada should be repulsed. The defeat of Spain was in his best interests as well as those of Elizabeth, which might not have been altogether the case had his mother been still alive. Therefore, while holding his Catholic nobles as it were in reserve, he confirmed his alliance with Elizabeth, put his kingdom in a state of defence and awaited events. The outcome was the total destruction of Philip's great fleet by Elizabeth's seamen and by the storms which came to their assistance. A crisis of survival had been mercifully averted.

In the period of calm which followed, the King of Scots negotiated his marriage. It had been spoken of as early as 1582, and various prospective brides had been mentioned, including the King's cousin, Lady Arbella Stuart, the daughter of Lord Charles Stuart. The two most seriously considered, however, were Catherine of Navarre, the sister of the future Henri IV of France, who was a Calvinist, and Anne of Denmark, the daughter of King Frederick II, who was a Lutheran. Community of religion suggested the desirability of the French marriage, which was urged by Thirlestane. But long-established trade relations between Scotland and Denmark made a good case for the Danish marriage which might bring new commercial advantages. As for the Princesses themselves, Catherine of Navarre was eight years older than James and notoriously plain, while Anne of Denmark was eight years younger, and if not beautiful at least possessed of youthful freshness.

James finally chose Anne of Denmark, to whom he was married by proxy on 20 August 1589. A stormy September delayed Anne's passage to Scotland, and the following month James, delighted perhaps by an excuse to leave the intricacies of internal politics, voyaged to Denmark to bring her home. Like James v he allowed the pleasures of a foreign court to delay him over the winter. It was May Day 1590 when he returned with his bride to Leith.

Many portraits exist of Anne of Denmark, which show her first as a slender young girl and later as a statuesque but not unhandsome woman. In youth her fair skin and bright gold hair aroused general admiration. She had an agreeable disposition, a talent for friendship and an affection for animals. It was unfortunate that her intelligence in no way matched her husband's.

James had been taught by George Buchanan to hold women in contempt as indisputably the mental inferiors of men. Since his friendships and emotional attachments were always with men, he did not discover for himself that there were many exceptions to Buchanan's rule. It was a pity that when dynastic necessity forced a heterosexual relationship upon him he did not find an intelligent wife; had he done so she would have disabused him of Buchanan's error and might have been a great consolation to him.

As it was, the marriage was not unsatisfactory. Anne of Denmark produced an heir to the throne, Prince Henry, in 1594, a daughter, Elizabeth (the future Queen of Bohemia) in 1596, and a second son, Charles (the future Charles i), in 1600. Other children who were born to the King and Queen, the last in 1607, died in infancy. The relationship of James and his Queen was usually agreeable, sometimes toubled by domestic discord; it grew friendlier though more attenuated in their later years.

James vi had been seventeen when he was described as 'un vieux jeune homme', but the description would have suited him equally well throughout his twenties. He had a rather poor physique, but he was hardier than he looked, and though he lacked the stomach for martial sports, he was a tireless and a reckless horseman. When he was a child

James, like his mother, had fair red hair, which darkened as he grew older to blackish brown. The portraits of him painted during the later years of his reign in Scotland show a dark young man with a wary and disillusioned expression, and secretive, harassed eyes.

There was much to harass him, for the lull which had followed the defeat of the Armada, and permitted him to spend a winter in Denmark, was short-lived. He returned to a multitude of troubles, of which the most sensational was the affair of the North Berwick witches.

It appeared that the storms which had delayed the Queen in Denmark the previous year had not been ordinary autumnal storms but the work of witches determined to prevent the King's marriage. The witchcraft trials had been going on for some time before one of the accused confessed that the black magic rituals for which they were being tried had been undertaken at the behest of the Earl of Bothwell. When the King had put to sea himself the witches had bound live cats to portions of dead bodies which they had thrown into the sea to raise storms for his destruction. Equally ineffectively but even more treasonably, they had made a wax image of the King, which the members of the coven had passed from hand to hand reciting the incantation, 'This is King James the Sixth, ordained to be consumed at the instance of a nobleman, Francis, Earl of Bothwell.'

The nobleman in question was not only the nephew of Mary's third husband, he was also the son of one of the bastards of James v. When one of the witches confessed that they had attempted to compass the King's death 'that another might rule in his Majesty's place', it was obvious who that other was intended to be.

James was appalled and fascinated by the details of the witches' confessions. These confessions made it clear that the witches were not practising half-forgotten rituals of some pagan fertility cult. They were worshipping the Devil. In the intensely religious atmosphere of post-Reformation Scotland it was probably to be expected that some extreme forms of religious mania would arise. Satanic religion was perhaps the desperate resort of those who accepted the Calvinistic doctrine of predestination but were unable to apply to themselves the comforting conviction of assurance.

In the context of the times such people could not be seen as mentally disturbed; unless they were patently mad they were culpable for what they did. To James, who was a man of deep religious certainty, their religious practices were treason to God in exactly the same way as their magical practices were treason to himself. He conceived it his duty to prevent the mass of his subjects from being ensnared by the temptations of the Devil, and induced to worship him to their certain destruction. To this end he wrote a book, *Daemonologie*, which was published in 1597. The conclusion embodies the explanation which he had found for the outbreak of Satanism in Scotland: 'The consummation of the world, and our deliverance drawing near, makes Satan to rage the more in his instruments, knowing his kingdom to be so near an end.' Anxious as he was to preserve his subjects, he had a Christian conviction of Satan's inevitable defeat.

The smaller matter of the defeat of the Earl of Bothwell presented an immediate problem of the greatest difficulty. Bothwell's activities and aspirations were multifarious and unbalanced. His aspiration to the throne was an incorporeal dream. In the event of the King's death legitimate Hamiltons and Lennox Stuarts would have contended for it before an illegitimate offshoot of the Royal Stewarts would have been admitted. But the means by which Bothwell sought the King's death were indisputably treasonable. Nonetheless, despite the seriousness of the crimes alleged against him, it was impossible for the King to bring the Earl of Bothwell to justice: the traitor and Satanist was the champion of the Kirk.

The problem of Bothwell was complicated by the religio-political background. The Kirk had a use for Bothwell, the most unsavoury of its allies, to counterbalance the Catholic Earls upon whom, from the extreme Protestant viewpoint, the King looked with too much favour.

The King's extraordinary indulgence to them, especially to Huntly, had been revealed in February 1589, when a letter from Huntly to Philip II, expressing regret at the defeat of the Armada and promising support in the event of a future invasion, had been intercepted in England and made public. The King had been forced to make a show of disapproval, and Huntly had been briefly imprisoned. But James still did not wish to show himself as an overt enemy of Catholicism, in case he should require the support of English or continental Catholics to secure the English throne on Elizabeth's death. Huntly had been soon restored to his former degree of favour.

The King's attitude to him was ambivalent. Apart from his political reasons for treating Huntly's intrigues with leniency, the King had a fondness for him that was half emotional and half familial. Huntly was married to Lady Henriette Stuart, one of Esmé Stuart's daughters, which brought him into the circle of the King's family affection. However, the King's warmth of feeling and Huntly's political usefulness were both strained by two public scandals in 1592. The first was the murder of the 'Bonnie Earl of Moray' and the second was the affair of the 'Spanish Blanks'.

The 'Bonnie Earl' was James Stewart of Doune who had married the elder daughter of the Regent Moray and inherited the title in right of his wife. The Earls of Moray and Huntly had a long-standing feud, which dated from Mary, Queen of Scots's creating her half-brother Earl of Moray in defiance of the fourth Earl of Huntly's expectations. The Gordons had not regarded the Battle of Corrichie as decisive. Early in 1592 James announced his intention of settling the feud, and Moray came to his house of Donibristle, on the north shore of the Forth near Aberdour, in readiness to meet his enemy. On the night of 7 February Huntly crossed the Forth, set fire to Donibristle and murdered Moray as he fled from the blazing ruins. The savage incident was immortalized in the well-known ballad *The Bonnie Earl o' Moray*:

> *Ye Highlands and ye Lawlands*
> *Oh where have you been?*
> *They hae slain the Earl o' Moray*
> *And laid him on the green.*

There was a great outcry against Huntly, and much murmuring against the King, who, it was thought, since he favoured Huntly, might well have intended Moray's death rather than the ending of the feud. The ballad, however, exculpated the King, imputing to him the words

> *Now wae be to you, Huntly!*
> *And wherefore did ye sae?*
> *I bade you bring him wi' you,*
> *But forbade you him to slay.*

The uproar over the 'Spanish Blanks' followed at the end of the year. It was once again a question of intercepted letters, or rather, blank pieces of paper. The blank sheets, however, bore the signatures

248

of the Earls of Huntly, Errol and Angus (another Angus, the tenth earl, who was a Catholic), and were on their way to Philip II in the hands of one George Kerr. The unfortunate Kerr confessed under torture that there was indeed a new Spanish invasion plot, the details of which were to be outlined on the blanks in due course.

Again James showed a degree of leniency which seriously alarmed the Kirk. He made the gesture of marching on Aberdeen in force, but when Huntly and his allies withdrew into Caithness he did not pursue them. In the summer of 1593 the Parliament which was expected to pass an act of forfeiture against them did not do so; instead, the next Parliament in November passed an act of oblivion for their misdeeds, on condition of their formally submitting to the Kirk.

Bothwell, in the meantime, had been pursuing a wild course of action, apparently with the intention of terrorizing the King into restoring him to favour and admitting him to power. He had a great contempt for Thirlestane whom he called the 'puddock stool of a night'. In the spring of 1591, after the revelation of his patronage of the North Berwick witches, Bothwell had been arrested and imprisoned. In June he had escaped, and been 'put to the horn', or declared an outlaw. Thereafter began his career of terrorism. In December 1591 he carried out a night attack on Holyroodhouse, but escaped before he could be rearrested. In June 1592, after he had been forfeited by Parliament, he made an attack on Falkland, and again escaped. In July 1593 the Parliament which took no action against Huntly confirmed the forfeiture of Bothwell, and immediately after he forced his way into Holyroodhouse again. On this occasion he entered the King's bedchamber carrying a naked sword which he laid at the King's feet. He may have had some idea of demanding the King's favour, and illustrating that he could use force but would not; but his mental processes were clearly deranged, and the King disliked symbolic actions which involved the use of naked swords.

Repetition of his efforts, however, diminished Bothwell's power of terror. The King could be frightened, but not as frightened as his detractors liked to believe; fear did not cause him to alter his policy.

The more extreme members of the Kirk countenanced Bothwell's wild escapades, on the grounds that he was a 'sanctified scourge' who might cause the King to 'turn to God', in other words, cease from favouring the Catholic Earls. James did indeed woo the Kirk with a more conciliatory ecclesiastical policy. The 'Golden Act' of 1592 permitted the assemblies which the 'Black Acts' had forbidden. The Kirk was at last officially permitted to develop its Presbyterian organization.

In 1594 the interests of the King and the Kirk temporarily coalesced. In the spring Bothwell carried out a last futile attack upon the King, and when it failed he took refuge with Huntly. He had claims of kinship upon Huntly. His uncle the previous Earl of Bothwell, before his marriage to the Queen of Scots, had been married to Huntly's aunt, Lady Jean Gordon. This link between the leader of the Catholic Earls and the Kirk's 'sanctified scourge' exhausted the King's patience with Huntly and turned the Kirk against Bothwell.

In the autumn of 1594 the King mustered an army and marched into Aberdeenshire, taking Andrew Melville with him. Melville, of course, regarded Huntly as the principle enemy, whereas in the King's view that rôle belonged to Bothwell. A skirmish took place in Glenlivet between Huntly's forces and the advance guard of the King's army led by the young Earl of Argyll. Huntly had the best of it, but the King's army continued to advance. The King appeared before Huntly's Castle of Strathbogie, which he threatened to blow up unless Bothwell were handed over to justice.

Apparently, in the face of a genuine threat, Huntly was not prepared to resist the King, who had always shown him remarkable indulgence. He let Bothwell escape, and then himself retired abroad. Bothwell fled first to Caithness, and in the spring of 1595 he too left the country. The difference was that Huntly returned to Scotland in 1596 and was received back into favour by the King, who insisted that he should make at least a formal gesture of conversion to Protestantism for the satisfaction of the Kirk; whereas Bothwell never returned, the rest of his life was spent as a wandering exile, and he died in Naples in 1624.

The King had emerged victorious from an intricate conflict; now a conflict of a different kind awaited him, with the Kirk. The enmity aroused by the 'Black Acts' and the reconciliatory effect of the 'Golden Act' might suggest that the King and the Kirk were quarrelling merely over ecclesiastical polity. As far as that polity was concerned, while Morton, Lennox, Gowrie and Arran had come and gone, the Kirk had quietly continued establishing its Kirk Sessions and the rest of its

Presbyterian organization, and holding its General Assembly. There had been several confrontations between the Kirk and the government on the subject of episcopacy, but Bishops also had continued to exist. The 'Black Acts' had strongly asserted the King's wishes, the 'Golden Act' had conceded a part of what the Kirk desired. The word 'Presbytery' had become something of a shibboleth, and the fact that the 'Golden Act' authorized Presbyterian organization gave the Kirk a deep satisfaction which was not really warranted by the limited concessions which the act contained.

To Andrew Melville, however, the conflict between the King and the Kirk (at least the Kirk that Melville envisaged) was something much more profound than a disagreement over ecclesiastical polity. It was a religious conflict, and Melville's God was not a God of compromise. Melville sought nothing less than theocracy, and he summed up his own religio-political views in the well-known words which he addressed to the King: 'Sir, I must tell you, there are two Kings and two Kingdoms in Scotland. There is Christ Jesus the King, and his Kingdom the Kirk; whose subject King James the Sixth is, and of whose Kingdom not a King, nor a lord, nor a head, but a member.'

Few men have ever summed up their beliefs so succinctly. He made it perfectly clear that the Melvillian theocracy would have meant the supremacy of the Kirk over the state and of the ministry over the King.

James held his own belief equally strongly. He had had his views on kingship tempered by resistance to Buchanan years before. He did not, indeed, see Kings as other than the servants of God, but whereas to Melville a King was 'God's sillie vassal' (i.e. God's simple servant), to James a King was God's lieutenant. There was no question of two kingdoms; Kirk and State should be alike subject to the King.

It was as a question of ecclesiastical polity that the conflict was fought out, for Melville proposed to use the General Assembly as the instrument of his theocracy, and the King proposed to use Bishops as the instruments of monarchical supremacy. In the middle 1590s it might have appeared that Melville possessed the advantage, for the General Assembly was an admirable instrument of opposition to the government, and episcopacy was in an extremely enfeebled condition. The King, however, was in a stronger position than appeared, for he had certain undisputed powers over the General Assembly itself, which he used most adroitly.

The 'Golden Act' was not so golden from Melville's viewpoint, in that it gave the King the power of deciding where the General Assembly should meet. Melville's partisans were mostly in the southeast of the country. If the Assembly met in Edinburgh or St Andrews Melville could be confident of dominating it; if the King decided that it should meet in Aberdeen, Montrose or Perth, ministers from the north, to whom Melville's programme appeared too radical, would be in a majority. The King also exhibited his power over the Assembly by using his prerogative of arranging the date of its meeting to suit his own policy.

In December 1596 James was able to take advantage of a riot which occurred in Edinburgh as a means of extending his influence over the Kirk. An inflammatory sermon against the King and certain of his counsellors led to a demonstration outside the Tolbooth, where, when the sermon concluded, the King was with the Lords of Session. When order had been restored, the King warded the ministers of Edinburgh in the castle and levied a fine of 20,000 marks on the city as a punishment for disorder. He used the riot as an occasion to insist that ministers should not be appointed in Edinburgh and other leading towns without his consent.

The General Assembly of 1597 showed a new docility by appointing a commission to advise the King on ecclesiastical affairs, a very different state of being from dictating to the King as Melville would have wished. The commission proved to be greatly to the King's advantage, as yet another means by which he could exert his influence upon the Kirk.

His next step was to break down the division between Kirk and State, General Assembly and Parliament, by securing the representation of the Kirk in Parliament. Such representation would offer benefits, for the enactments of the General Assembly did not have the force of law; representation in Parliament could obtain the Kirk beneficial legislation. Traditionally, the clerical estate in Parliament consisted of the Bishops; in 1597 James won the Kirk's agreement that he should appoint ministers to vacant sees and that they should sit in Parliament. In 1600 three 'Parliamentary Bishops' were appointed, to Aberdeen, Ross and Caithness, though their status within the Kirk was still only that of ministers. Thus, as David Calderwood put it, 'the Trojan horse, the Episcopacy was brought in busked and covered with caveats, that the danger and deformity might not be seen'. Ten years later the General Assembly, slowly and patiently tamed, accepted episcopacy as officially part of the Kirk. Bishops, appointed by the King, were servants of the state as well as ecclesiastical dignitaries. Their acceptance by the General Assembly brought the Kirk within the structure of the State, and precluded Melvillian theocracy.

While James repudiated the concept of Kirk and State as two 'Kingdoms', he accepted ecclesiastical and secular government as twin areas of responsibility. In each area he sought to create and employ a corpus of able and efficient servants who were answerable only to himself.

Maitland of Thirlestane died in 1595. The King had been very young when Thirlestane joined the coalition formed after the fall of Arran. He had been out of office for a time, but for the most part of a decade he had been the King's chief minister, and had perhaps regarded himself as the King's mentor as much as his minister. James lamented his death with a sonnet – 'How rare a man leaves here his earthly part' – which was carved upon his tomb. Nonetheless James showed a certain relief at being liberated from Thirlestane's didacticism. He declared it his intention to employ in future only such ministers 'as he could correct and were hangable'. He chose them sufficiently well never to need to hang any of them.

The group of men customarily regarded as Thirlestane's successors were eight in number, hence their group nickname 'the Octavians'. They included Walter Stewart, prior of Blantyre, who had shared the King's education; Sir Peter Young, his erstwhile tutor, now knighted; Alexander Seton, Lord Urquhart, President of the Court of Session, and later Earl of Dunfermline and Chancellor; and Thomas Hamilton, whom the King called familiarly 'Tam o' the Cowgate', after the part of Edinburgh in which he lived. He was distantly related to the royally-connected Hamiltons on his father's side; his mother came from the Edinburgh merchant family of Heriot. He was a great Crown servant of a new kind; assuredly hangable, but invaluable. The other Octavians were of similar background; well connected but dependent upon the King.

Initially they were appointed as a commission to put the King's finances in order. The commission itself was short-lived and ineffective, but the individuals continued to hold public office or to serve the King personally. None of them was a favourite. Alexander Lindsay, Lord Spynie, had the reputation of 'the King's best loved minion', but he had little influence in politics. During the 1590s James was less amenable to the influence of a single individual than at any other time in his life. During his adolescence and early manhood Lennox and Arran had been all-powerful. The influence of the Master of Gray had been brief; he was perhaps too closely connected with the death of Mary, Queen of Scots for the King to take pleasure in his presence after it. Huntly, as part-favourite, part-kinsman, had seemed at least to his enemies alarmingly powerful. After James had become King of England he would submit to the influence of Somerset and ultimately to the complete domination of Buckingham. But during the last years of his reign in Scotland he allowed supreme power to no-one but himself.

These last years witnessed a decline in violence, and a remarkable increase in respect for the law. The King, with his detestation of violence, had a fervent personal desire to make his subjects live at peace with one another. The inherited vendetta could present an almost indissoluble problem, and even the would-be peacemaker did not always escape without blame, as the affair of the 'Bonnie Earl of Moray' had illustrated. But slowly James persuaded his nobility to settle quarrels by the law instead of perpetuating them in blood feuds.

To improve the quality of justice was a problem for which James was aware there was no easy solution. The problem was partly financial; it went back to the venal manner in which James v had handled the foundation of the College of Justice. The royal judges were still underpaid or even unpaid. The local courts which existed under heritable jurisdictions were not impartial; James considered them indeed 'the greatest hinderance to the execution of our laws'. He could think of no remedy but gradually to eliminate them as occasion offered, and 'dispone them never heritably again'.

In the Highlands he tried to break away from the dangerous policy of building up the power of one family or clan as a means of controlling its neighbours. He sought instead to make the chiefs answerable for the good behaviour of their followers. In the Isles and in Orkney he employed Bishops Andrew Knox and James Law respectively as the instruments of royal authority. The Borders witnessed some violent incidents during the last years of the reign in Scotland; after 1603 they ceased ineluctably to be a problem area. After his accession to the English throne James wished them to be regarded as the 'Middle Shires' of his united kingdom, but they never have been.

His achievement in improving the condition of his native country was summed up in a eulogy addressed to him by its Chancellor in 1617:

'I show that the blessings of justice and peace, and the fruits arising thereof, did so oblige every one of us as nothing in our power could equal it; desiring that it might be remembered, that whereas the Islanders oppressed the Highlandmen, the Highlanders tyrannized over their lowland neighbours . . . the Borderers triumphed in the impunity of their violences to the ports of Edinburgh; that treasons, murders, burnings, thefts . . . and barbarities of all sorts were exerced in all parts of the country . . . Edinburgh being the ordinary place of butcherly revenge, and daily fights; . . . noblemen, barons, gentlemen, and people of all sorts being slaughtered, as it were, in public and uncontrollable hostilities . . . [these] and all other abominations, which settled by inveterate custom and impunity, appeared to be of desperate remedy, had been so repressed, punished and abolished by your Majesty's wisdom, care, power and expenses, as no other nation in earth could now compare with our prosperities. . . .'

Even if the contrast were exaggerated to enhance the compliment, the King's achievement was still great enough to deserve eulogy.

Perhaps it was not surprising that as the sixteenth century approached its end the King felt a certain satisfaction in what he had done; felt, indeed, that he had the measure of his people and had learnt to rule them for their betterment. He decided to write a book which would crystallize his experience for the benefit of his son Prince Henry. The book was *Basilikon Doron* (i.e. The Kingly Gift). He dedicated it to the Prince with a sonnet which is well known, but worth quoting because it perfectly summarizes the King's view of kingship:

God gives not Kings the style of Gods in vain
For on his throne his sceptre to they sway,
And as their subjects ought them to obey

So Kings should fear and serve their God again.
If then ye would enjoy a happy reign
Observe the statutes of your heavenly King,
And from his Law make all your laws to spring,
Since his lieutenant here ye should remain.
Reward the just, be steadfast true and plain;
Repress the proud, maintaining aye the right,
Walk always so as ever in his sight
Who guards the godly, plaguing the profane.
And so ye shall in princely virtues shine
Resembling right your mighty King Divine.

James stressed upon Prince Henry his duty 'to know and love God, whom-to ye have a double obligation; first, for that he made you a man; and next, for that he made you a little God to sit on his throne and rule over other men'.

He recommended his son to remember that Parliaments 'have been ordained for making of laws . . . abuse not their institution in holding them for any man's particulars'. In other words, they should be used for legislation, and not for acts of forfeiture against individuals; this was in essence a recommendation of his own authoritative pursuit of a *via media*, and the avoidance of partisan measures.

On the subject of creating respect for the royal authority, he observed, 'Whon ye have by the severities of justice once settled your countries, and made them know that ye can strike, then may ye thereafter all the days of your life mix justice with mercy, punishing or sparing, as ye shall find the crime to have been wilfully or rashly committed, and according to the by-past behaviour of the committer.'

To this eminently practical advice he added a list of 'horrible crimes that ye are bound in conscience never to forgive': witchcraft, wilful murder, incest, sodomy, poisoning and false witness. The King's biographers seldom fail to comment with surprise that considering the nature of his own private life he classed sodomy as an unforgivable crime. Presumably he felt that there was an essential distinction between permissible and impermissible acts. However, he was capable of giving counsels of perfection which he clearly did not carry out: 'Let not your Chamber be throng and common in the time of your rest, as well for comeliness as for eschewing of carrying reports out of the same . . . but behave yourself so in your greatest secrets as ye need not be ashamed, suppose they were all proclaimed at the Mercat Cross.'

Whether or not James practised all that he preached, most of his recommendations were based on practical commonsense. His comments on various classes of his subjects were shrewd and humorous. The nobility, he observed, have 'a feckless, arrogant conceit of their greatness and power', and a senseless pleasure in feuding: 'They bang it out bravely, he and all his kin against him and all his.' Of the merchants he wrote: 'They transport from us all things necessary; bringing back sometimes unnecessary things, and at other times nothing at all. They buy for us the worst wares, and sell them at the dearest prices'; of the craftsmen: '[They] think we should be content with their work, how bad and dear soever it be: and if they in anything be controlled, up goeth the Blue Blanket' (the craftsmen's banner, initially the citizen's banner, for the origin of which see chapter five).

Basilikon Doron was first published in a limited edition for the King's intimates; it became an international best-seller upon the accession of James to the English throne.

Before that peaceful event, the good order which James had imposed upon Scotland was disturbed by a violent occurrence, the inexplicable 'Gowrie Conspiracy' of 1600.

On 4 August of that year the King visited Gowrie House in Perth, at the invitation of the two sons of that Earl of Gowrie who had been executed in 1584. Apparently the King was lured to Perth by a story of a man who had been found about to bury a hoard of gold coins; the implication possibly was that he would be presented with the treasure. Despite certain reservations concerning the Ruthven family which were the natural consequence of the 'Raid of Ruthven', James allowed himself to be escorted upstairs alone by the younger of Gowrie's sons, ostensibly to interview the would-be interrer of the treasure; and, on his own account, he realized that he was about to be murdered as an act of revenge for the execution of the young man's father. He shouted for help, and his rescuers killed both the Ruthven brothers; consequently, the King's version of the story was the only one preserved for posterity. Whether the King was saved from a regicidal conspiracy or whether the Ruthven brothers were the chance victims of the King's nervous terrors remains a mystery.

This alarm was parenthetical to James's interests at the opening of the seventeenth century; uppermost in his mind was the question of the English succession. Throughout his reign, but especially since the execution of his mother, the hope of succeeding Elizabeth had underlain all his thought. To secure his rights as far as he was able, and to ensure that, if they were not acknowledged by Elizabeth, the inheritance was not snatched from him at her death, became almost an obsession with him.

If James VI and his mother had had no common interest during her lifetime, they had the same ambition. Mary's insistence upon her claim had been an embarrassment to her son while she lived; after her death, her indomitable assertion of it proved a great asset to him. He inherited her insistence upon hereditary right. His anxiety arose from the fact that Henry VIII had made a will excluding the descendants of Margaret Tudor from the succession, and adopting the descendants of his younger sister Mary, who had been married first to Louis XII of France, and then to Charles Brandon, Duke of Suffolk. The first marriage had been childless; the descendants of the second were represented by Edward Seymour, Lord Beauchamp and by the daughters of the Earl of Derby. (The claim of the Lady Arbella Stuart was, of course, inferior to that of James in the same line.)

The power of a dead man, even of a King, to impose his will upon posterity is notoriously weak. The will of Henry VIII could not make obscure members of the English nobility preferable to a King of proved ability, whose accession would unite two kingdoms.

At the beginning of the seventeenth century the long reign of Elizabeth was approaching its end. While James had survived whatever threat the 'Gowrie Conspiracy' implied, Elizabeth had triumphed over the attempted coup of her presumptuous favourite the Earl of Essex. James had not neglected to cultivate Essex in the days of his power. After his execution the most powerful man in England was Sir Robert Cecil, the son of Elizabeth's chief minister, Lord Burghley. Cecil, watching the old Queen's decline, in his turn cautiously began to cultivate the King of Scots. He took it upon himself circumlocutively to assure the King that the presiding interests in England would not permit a succession dispute to arise, and therefore, 'We do neither presume to indent with you for future favours . . . because we think it not ingenious to recommend to Honour itself the things which Honour requireth. With which conclusion,' Cecil wrote meaningfully, 'I humbly kiss your royal hands.' Thereafter it behoved James only to wait.

In that year of reassurance, 1601, the English poet and diplomat Sir Henry Wotton visited Scotland, and recorded his impressions of the King that Scotland knew and England waited to know.

> 'The King [he wrote], though born in 1566, does not appear to be more than twenty-eight years old. He is of medium stature and of robust constitution; his shoulders are broad but the rest of his person from the shoulders downward is rather slender. In his eyes and in his outward appearance there is a natural kindliness bordering on modesty. He is fond of literary discourse, especially of theology, and is a great lover of witty conceits. His speech is learned and even eloquent. In imitation of his grandfather, James V, he wears his hair cut short. About food and clothing he is quite indifferent. He is patient in the work of government, makes no decision without obtaining good counsel, and is said to be one of the most secret princes of the world. . . .'

Such was his reputation when the fulfilment of his ambitions was granted at last.

On 24 March 1603 Elizabeth died. Whether she acknowledged as her heir 'our cousin of Scotland', whether she made a sign of assent when asked to name him, or whether she maintained her silence to the last, is uncertain. Cecil, however, kept his promise. James VI of Scotland was proclaimed Elizabeth's successor, 'now become also our only lawful, lineal and rightful liege lord, James the First, King of England'. That 'augmentation', he once perceptively declared, would be one of 'cares and heavy burdens'; but he made haste to embrace it, taking a public farewell of his subjects on 3 April, and on 5 April beginning his southward journey into England.

When he left his native kingdom James promised to return to it frequently; but that promise he did not keep, for he returned only once, in 1617. His achievement as King of Scots had been most creditable; as King of England it was very much less so. It is impossible to avoid the impression that the fulfilment of his ambitions had been to gain England, and that he did not exert himself comparably to govern it. Possibly he had spent himself on his Herculean labours in Scotland and at the age of thirty-seven was already tiring; possibly, despite his remark on the subject of the 'augmentation', he regarded England as the reward of his labours and not as a new and separate challenge.

Whatever the reason, although the history of his reign in England is not a tale of unmitigated failure, it is a tale of promise unfulfilled and ultimately of discreditable decline. The final impression, caused by the deterioration of his health, appearance and intellectual powers during the last years of his life, and his surrender to the domination of his last favourite, the infinitely venal and incompetent Buckingham, all but engulfed the memory of his successful early years and his admirable record as the last King of a separate kingdom of Scotland.

James I of England neither forgot nor neglected Scotland, but his non-residence was a disservice to his country, the more so in that it was imitated by his successors to whom Scotland began to seem but an appanage of their larger domain. At first, indeed, it seemed a just and wonderful reward, that after the indomitable defence of their country against English domination that the Stewart Kings had so long sustained, one of them should become at last the 'lawful, lineal and rightful' King of England. But in the course of the next century it began to appear that the prophecy of Henry VII had been fulfilled: 'It ever happens that the less becomes subservient to the greater, the accession will be that of Scotland to England . . . as a rivulet to a fountain.'

The Union of Crowns under James VI and I was a partial incorporation of the two kingdoms; the Union of Parliaments just over a century later was intended to complete the process. Whether it was beneficial or detrimental to Scotland has been a matter of controversy ever since. Sir John Clerk of Penicuik, at the time of the Union of Parliaments, in a way presented both views. He pleaded the desirability of a complete incorporation, on the grounds that since the process had been partly carried out there was little point in not completing it. Yet at the same time he presented the opposing view, when he referred to the Union of Crowns as 'the only source and spring of our misfortunes, for thereby, the seat of our Kings being removed from us, we are deprived of the golden influences which attend the Court of Princes'.

Appendix: Translations of Scottish Texts

(p. 96)
One thing more amazes all good men: when the Great Council, with your own consent, orders that strict justice shall spare nobody, only a short time afterwards you change your mind, and immediately you send a letter commanding the contrary, ordering that no more be said of your previous wishes. And at that everyone says your favour has been bought.

(p. 101)
A mournful season and a sombre piece of writing match each other and should go together. So it was when I began to write this tragedy. The weather was bitter. It was mid-Lent, when Aries sends down showers of hail from the north, and I could scarcely protect myself from the cold. . . . I mended the fire and wrapped myself up, and took a drink to cheer my spirits and keep out the cold. Then, to shorten the winter night I left all other occupations and took up a book, written by the worthy and glorious poet Chaucer, about fair Cressida and worthy Troilus.

(p. 141)
Sire, you have many servants, and a great variety of court officials. You have churchmen, courtiers and skilled craftsmen, and doctors of law and medicine; you have seers, rhetoricians and philosophers, astrologers, artists and orators; you have men-at-arms, valiant knights, and many other such worthy people; you have musicians, minstrels and merry singers, horsemen, *cawandaris* [word of unknown meaning] and dancers; you have carvers and carpenters and men to mint your coins; you have builders of boats both large and small, masons laying [stone] on the land and shipwrights hewing [timber] on the shore; you have glaziers, goldsmiths and jewellers, printers, painters and apothecaries.

(p. 143)

Damian attempted to make the Quintessence [which, it was believed, would transmute base metals into gold] and failed, and, when he saw that his efforts were futile, he made himself some plumage and announced that he was going to fly to Turkey. But when he took to the air all the birds that saw him wondered what he could be. All the time the pigeons tugged at him, the rooks tore at him, the ravens dragged at him and the hooded crows pulled out his hair. The skies were no place for him. He cast off his shining plumage, shook himself free of it, and fell into a marsh, up to the eyes in mud.

Books for Further Reading

1 CHRONICLES, EARLY HISTORIES AND MEMOIRS MENTIONED OR QUOTED IN THIS BOOK

The Agricola and the Germania, Tacitus, trans. H. Mattingly, revised S. A. Handford (Penguin Books, 1970).

The Bruce, John Barbour, trans. and ed. A. A. H. Douglas (Maclellan, 1964).

The Original Chronicle of Andrew of Wyntoun, ed. F. J. Amours (Scottish Text Society, 1903–14).

The Chronicles of Scotland, Hector Boece, trans. John Bellenden, 1531, ed. Edith C. Batho and H. Winifred Husbands (Scottish Text Society, 1905).

Historie and Cronicles of Scotland, 1437–1575, Robert Lindsay of Pitscottie, ed. Aeneas J. G. Mackay (Scottish Text Society, 1899–1911).

History of Scotland, 1437–1561, John Lesley, ed. Thomas Thomson (Bannatyne Club, c. 1918).

History of the Reformation in Scotland, John Knox (Wodrow Society, c. 1833).

History of the Kirk of Scotland, 1524–1625, David Calderwood (Wodrow Society, 1678).

History of Scotland, George Buchanan. Anon. trans. (Edinburgh, 1752).

The Tyrannous Reign of Mary Stewart, W. A. Gatherer (a translation of the portion of Buchanan's *Rerum Scoticarum Historia* which concerns Mary, Queen of Scots) (Nelson, 1958).

Book of the Ladies: Illustrious Dames, Pierre de Bourdeille, Abbé de Brantôme, trans. Catherine Prescott Wormley (Heinemann, 1899).

Historical Memoirs of the Reign of Mary Queen of Scots and of King James VI, Lord Herries (Abbotsford Club, 1830).

Memoirs of his Own Life, Sir James Melville of Halhill (Chapman and Dodd, Abbey Classics, 1922).

The Memoirs of Sir James Melville of Halhill, ed. Gordon Donaldson (Folio Society, 1969).

History of Scotland, William Drummond of Hawthornden (London, 1655).

2 STEWART WRITINGS

The Kingis Quair, James I, ed. Mackay Mackenzie (Faber and Faber, 1939).

Queen Mary's Book (Mary, Queen of Scots), Mrs P. Stewart-Mackenzie Arbuthnot (Bell, 1907).

The Silver Casket: *being love-letters and love-poems attributed to Mary Stuart, Queen of Scots . . .*, introd. and trans. Clifford Bax (Home and Van Thal, 1946).

The Poems of James VI of Scotland, ed. J. Craigie (Scottish Text Society, 1944).

Basilikon Doron, James VI, ed. J. Craigie (Scottish Text Society, 1944).

Monarchs and the Muse: Poems by Monarchs and Princes of England, Scotland and Wales, ed. Sally Purcell (Carcanet Press, 1972).

3 SELECTIONS OF CONTEMPORARY SOURCE MATERIAL

A Source Book of Scottish History, W. Croft Dickinson, Gordon Donaldson, Isabel Milne (Nelson, 1953).

Scottish Historical Documents, Gordon Donaldson (Scottish Academic Press, 1970).

Scottish Pageant, Agnes Mure Mackenzie (Oliver and Boyd, vols I and II, 1946 and 1948).

4 SCOTTISH POETRY

A Choice of Scottish Verse, 1470–1570, ed. John and Winifred MacQueen (Faber and Faber, 1972).

Late Medieval Scots Poetry, ed. Tom Scott (Heinemann, 1967).

Ballattis of Luve: the Scottish Courtly Love Lyric, 1400–1570, ed. John MacQueen (Edinburgh University Press, 1970).

Oxford Book of Scottish Verse, ed. John MacQueen and Tom Scott (Oxford University Press, 1966).
Oxford Book of Ballads, ed. Sir A. Quiller-Couch (Oxford University Press, 1910).

5 HISTORIES OF THE STEWARTS AND OF SCOTLAND

Scottish Kings, Gordon Donaldson (Batsford, 1967).
The Royal Stewarts, T. F. Henderson (Blackwood, 1914).
The Rise of the Stewarts, Agnes Mure Mackenzie (Macclehose, 1935).
Scotland from the Earliest Times to 1603, W. Croft Dickinson (Nelson, 1961).
Scotland: James V to James VII, Gordon Donaldson (The Edinburgh History of Scotland, Vol. III, 1965).
A Short History of Scotland, P. Hume Brown, new ed. H. W. Meikle (Oliver and Boyd, reprint 1961).
History of Scotland, Andrew Lang (4 vols, 3rd ed., Blackwood, 1903–7).
Scotland the Nation, Rosaline Masson (Nelson, 1934).
A History of Scotland, Rosalind Mitchison (Methuen, 1970).
The Scottish Nation, ed. Gordon Menzies (BBC Publications, 1972).

6 BIOGRAPHIES

James I, King of Scots, E. W. M. Balfour Melville (Methuen, 1936).
No full-length biography of either James II or James III has yet been written; much information about both of them can be found in Annie I. Dunlop's *The Life and Times of James Kennedy, Bishop of St Andrews* (Oliver and Boyd, 1950).
King James IV of Scotland, R. L. Mackie (Oliver and Boyd, 1958).
James V, King of Scots, Caroline Bingham (Collins, 1971).
The Sisters of Henry VIII, Hester W. Chapman (for biography of Margaret Tudor) (Jonathan Cape, 1969).
Lives of the Queens of Scotland, Agnes Strickland (Blackwood, 1850–8).
Mary, Queen of Scots, Antonia Fraser (Weidenfeld and Nicolson, 1969).

The Enigma of Mary Stuart, Ian B. Cowan (Gollancz, 1971). (This is not a biography, but a study of biographical writing on Mary, and of the fluctuations of her reputation.)

The Making of a King: the Early Years of James VI and I, Caroline Bingham (Collins, 1968).

King James VI and I, D. H. Willson (Jonathan Cape, 1956).

James I (i.e. James VI and I), David Mathew (Eyre and Spottiswoode, 1967).

1. THE ROYAL HOUSE OF SCOTLAND

showing the conflicting claims of Balliol and Bruce

DAVID I, KING OF SCOTS
1124–53

|
Henry

MALCOLM IV   WILLIAM   David, Earl of Huntingdon
['the Maiden']   ['the Lion']   d. 1219
1153–65   1165–1214

ALEXANDER II
1214–49

ALEXANDER III   Margaret   Isabella
1249–86   m.   m.
                       Lord of Galloway   Lord of
                       | Annandale
                       Devorgilla
                       m.   Robert the Bruce
Margaret   m. 1   John Balliol
[Sister of Edward I,   Robert the Bruce
King of England]   JOHN BALLIOL
                                                   ROBERT I
Yolande de Dreux   ['the Bruce']
m. 2
d.s.p.   Walter 'the Stewart' m. Marjey

Erik II,   m. Margaret   ROBERT II
King of Norway   →

Margaret
['the Maid of Norway']
d. 1290

11. EARLY STEWARTS

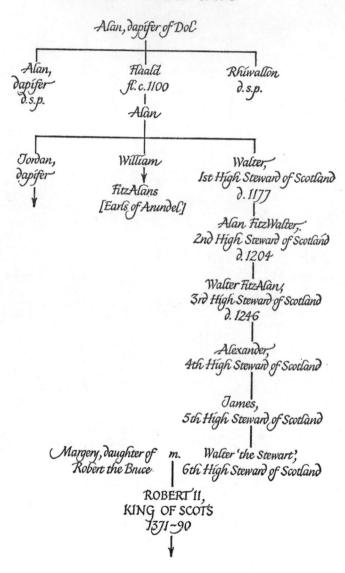

Alan, *dapifer of Dol*

Alan, *dapifer* d.s.p. — Flaald *fl. c. 1100* — Rhuwallon *d.s.p.*

Alan

Jordan, *dapifer* — William — Walter, 1st High Steward of Scotland *d. 1177*

FitzAlans [Earls of Arundel]

Alan FitzWalter, 2nd High Steward of Scotland *d. 1204*

Walter FitzAlan, 3rd High Steward of Scotland *d. 1246*

Alexander, 4th High Steward of Scotland

James, 5th High Steward of Scotland

Margery, daughter of Robert the Bruce   *m.*   Walter 'the Stewart', 6th High Steward of Scotland

ROBERT II, KING OF SCOTS 1371–90

III. DESCENDANTS OF KING ROBERT II

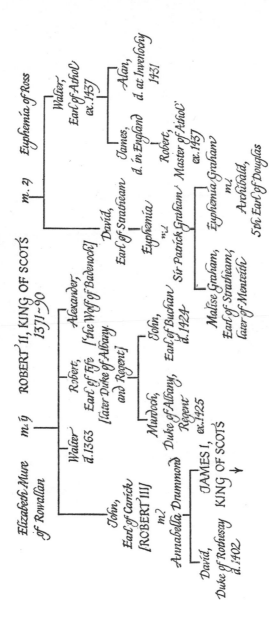

Elizabeth Mure   m.1   ROBERT II, KING OF SCOTS   m.2   Euphemia of Ross
of Rowallan   1371~90

Walter   Robert,   Alexander,   Walter,
d.1363   Earl of Fife   [the Wolf of Badenoch]   Earl of Athol
                [later Duke of Albany   ex.1437
                and Regent]

John,   John,   David,   James,   Alan,
Earl of Carrick   Earl of Buchan   Earl of   d. in England d. at Inverlochy
[ROBERT III]   Murdoch,   d.1424   Strathearn   1431
m.2   Duke of Albany,
                 Regent   Euphemia   Robert,
Annabella Drummond ex.1425   m.2   Master of Athol'
                                                      ex.1437
                 Malise Graham,   Sir Patrick Graham
David,   Earl of Strathearn,   Euphemia Graham?
Duke of Rothesay later of Menteith   m.
d.1402   Archibald,
         JAMES I, KING OF SCOTS   5th Earl of Douglas
         ↓

[In addition to the sons named on this genealogical table, Robert II had
seven legitimate daughters and eight illegitimate sons, giving him a
total of twenty-one children.]

IV. EARLS OF DOUGLAS

The Earldom was created in 1357, and the 1st Earl was a nephew of 'The Good' Sir James Douglas, the faithful supporter of King Robert I. On the death of the 2nd Earl without issue, the earldom was conferred on Archibald 'the Grim', the illegitimate son of 'the Good' Sir James.

Archibald ['the Grim'], 3rd Earl of Douglas

Archibald, 4th Earl of Douglas and Duke of Touraine d. 1424

m.

Margaret, daughter of King Robert III

Archibald, 5th Earl of Douglas d. 1439

m.

Euphemia Graham

William, 6th Earl of Douglas — David — Margaret ['the Fair Maid of Galloway']

Victims of the 'Black Dinner' 1440

James ['the Gross'], 7th Earl of Douglas d. 1443

William, 8th Earl of Douglas, murdered by James II, 1452

m.

James, 9th Earl of Douglas, m. his elder brother's widow, 'the Fair Maid of Galloway' d. 1488

Archibald, Earl of Moray d. 1455

Hugh, Earl of Ormond ex. 1455

John of Balveny ex. 1463

V. ROYAL STEWARTS, LENNOX STEWARTS [or STUARTS] AND HAMILTONS

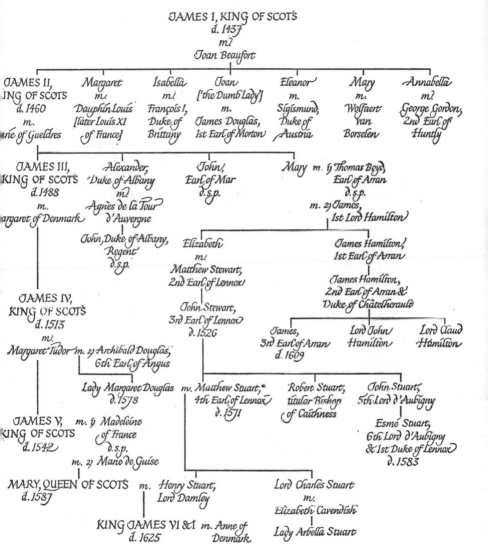

JAMES I, KING OF SCOTS
d. 1437
m.
Joan Beaufort

JAMES II, ING OF SCOTS d. 1460 m. *..rie of Gueldres* | *Margaret* m. *Dauphin Louis [later Louis XI of France]* | *Isabella* m. *François I, Duke of Brittany* | *Joan* ['the Dumb Lady'] m. *James Douglas, 1st Earl of Morton* | *Eleanor* m. *Sigismund, Duke of Austria* | *Mary* m. *Wolfaert Van Borselen* | *Annabella* m. *George Gordon, 2nd Earl of Huntly*

JAMES III, KING OF SCOTS d. 1488 m. *..argaret of Denmark* | *Alexander, Duke of Albany* m. *Agnes de la Tour d'Auvergne* | *John, Earl of Mar* d.s.p. | *Mary* m. 1) *Thomas Boyd, Earl of Arran* d.s.p. m. 2) *James, 1st Lord Hamilton*

John, Duke of Albany, Regent d.s.p.

Elizabeth m. *Matthew Stewart, 2nd Earl of Lennox*

James Hamilton, 1st Earl of Arran

JAMES IV, KING OF SCOTS d. 1513 m. *Margaret Tudor* m. 2) *Archibald Douglas, 6th Earl of Angus*

John Stewart, 3rd Earl of Lennox d. 1526

James Hamilton, 2nd Earl of Arran & Duke of Châtelherault

James, 3rd Earl of Arran d. 1609 | *Lord John Hamilton* | *Lord Claud Hamilton*

Lady Margaret Douglas d. 1578 m. *Matthew Stuart,* 4th Earl of Lennox* d. 1571 | *Robert Stuart, titular Bishop of Caithness* | *John Stuart, 5th Lord d'Aubigny*

JAMES V, KING OF SCOTS d. 1542 | m. 1) *Madeleine of France* d.s.p. m. 2) *Marie de Guise*

Esmé Stuart, 6th Lord d'Aubigny & 1st Duke of Lennox d. 1583

MARY, QUEEN OF SCOTS d. 1587 m. *Henry Stuart, Lord Darnley*

Lord Charles Stuart m. *Elizabeth Cavendish*

KING JAMES VI & I d. 1625 m. *Anne of Denmark*

Lady Arbella Stuart

* The 4th Earl of Lennox and his brother John, Lord d'Aubigny, took French nationality in 1537. From this event dates the French [Stuart] spelling of the surname of this branch of the family. I have given the same spelling to their brother Robert for the sake of clarity.

Index